Web 2.0 Architectures

Web 2.0 Architectures

James Governor, Dion Hinchcliffe, and Duane Nickull

O'REILLY®

Beijing · Cambridge · Farnham · Köln · Sebastopol · Taipei · Tokyo

Web 2.0 Architectures

by James Governor, Dion Hinchcliffe, and Duane Nickull

Published by O'Reilly Media, Inc., 1005 Gravenstein Highway North, Sebastopol, CA 95472.

O'Reilly books may be purchased for educational, business, or sales promotional use. Online editions are also available for most titles (*http://my.safaribooksonline.com*). For more information, contact our corporate/institutional sales department: (800) 998-9938 or *corporate@oreilly.com*.

Editors: Simon St.Laurent and Steve Weiss
Production Editor: Loranah Dimant
Copyeditor: Rachel Head
Proofreader: Loranah Dimant

Indexer: Lucie Haskins
Cover Designer: Karen Montgomery
Interior Designer: David Futato
Illustrator: Robert Romano

Printing History:

May 2009:   First Edition.

ISBN: 978-0-596-51443-3

[M]

1241189917

**Adobe
Developer
Library**

Adobe Developer Library, a copublishing partnership between O'Reilly Media Inc., and Adobe Systems, Inc., is the authoritative resource for developers using Adobe technologies. These comprehensive resources offer learning solutions to help developers create cutting-edge interactive web applications that can reach virtually anyone on any platform.

With top-quality books and innovative online resources covering the latest tools for rich-Internet application development, the *Adobe Developer Library* delivers expert training straight from the source. Topics include ActionScript, Adobe Flex®, Adobe Flash®, and Adobe Acrobat®.

Get the latest news about books, online resources, and more at *http://adobedeveloper library.com*.

Table of Contents

Preface

"Web 2.0 is the business revolution in the computer industry caused by the move to the Internet as a platform, and an attempt to understand the rules for success on that new platform. Chief among those rules is this: build applications that harness network effects to get better the more people use them."

—Tim O'Reilly

If you're in the technology industry or your business uses the Internet, chances are you've heard of Web 2.0. But what exactly is it?

Some people think of Web 2.0 as the assimilation of human participation into web architecture, while some define it as a natural progression of the Internet. Others claim that Web 2.0 is actually what the first generation of the Internet strived to be. There are many different definitions and examples. While researching this book, we encountered people who vehemently denied the existence of Web 2.0, and others who spoke of it as though it were as tangible as the very earth on which they stood.

Controversy aside, it's hard not to recognize that the Internet has evolved dramatically, creating a genuine sense of excitement about what's happening in cyberspace. This book delves into the sources of that excitement, examining the design patterns and models behind things deemed "Web 2.0" and exploring how the Internet grew from its humble origins to its current state. During this journey, you will take a dive into the way architects think, learn how to separate fact from hype and pragmatic views of technology from empty buzzwords, and seek truth.

Why Web 2.0 Matters

Web 2.0 generally refers to a set of social, architectural, and design patterns resulting in the mass migration of business to the Internet as a platform. These patterns focus on the interaction models between communities, people, computers, and software. Human interactions are an important aspect of software architecture and, even more specifically, of the set of websites and web-based applications built around a core set of design patterns that blend the human experience with technology.

This book captures what Web 2.0 is by analyzing major changes in web resources uncontentiously deemed to be "Web 2.0" so that entrepreneurs, architects, and developers worldwide can reapply the knowledge to new business models. The format for that knowledge is expressed within this book as a set of patterns. Every website that implements Web 2.0 yields important clues regarding its core design patterns, models, and solutions that we can repurpose or leverage to solve other problems. This book lays out those patterns in such a way that readers can improve on and implement them over multiple technologies, families, and contexts.

This book often refers to "the new Internet," a term used to include Web 2.0 design patterns and associated technical evolutions, such as the rapid adoption of broadband. The new Internet is not being built as a product of speed increases alone, though. Easy-to-use developer technologies coupled with innovative design patterns from smart entrepreneurs are the primary drivers for new, innovative Internet applications. Continued performance improvements in technology, along with designers building visually compelling user experiences connected to sophisticated services, have made new patterns of interaction possible.

One of these, sometimes mistaken for Web 2.0 itself, is a development trend called Rich Internet Applications (the RIA design pattern is described in greater detail in Chapter 7). New sets of vendor tools and technologies, along with better application architectures, are putting RIA development capabilities at the fingertips of hobbyists. However, from an architect's perspective, how do you quantify "richness"? Is there a list of visual elements that are required, perhaps along with some optional elements? For an application to be rich, it must surely incorporate some functionality that defines it as being different from a non-RIA. But like beauty, the richness of an application lies in the eyes of the beholder. As with many other Web 2.0 concepts, the definition can be captured at best as a design pattern, with notes to aid implementers.

Beyond the development tools and techniques they use, much of the success of companies deemed to be "Web 2.0" is a by-product of a pattern of viral marketing, a scenario in which a new site is promoted far faster via word of mouth than any advertising executive could feasibly achieve via other channels. This phenomenon makes Web 2.0 a hot topic among venture capitalists. Entrepreneurs are creating Web 2.0 sites and applications that are so compelling that the users themselves do the marketing, enabling the little guys to enter into head-to-head competition on an even footing with large multinational corporations with huge advertising budgets. Enthusiastic users of a Web 2.0 site can bury a large corporation's expensive advertising efforts within months. A case in point is MySpace.com, which became the top web destination in early 2007 based largely on viral marketing and content created by its own users. Other companies, such as Twitter, Facebook, YouTube, and Flickr, share this pattern.

On these companies' sites, users both provide and consume the bulk of the data. The users are an integral part of the sites' overall conceptual architecture. These new Internet sites have changed in terms of how people experience them, too. Analysts predict that the bulk of first-time Internet users in the next decade might use wireless connections as their first means of connecting to the Internet.* Video gamers seek greater, more interactive experiences by gathering online to do battle with live opponents, mobile Internet users send messages via the Short Message Service (SMS) to keep in close contact with friends and family, and musicians separated by hundreds or thousands of miles are able to collaborate thanks to their Internet connections.† These are only a few examples of what this rich interconnected tool makes possible.

Web 2.0 represents more than just a change in Internet technology. It is a global change in how we engage with one another. Customer brand loyalty is at an all-time low. Competition is a mere click away for most companies. With the realization of social change comes a desire on the part of large enterprises to learn about the mechanisms behind Web 2.0. As enterprises race to gain a competitive edge over their global competitors, they're realizing that Web 2.0 design patterns can be a critical ingredient in their overall success or failure.

Streaming high-definition television (HDTV)‡ over the Internet is driving the convergence of television with the Internet. When more people watch a sporting event on the Internet than on TV, the incumbent media companies should be scared. When more people view a Volkswagen commercial featuring a girl named Helga on YouTube than watch many regularly scheduled television programs,§ TV executives should take note. When a homemade video of a baby laughing upstages the Helga video on YouTube,‖ and approaches the all-time best TV viewing figures for the Super Bowl,# it should become clear that the battle for the media is in a state of flux.

It's not just a multimedia issue, though. A key trend in Web 2.0 is the inclusion of the user as a core part of any model. Most Web 2.0 examples have breached the purely technical realm and include users as an integral part of their workflow. Online applications are more than mere software; they represent a process of engagement with users. Users provide key functionality and content in most Web 2.0 applications, helping to build a web of participation and collaboration. These design patterns drive young startups, while incumbent enterprises scramble to adapt to the threat posed to them by people who have built something better to engage the user.

These changes are also bringing democracy to several aspects of our lives, from shopping to news reporting and even politics. YouTube hosts debates in which ordinary

---

* See *http://ieeexplore.ieee.org/Xplore/login.jsp?url=/iel5/35/28348/01267107.pdf*.

† See *http://www.mixmatchmusic.com*.

‡ See *http://www.flashvideofactory.com/test/demofullscreen555.html*.

§ At press time, the Volkswagen video (*http://www.youtube.com/watch?v=cv157ZIInUk*) had received over 4.5 million views.

‖ At press time, the "Hahaha" video (*http://www.youtube.com/watch?v=5P6UU6m3cqk*) had received over 80 million views.

The 2008 American Football Super Bowl garnered over 97 million television viewers (see *http://www .contactmusic.com/news.nsf/article/super%20bowl%20audience%20sinks_1093563*).

citizens ask harder-hitting questions than journalists do; citizens in Baghdad blog war reports that give us unprecedented insight into what it means for a government to be overthrown and slowly rebuilt; and giant computer manufacturers lose control over their public relations when not only *Consumer Reports*, but also consumers reveal these companies' flaws on their own corporate websites' support forums.

Historically, those who control the media have the ability to greatly impact the future. A combined media impact can rouse a nation's population to question or overthrow its leaders. Recall, for example, media reports in the late 1990s regarding President Bill Clinton's possible romantic escapades with an intern, which resulted in widespread calls for his impeachment before the matter ever reached a court. Web 2.0 represents a social change that may, within our lifetimes, forever shift the power of the media. Attempts to retain control are getting more and more expensive.*

Web 2.0 nudges the balance of power toward the average person. Like the invention of the printing press several centuries ago, the Web 2.0 revolution is balancing the unequal powers between large corporations and individual rights, the mainstream press and the concerned community member, and the large government and a single citizen. Web 2.0 is providing the infrastructure that allows any information to be published, blogged, linked, mashed, streamed, and syndicated, among a host of other interactions.

Much of the excitement of analysts and the press over Web 2.0 is linked directly to the Internet's increasing scale, size, speed, and interconnectedness. The Internet is the largest single marketplace ever known to mankind. It connects together more digital information, humans, services, corporations, governments, and other endpoints than any previous infrastructure. It's becoming easier than ever to reach out and get your message to a sizeable proportion of today's approximately 1 billion Internet users practically overnight.

Users, businesses, and other organizations that deeply embrace the fundamental nature of the Web as a platform for intercommunication among all connected devices will be able to fully exploit the possibilities of Web 2.0. Once individuals start to understand the concept of patterns, they'll see patterns everywhere. Patterns of using the Internet to route telephone calls, create music asynchronously, and use software as a service are causing major disruptions within the relevant industries.

Entrepreneurs who can learn to recognize these patterns and reapply them have reaped substantial financial benefits in the process, and may yet reap more rewards even in an

---

* Many of the top Internet companies from the first iteration of the Web were acquired by or merged with large media conglomerates that were attempting to retain their control over the media. Examples include Disney acquiring Infoseek between 1998 and 1999, USA Networks acquiring $37 million worth of shares in Expedia in 2001, and the merger of AOL and Time Warner in the late 1990s. More recently, Google and Yahoo! have acquired many companies, and Yahoo! itself has been the object of recent takeover attempts. Investors spent much of 2007 speculating about how to invest in Facebook. Companies trying to acquire the next Google, YouTube, MySpace, or Facebook, however, may find a mismatch with previous media company business models. Most of the content driving those sites is not owned by any one entity, nor can the sites' contributors be constrained by non-competition clauses in a buyout contract.

economic downturn. The pace of innovation remains high. The pace at which new disruptive technologies† are being introduced is equally rapid. The rate at which young startup companies are replacing or upstaging large incumbent forces seems exponentially faster than at any other time in history. The signs of change—some more obvious than others—are upon us.

The Post That Led to This Book

Back in 2006, Tim O'Reilly posted the following on his blog (*http://radar.oreilly.com/ archives/2005/10/web_20_compact_definition.html*):

> I said I'm not fond of definitions, but I woke up this morning with the start of one in my head:
>
> Web 2.0 is the network as platform, spanning all connected devices; Web 2.0 applications are those that make the most of the intrinsic advantages of that platform: delivering software as a continually updated service that gets better the more people use it, consuming and remixing data from multiple sources, including individual users, while providing their own data and services in a form that allows remixing by others, creating network effects through an "architecture of participation," and going beyond the page metaphor of Web 1.0 to deliver rich user experiences.

This seemed to us the most meaningful definition that Tim had offered to date, but it still stops short of fully defining Web 2.0, and it remains broad enough to support many interpretations. It also creates a path for follow-up work—specifically the development of design patterns and models that illustrate the abstract concepts behind Web 2.0.

Developing Web 2.0 Patterns

During a conference brainstorming session in 2003, web pioneer Dale Dougherty observed that far from having "crashed" after the dot-com bust, the Internet was thriving and had become more important than ever. He was excited about the wide range of new applications coming online and the high frequency with which they were appearing. What's more, the conference participants noted that the companies that had survived the Internet industry's 2000–2002 collapse seemed to have some things in common. These observations led to the development of the concept of "Web 2.0."

---

† The terms *disruptive* and *disruptive innovation* are commonly used to note changes in which one technology starts to become deprecated in favor of a newer technology. The eventual retirement of one technology then offers opportunities to those who can provide the replacement technology. In this context, these terms refer to a concept of radical innovation defined in the 1997 best seller *The Innovator's Dilemma* (Collins), in which Harvard Business School professor Clayton Christensen discussed the nature of certain changes within established industries that were so radical that they led to discontinuity within those industries. Some of these changes even unexpectedly reinforced the incumbent technology's position. For example, Christensen analyzed the disk drive industry as a rapidly changing, technologically discontinuous model.

To foster a better understanding of Web 2.0, Tim O'Reilly compiled a list comprising companies deemed Web 1.0 and those deemed Web 2.0, explaining his reasoning in his article "What Is Web 2.0."[‡] This list of companies, discussed in Chapter 1 and Chapter 3, is among the most widely published artifacts used to explain Web 2.0, and it provided us with an excellent set of examples from which to draw patterns of common experience.

While we were mining the examples in Tim's list, a set of abstract patterns emerged. Although the names we use in this book might not match precisely the patterns Tim discussed in his article,[§] the concepts remain aligned. For example, we have renamed Tim's "Cooperate, Don't Control" pattern "Participation-Collaboration." We developed the patterns using a single template, explained in Chapter 6, to express all of them in a consistent and unambiguous format. We present the patterns in that template format as a set of reusable artifacts to help developers, businesspeople, and futurists understand and use them.

We also defined an abstract model based on commonalities across the patterns, discussed in Chapter 4, which represents the evolution of the core model for Internet applications. Unlike the client/server model, often considered the core model for the first iteration of the Internet, this new Web 2.0 model captures the ways in which servers, clients, and users have evolved in the past decade. The abstraction makes it easier to find similarities at different scales in different environments. Although it can describe the interaction between an enterprise and a customer, it's equally applicable to a cell phone providing a Bluetooth-enabled device with some data, as well as to hundreds of other potential applications.

Chapter 5 contains a more formal abstract Web 2.0 reference architecture. Similar to the model in Chapter 4, the reference architecture is abstracted from all the technologies, protocols, standards, vendor products, and other dependencies that may impact its durability. It doesn't rely on any one flavor of these things, so you can use it among a very wide cross section of technological choices.

Although architects or developers could optionally build more specialized architectures, that is beyond the scope of this book. Figure P-1 depicts the relationships between the Web 2.0 design patterns, models, and reference architecture artifacts.

In several places in this book, it might seem as though the patterns we're discussing are directly tied to a particular enterprise or other large corporate player. That's not the intent, nor should readers infer such relationships from models or reference architectures. In fact, the beautiful truth about patterns is that they don't depend on any specific implementation, and instead can be used as development or architecture guides in multiple technologies. Patterns let you share, reuse, and combine knowledge across

---

[‡] See *http://www.oreilly.com/pub/a/oreilly/tim/news/2005/09/30/what-is-web-20.html*.

[§] See *http://www.oreilly.com/pub/a/oreilly/tim/news/2005/09/30/what-is-web-20.html?page=5*.

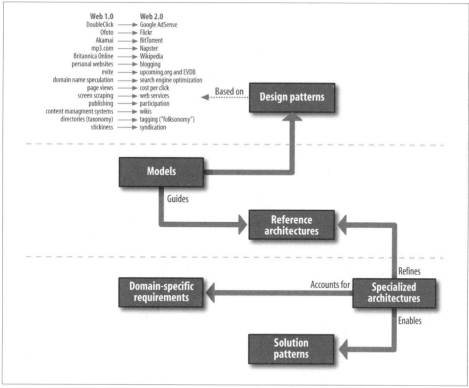

Figure P-1. The relationships between the Web 2.0 design patterns, models, and architecture artifacts

multiple disciplines, even extending beyond the technology realm and into the business world.

How to Use This Book

Chapters 1–6 explore Web 2.0 from the perspective of software architects. They explain the architectures, patterns, models, and other methodologies we used to categorize information we encountered regarding Web 2.0. Each chapter explores Web 2.0 examples to demonstrate the core concepts in greater detail. Readers who are not familiar with the conventions used by software architects should read these chapters sequentially.

Chapter 7 provides a catalog of core Web 2.0 architectural patterns. We present the patterns in a specific order, with broad-base patterns first (such as Service Oriented Architecture, or SOA), followed by more specific patterns that build on those base patterns (e.g., the Mashup pattern, which depends on SOA). Architects and those familiar with the concepts of architectural patterns may want to read Chapter 7 right away. Keep in mind, however, that the list of patterns discussed in this book is far from exhaustive.

Chapter 8 looks ahead to where the application of these patterns and the knowledge of Web 2.0 may take us as a society.

Scattered throughout the book are sidebars called "Entrepreneur Alert." We hope that these will stimulate your thought processes, help you to reapply the patterns to new business domains, and invite you into uncharted territory.

Conventions Used in This Book

The following typographic conventions are used in this book:

Italic
> Used for emphasis, new terms where they are defined, URLs, and email addresses.

`Constant width`
> Used for code samples and for HTML and XML elements.

 This icon signifies a tip, suggestion, or general note.

 This icon indicates a warning or caution.

Using Code Examples

This book is here to help you get your job done. In general, you may use the code in this book in your programs and documentation. You do not need to contact us for permission unless you're reproducing a significant portion of the code. For example, writing a program that uses several chunks of code from this book does not require permission. Selling or distributing a CD-ROM of examples from O'Reilly books *does* require permission. Answering a question by citing this book and quoting example code does not require permission. Incorporating a significant amount of example code from this book into your product's documentation *does* require permission.

We appreciate, but do not require, attribution. An attribution usually includes the title, author, publisher, and ISBN. For example: "*Web 2.0 Architectures*, by James Governor, Dion Hinchcliffe, and Duane Nickull. Copyright 2009 James Governor, Dion Hinchcliffe, and Duane Nickull, 978-0-596-51443-3."

If you feel your use of code examples falls outside fair use or the permission given above, feel free to contact us at *permissions@oreilly.com*.

Safari® Books Online

When you see a Safari® Books Online icon on the cover of your favorite technology book, that means the book is available online through the O'Reilly Network Safari Bookshelf.

Safari offers a solution that's better than e-books. It's a virtual library that lets you easily search thousands of top tech books, cut and paste code samples, download chapters, and find quick answers when you need the most accurate, current information. Try it for free at *http://my.safaribooksonline.com*.

How to Contact Us

We have tested and verified the information in this book to the best of our ability, but you may find that features have changed (or even that we have made mistakes!). Please let us know of any errors you find, as well as your suggestions for future editions, by writing to:

O'Reilly Media, Inc.
1005 Gravenstein Highway North
Sebastopol, CA 95472
800-998-9938 (in the U.S. or Canada)
707-829-0515 (international/local)
707-829-0104 (fax)

We have a website for the book, where we'll list examples, errata, and any plans for future editions. You can access this page at:

http://www.oreilly.com/catalog/9780596514433/

To ask technical questions or comment on the book, send email to:

bookquestions@oreilly.com

For more information about our books, conferences, software, Resource Centers, and the O'Reilly Network, see the O'Reilly website:

http://www.oreilly.com

Acknowledgments

We want to acknowledge Tim O'Reilly for bringing the revolution of the new Internet into focus. We also want to thank our families for giving us the time to work on this project, and our employers—Adobe, RedMonk, and Hinchcliffe & Company—for allowing us to dedicate our minds and resources to the book. Thanks also to our friends and others who have helped us over the years, whether they know it or not. These include the bloggers who expressed their opinions, the entrepreneurs who took ideas further than anyone expected, the standards world that created rules for allowing us to interoperate, the visionaries who broke those rules into little pieces to make something new, and you for taking the time to read this book.

Without naming everyone, there are some individuals who have played an especially important part in allowing this work to happen—our gratitude goes out to all of you.

Duane's Acknowledgments

I would like to thank Kevin Lynch, Michele Turner, and Jeff Whatcott from Adobe for letting this book take precedence over filing status reports (☺); my wife, Bettina Rothe, and my children for putting up with me during the process; Ted Patrick, James Ward, Prayank Swaroop, Alex Choy, Kumar Vora, the entire Adobe Platform Business Unit, Enrique Duvos, Ivan Koon, Eugene Lee, Waldo Smeets, John Hogerland, Ben Watson, Matt Mackenzie, Melonie Warfel, Ed Chase, Diana Helander, David Mendels, and Ben Forta and the Adobe Technical Evangelism team for challenging my intellect and generally being great people to work with; Rom Portwood for the blue hair idea and the Balvenie 21-year Portwood finish; Bobby Caudill (when is that demo tape coming???); Andre Charland (Nitobi and constant blogger); my bands 22nd Century (*http://www .mix2r.com/audio/by/artist/22nd_century*) and Stress Factor 9 (*http://www.myspace .com/stressfactor9*); the guys and girls at Weissach for keeping the Porsche "tuned"; Matt and Trey, the creators of *South Park*, for inspiring me to reach for something lower and not be afraid, and Beavis and Butthead for inspiring me to create things that truly do not suck; Dilbert creator Scott Adams; Sim Simeonov, Danny Kolke, Greg Ruff, Ajit Jaokar, Jeremy Geelan, Tim Bray, and Mark Little (for taking time out of his busy schedule to help edit this book); Yefim Natis (Gartner); the entire staff at OASIS and UN/CEFACT; Bruce D'arcus (the guy whom I like the most despite the fact that we never agree ☺); Audrey Doyle; Gary Edwards; David RR Webber; Colleen Nystedt (friend, movie producer, and creator of MovieSet.com); Bob Sutor; Christian Heumer; Birgit Hoffmeister (for teaching me about modeling); Brian Eisenberg; Arofan Gregory (how was that Barcelona-ian brandy?); all the people involved in the creation of this book and O'Reilly Media for taking on the project; John Sowa for making sense of propositional algebra; Adam Pease for SUMO and for being an upstanding, approachable academic; David Luckham for sharing good Scotch over discussions on CEP; Gary Dunn; Dick Hardt (my Porsche is *almost* as fast as yours); Guy Kawasaki; Bob Glushko; Shantanu Narayen and Bruce Chizen, Adobe Systems CEOs, for inspiring me on a great humanitarian level and showing that corporate success and good community go hand in hand; all of Adobe PR for putting up with my antics; Johnny Rotten, Jim Morrison, and Kurt Cobain (for their immense wisdom and teaching me that speaking the truth is never wrong); Peter Brown (who gets stuck with the next wine bill); Pam Deziel (I'll invite you to wine if it's Peter's turn to buy); Marc Straat; Marc Eaman for drinking beer to help lower my wine bills and reminding me that old guys can play great ice hockey; Chuck Myers for not questioning my wine bills; and my friends and colleagues who have helped me over the years in this high-tech life.

James's Acknowledgments

Although I have been a professional writer for more than 12 years, I have never worked on a book before. I must therefore thank Duane Nickull, who asked me to contribute to this project. Duane is one of the brightest people I have ever met (I keep the term *godlike genius* in my back pocket for him). I am glad Adobe gave him the time to pursue his ideas. This book is very much Duane's, and as such I can only hope that my small contributions don't detract from the overall quality. We didn't always see eye to eye over Duane's early drafts; it could be that my most important contributions were not sections I wrote, but pushback I provided.

The Synchronized Web idea came together on a great night at JavaOne 2006 in San Francisco at a party for JavaDB, organized by Rebecca Hansen with David Van Couvering. My partners in crime that night were David Berlind, Francois Orsini, and Patrick Chanezon. We were all enthused by the SynchWeb idea, so I figured it was not completely suboptimal. Slightly less than a year later, Robert Bruin, Sun Software's CTO, name-checked Synchronized Web in his JavaOne keynote speech.

Declarative Living and Tag Gardening are concepts I have been thinking about for some time. David Weinberger and Clay Shirky must take the primary credit for anything good in my ideas, and none of the blame for any shortfalls. A key phrase from Weinberger haunted me and inspired me, and really drove me to want to express my own ideas on the subject of the power of tags and how they apply to so much of what is good and useful in Web 2.0:

> Tagging instead creates piles of leaves in the hope that someone will figure out ways of putting them to use—perhaps by hanging them on trees, but perhaps creating other useful ways of sorting, categorizing, and arranging them.

David and Clay are the tree. I am adding a few leaves.

Just after agreeing to work on this book, I picked up Peter Morville's *Ambient Findability: What We Find Changes Who We Become* (*http://oreilly.com/catalog/9780596007652/*) (O'Reilly). It was like being punched in the solar plexus, the book was so good. Morville captures many of the same ideas I wanted to, but with a degree of technical aptitude and scholarship I couldn't hope to match. *Ambient Findability* remains a high bar for me, and a book I wish I had written. Thanks, Peter.

Other works that strongly influenced my thinking include John Battelle's *The Search* (Portfolio) and Chris Anderson's *The Long Tail* (Hyperion). If you haven't read these books, perhaps because you thought "I already read the blog," I advise you to think again. Both works are excellent, solid in their own right, and add a great deal of depth and thinking to the expected central ideas. Declarative Living feeds Battelle's Database of Intentions.

Ludwig Wittgenstein's theories of language games and communities of practice were another inspiration.

Many of my thoughts were firmed up in conversations with Stephen O'Grady, co-founder of RedMonk, whom I have to thank for not firing me when I needed to spend a bit of work time on the project, even though the majority of the work was done on my own time.

I didn't take too much time away from my family to make my contributions, but I can't thank my wife enough for making life such a pleasure, and for supporting me in all my endeavors. Natalie is enough of a Luddite to keep me sane, but not enough to drive me nuts; we dorks need "civilians" in our lives. Watching my son, Farrell, learn language has been like watching Tag Gardening in action. Fantastic. Thanks boy.

Finally, I want to thanks the hundreds, if not thousands, of bloggers who constantly make me smarter on a dizzying range of subjects. You all helped. My blog roll on Monkchips names many of you. Last, but definitely not least, thanks to everyone who commented on "early drafts" of my ideas on my blog. Alex Barnett, Danny Ayers, Berkay Mollamustafaoglu, Roo Reynolds, and Isabel Wang deserve a particular mention here. After all, good ideas only make sense in communities.

Wait! How could I not thank the people who built the services that have inspired so many of us—Josh Shacter of Delicious, and Caterina Fake and Stewart Butterfield of Flickr? These people didn't write the book; they created the future.

Dion's Acknowledgments

Working on a book can be one of the most difficult projects, and one of the most (potentially) rewarding. I'd like to thank Duane Nickull for the gracious invitation to work on this book with him and James Governor. Of course, no book on Web 2.0 could omit thanks to O'Reilly Media and Tim O'Reilly for their groundbreaking work on bringing the concepts to the world. It's been amazing to watch the rise of the next generation of the Web, and the blogosphere, of course, is one of the most fertile grounds for tracking new ideas and having open conversations about the disruptive trends and powerful new ideas that seem to emerge continuously in the living laboratory of the Web. My travels through the blogosphere in my researching and thinking around Web 2.0 have included the likes of Andrew McAfee, Nick Carr, Michael Arrington, Richard MacManus, Paul Kedrosky, Brady Forrest, Chris Pirillo, Robert Scoble, Om Malik, Alex Barnett, David Ing, Dave Orchard, Mark Baker, Dare Obasanjo, Rod Boothby, Stowe Boyd, John Musser, Richard Monson-Haefel, Tim Bray, Steve Vinoski, Jeff Schneider, Sam Ruby, Martin Fowler, Stefan Tilkov, Don Box, Mark Nottingham, Phil Windley, and hordes of other online voices that have informed my work and ideas over the years.

Of course, I have to thank the folks who got us here and who make the Web in its current incarnation possible. Sir Tim Berners-Lee comes at the top of this list of giants. So too do Thomas Erl, the grand maven of SOA; Dave Winer, the genius behind many of the technologies we call Web 2.0; Roy Fielding, the brains behind HTTP and REST; Jesse James Garrett, the man behind the term *AJAX*; and hundreds of others too numerous to mention who all contribute to the global network that has changed our lives and businesses forever. Last, but certainly not least, thanks to the vast audience of participants on the Web itself, who have been creating it and shaping it over the past 15 years and have finally claimed it for themselves. It's our Web now, and we haven't looked back.

Naturally, no work of writing could be complete without those who make our personal and professional lives possible. I'd like to thank Kate Allen in particular, who has been my long-suffering business partner as we built an entire business around the world of Web 2.0, and who is principally responsible for all of the time that I was able to put into this book.

CHAPTER 1

An Architect's View of the Web

"If you build it…they will come."
—from *Field of Dreams*

"Quick, they're coming. Build something."
—motto for new Internet startups

Understanding Web 2.0 design patterns and the architectural processes behind them will give you an edge over your competition. The abstraction and identification of artifacts, tools of the architect's trade, will help you to separate fact from hype.

Looking for Web 2.0

If you picked up this book looking for a simple definition of Web 2.0, you'll be disappointed. There is no single, commonly accepted definition, nor is there likely to ever be one. To understand why, you need to study the evolution of the term and the philosophy of its creator, Tim O'Reilly.[*]

Why is it difficult to define Web 2.0? The Internet is changing so fast that by the time a definition was documented, it would be out of date. The Web is very dynamic and is built on a constant churn of incremental updating at every level, from blog content and comments to infrastructure.

Capturing a static or structural view of the Internet would not tell the whole story either. Web 2.0 is about more than how the technology works; it's also about how the technology is used and its real-world effects. Consider the elation a user might feel upon being "favorited" on MySpace.com. How would you document that in a formal architecture? How can you quantify the emotions of humans as part of the machine?

---

[*] To disambiguate references to Tim O'Reilly and O'Reilly Media, we'll use Tim's full name at first mention in each chapter and then refer to him informally as "Tim" throughout the remainder of that chapter. All references to "O'Reilly" refer to the corporate entity.

Fact: No formal architecture or specification exists to explicitly define Web 2.0, nor is there ever likely to be one.

Use of the term "Web 2.0" has spiraled out of control as thousands of technology companies have applied it to their products and services as proof of their being on the cutting edge. These companies have not, however, bottled some magic solution.

Fact: You cannot buy Web 2.0 for your enterprise.

Companies may imply that they are selling you Web 2.0 by linking the term to specific technologies. Some of them remind us of circus hucksters, standing high on a soapbox announcing their wares: "Want to buy Web 2.0 stuff for your company? Don't get left behind! Step right up! No pushing; we've got plenty to go around!" (If you ever encounter this sort of behavior, please run as fast and as far as you can.) Sadly, Web 2.0 is not something you can buy or install to suddenly become the hippest of the hip.

To understand why this is, it's important to examine the roots of the term. Tim first coined the term back in 2003 when planning a conference.[†] The first public use of the term seems to have been at an O'Reilly conference in 2004, where it immediately resonated with the audience.[‡] "Web 2.0" became an overnight sensation, one of the most-hyped technology terms in the industry. Everyone from analysts to the press seemed to jump on the bandwagon without worrying about a strict definition, or what the term might mean to others. Because every person who used the term probably had a slightly different opinion about what it meant, the chances of solidifying a formal definition slipped further away with every repetition, with those who were fresh to the term inferring its meaning based largely upon where they heard it.

In September 2005, Tim wrote a paper to further clarify Web 2.0.[§] Rather than attempting to define the concept as a static architecture or some other type of specification, he illustrated what various examples of Web 2.0 meant by comparing them to similar examples in previous websites, technologies, or models. Figure 1-1, a table from Tim's paper, has become perhaps the most widely used explanation of Web 2.0. The table compares what the old Web had to offer to the more recent evolution (bear in mind that much has changed since this chart was created).

After presenting this list, Tim continued:

> The list went on and on. But what was it that made us identify one application or approach as "Web 1.0" and another as "Web 2.0"? (The question is particularly urgent because the Web 2.0 meme has become so widespread that companies are now pasting it on as a marketing buzzword, with no real understanding of just what it means. The question is particularly difficult because many of those buzzword-addicted startups are definitely not Web 2.0, while some of the applications we identified as Web 2.0, like Napster and BitTorrent, are not even properly Web applications!) We began trying to

[†] See *http://radar.oreilly.com/archives/2006/05/controversy_about_our_web_20_s.html.*

[‡] See *http://en.wikipedia.org/wiki/Web_2.*

[§] See *http://www.oreilly.com/pub/a/oreilly/tim/news/2005/09/30/what-is-web-20.html.*

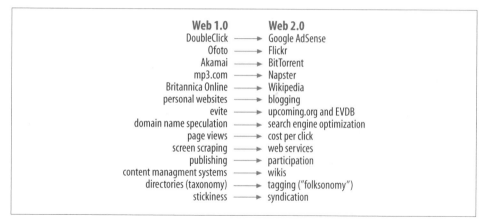

Figure 1-1. Tim's list of Web 1.0 versus Web 2.0 examples

tease out the principles that are demonstrated in one way or another by the success stories of Web 1.0 and by the most interesting of the new applications."[*]

If you look beyond the examples themselves, you can distill a set of core patterns and abstract models. These patterns are the best way to clarify what Web 2.0 is. The following section offers a brief summary of the Web 2.0 patterns (Chapter 7 goes into much greater detail). To decouple the patterns from any specific implementations, we have abstracted them to a level in which they are no longer connected to any specific standards, protocols, products, businesses, or technologies.

Common Web 2.0 Architecture Patterns

Most of the Web 2.0 patterns we've identified can be abstracted on three levels, ranging from the most concrete (idiom) to the most abstract (high-level design pattern). Consider the following three statements:

1. A company uses a PDF form to collect user input from one of its customers.

2. An organization uses an electronic form to collect data from a person.

3. An entity uses an electronically encoded artifact to convey data between other entities and itself.

Each statement is true and accurate with respect to the same real-world example, yet the patterns become more abstract (and hence more easily repurposed) toward the bottom of the list. In the first pattern statement, the technology is constrained to PDF and the form users are specified as customers. The second pattern statement allows the pattern to be implemented in other technologies besides PDF and allows human users other than customers of a company. The third pattern statement can be applicable to

---

[*] From *http://www.oreillynet.com/pub/a/oreilly/tim/news/2005/09/30/what-is-web-20.html*.

electronic artifacts beyond mere forms and accounts for both machine and human users, regardless of whether they're actual customers.

With that in mind, here's a brief list of the Web 2.0 patterns in this book, sorted roughly from the most abstract to the most concrete:

Service-Oriented Architecture (SOA)
SOA (defined by the OASIS Reference Model for SOA[#]) is an architectural paradigm, a way of architecting a framework for matching needs and capabilities. A key feature of SOA is support for integrating services that are owned and managed independently. SOA is a core pattern underlying Web 2.0, and several other patterns (such as the Mashup pattern and the Software as a Service pattern) rely on it. An application server offering a SOAP endpoint where consumers can invoke a service to get a stock quote is a classic example of this pattern.

Software as a Service (SaaS)
SaaS delivers computational functionality to users without them having to persist the entire application or system on their computers. It applies SOA to the realm of software, shifting away from the older model of locally installed, self-contained software. SaaS has evolved largely from the advent of web-aware applications. The website at *http://createpdf.adobe.com* is a good example of Software as a Service because you can use it to turn an HTML document into a PDF document without having to install any software on your local system. This example is also a specialized type of SOA. The ultimate expression of this pattern could be virtualization, the core pattern behind cloud computing.

Participation-Collaboration
The Participation-Collaboration pattern focuses on self-organizing communities and social interactions among Web 2.0 participants. It embraces reuse of content, fractional updates or contributions to collective works, the constant beta, trusting your users, and making the user a core part of the architecture and model for Web 2.0. Wikipedia is perhaps one of the most cited examples of this pattern, as many people contribute to it. This is also known as *harnessing collective intelligence*.

Asynchronous Particle Update
This is the core pattern behind Asynchronous JavaScript and XML (AJAX), yet it can also be implemented in other technologies. Rather than forcing a complete object (page view) update, a smaller part of the whole can be updated asynchronously. This pattern has several variations that could trigger such an update, including timeouts, user activity, changes in state, and preset parameters. These triggers can happen on a server or a client, or in some other locale, such as in cloud computing.

[#] See *http://www.oasis-open.org/committees/tc_home.php?wg_abbrev=soa-rm*.

Mashup

The Mashup pattern relies on services (see SOA), aggregating content or computational resources from multiple sources, and mixing them together to create something new. Commonly, in the resulting view two or more applications appear to be working together. An example of a mashup is a Google map with financial data overlaid on it.

Rich User Experience (RUE)

Synonymous with a Rich Internet Application (RIA), a RUE is a replication of the complete, real-world interaction between two entities, rather than some part of that interaction. The RUE pattern combines several aspects, including visual presentation, contextually relevant information, and applications that are modeled to understand the complete scope of possible interactions between users and software. An offline example might be a conversation with an employee at a travel agency, wherein each party learns from and reacts to the other; in contrast, picking up a brochure from a travel agency to study on your own does not constitute a RUE.

The Synchronized Web

In this pattern, multiple applications or users share the same state or view of the same state. Online video gamers commonly use this pattern (to be able to play games together online), but it has evolved far beyond such applications. It is an essential pattern that supports multiple forms of interaction, including request/response, subscribe/push, probe and match, pull, and others.

Collaborative Tagging

Commonly referred to as *folksonomy*, a term coined by Thomas Vander Wal, Collaborative Tagging refers to the ability of users to add "labels" (or tags) to link resources with semantic symbols that themselves are grounded in a conceptual domain (ontology). Major top-down efforts to create a semantic web have failed to take hold, yet in the meantime, the rise of Collaborative Tagging has added a new aspect to the creation of a common semantic layer for the Internet. The website at *http://del.icio.us*, where users can apply labels to public bookmarks, is a prime example of the Collaborative Tagging pattern.

Declarative Living and Tag Gardening

In the real world, people make statements about just about everything. Declarative Living is the act of encoding those declarations in syntax that a machine can process, and making them visible to other entities on the Web. Tag Gardening is the act of harvesting the declarations to learn about the users' collective state. This pattern is grounded in the Collaborative Tagging pattern. An example is Twitter (*http://www.twitter.com*), where users make declarations about their daily activities that others can access. Even social networks such as Facebook, where people simply "declare" existing social structures, are a specialized form of this pattern.

Semantic Web Grounding

The Semantic Web Grounding pattern assembles interactions that monitor the links between declarations (e.g., "semantic tags") and resources, as well as how users interact based on those artifacts. It facilitates self-learning, self-healing software, as observing the patterns of interactions can lead to inferences about the relevancy of semantic declarations. Google Search is probably the best-known example of this pattern, although many adaptive learning software systems embrace it as well.

Persistent Rights Management

Persistent Rights Management is a pattern of users retaining their Create, Read, Update, Delete (CRUD) rights on every copy of a digital artifact. As opposed to simply securing the location of the original copy, this pattern bestows author rights on all copies of a work. People sometimes confuse Digital Rights Management (DRM) with this pattern, but although DRM is similar, there are differences. DRM is a subset of Persistent Rights Management[*] addressing read access to digital files,[†] whereas Persistent Rights Management encompasses finer-grained rights that owners might need to control, including printing, viewing, modifying, and more.[‡] Adobe LiveCycle Rights Management Server and Microsoft's Rights Management Server are both adopters of this pattern.

Structured Information

The advent of XML and the ability to apply customized tagging to specific elements has led to the rise of syntaxes commonly referred to as microformats. These are small formats with highly specialized abilities to mark up precise information within documents. The use of such formats, in conjunction with the rise of XHTML, lets Internet users address content at a much more granular level than ordinary HTML. The XML Friends Network (XFN) format is a good example of this pattern.

Chapters 3 and 7 of this book illustrate how these abstract patterns are distilled from examples. The patterns themselves capture and express the inner workings of each example and can be used to determine whether other websites embrace the same patterns. To infer the most knowledge from these patterns, it helps to understand the role that patterns and architecture play in Web 2.0.

Capturing Web 2.0 Knowledge with Patterns and Architecture

To understand Web 2.0 in pragmatic terms, it helps to review how architects think and work. Architects often see things that are not visible to the naked eye. An architect staring at a skyscraper might be admiring the hidden structural aspects of the building that give it extra rigidity or allow it to move slightly in adverse weather conditions. Architects often admire the whole, while also being able to appreciate the individual

---

[*] See *http://www.adobe.com/products/livecycle/rightsmanagement/*.

[†] See *http://en.wikipedia.org/wiki/Digital_rights_management*.

[‡] See *http://xml.coverpages.org/MicrosoftRMS.html*.

parts of a system and their integration into a cohesive unit. Seeing and understanding hidden qualities and aspects of a structure or system often lead to the repurposing of those aspects into new designs. By incorporating such design aspects into new projects, architecture continues to evolve.

About Architecture

There are "architects" in many different fields, working on everything from software systems to commercial buildings, bridges, airports, and much, much more. Architects design, describe, and document systems and their structure, including the internal components, the externally visible properties, and the relationships that exist between them. An architect typically describes and documents all of this in several *views* to account for static and dynamic behavior during all phases of development and use of a system or structure. These views are generally supplemented with other artifacts depicting additional *aspects* of the thing being architected. In the case of software, there may be a data model view, a technical infrastructure view, and views from various "actors" who will interface with the system. The term *actors* in this context refers to any "thing" that interacts with the system, including people or other systems.

Everything has architecture, so why is it so difficult to capture the knowledge of Web 2.0 as architecture?

Architecture encapsulates knowledge about a thing or class of things. Capturing this knowledge successfully requires architects to look beyond a specific implementation and document the concepts behind and relationships between each component in a system/thing in a manner that others can reuse for their purposes. Architects must look beyond what they see or what is visible and capture the axioms, tenets, and idioms in a manner that conveys the most knowledge possible.

Architects use a variety of conventions and formats to preserve knowledge, some of which are arcane and others of which are familiar to most of us. Blueprints are perhaps one of the most common formats, though they capture only part of the knowledge of a structure or system of structures. A blueprint of a building, for example, usually captures only the static structure; it does not describe how actual humans behave in the system. Architects cannot capture the required level of detail in blueprints alone; they use models and patterns of usage to convey additional knowledge that isn't portrayed in the normative architectural views.

In the software industry, a blueprint is usually synonymous with a component or technology view; it documents aspects that may not be visible to the naked eye. As with a building, the dynamics of how software is used may be just as important as its static structure. When studying Web 2.0, it's valuable to understand and apply these concepts. Web 2.0 is not just about the static architecture of the Internet; it's about the patterns of usage between a variety of things, whether human or machine, that use the Internet as a platform.

A Brief Introduction to Architectural Patterns

Patterns, in the context of this book, are abstract designs that may be applied to multiple and diverse manifestations of a common problem. Patterns may be expressed in many formats. However, they generally include three basic elements:

- A problem
- The context in which the problem occurs
- The solution to the problem

For different purposes, different templates for expressing patterns have been built to preserve knowledge in more specific formats. Chapter 6 goes into much greater detail about the process of creating patterns, but here's a brief explanation to get started.

Austrian-born American architect Christopher Alexander first documented the concept of architectural patterns in his 1970s books *A Timeless Way of Building* and *A Pattern Language: Towns, Buildings, Construction* (both from Oxford University Press). In the 1980s, Kent Beck and Ward Cunningham began to experiment with the idea of applying the patterns concepts to the art of software design and development. They presented their results at the annual Association for Computing Machinery OOPSLA (Object-Oriented Programming, Systems, Languages & Applications) conference, and the ideas rapidly spread throughout the IT sector.

Perhaps the best way to explain the concept of architectural patterns is to provide an example. Consider a pattern that captures the concepts of "pants," including legs, inseam, pockets, and other details. Such a pattern can be used to construct the pants in a variety of materials and/or for many different purposes. (Remember, this isn't a tightly defined sewing pattern, but a broader description.) For example, if the requirements are pants for warm weather, they can be made with very lightweight cotton, with higher legs for water-wading. For cold weather, the same pattern could be used to make pants that contain an inner lining and are composed of very dense material for thermal efficiency. Both products are easily distinguished from other products that follow the pattern of "skirt" or "shirt."

Both online and offline, the usefulness of patterns is often tied to their flexibility and reusability in different contexts. As an online example, YouTube implements patterns of Participation-Collaboration, Viral Marketing, and Semantic Web Grounding. It lets its users upload videos and tag them with comments and other terms. It allows URLs to be embedded in any website so that the linked videos can be displayed on that site. YouTube makes video publishers out of anyone who has content to contribute, and it helps people find multiple videos on similar subjects on demand. It doesn't take a rocket scientist to realize that a simple reapplication of the YouTube patterns for financial services research, cooking recipes, automobile repair information, or books might be a recipe for success.

While a pattern describes functionality shared across any number of implementations, patterns can evolve over time and adjust to meet different needs. Patterns are generally not versioned, and working from a template that allows aspects to be specialized helps others see how it's been implemented.

Consider the pattern of how musicians, engineers, and audio producers create a multitrack audio work. The pattern involves a producer acting as a centralized controller while music is captured from its analog form and converted into a digital form (with help from the skilled engineer), and then captured for persistence on some media device in the control room, where it is combined with other tracks to create a final audio product. The musician playing the instrument to add to the track listens to other tracks and then plays his part, which is recorded and added by the producer to the final mix, after some post-production tinkering.

Although this pattern is often implemented within the confines of a recording studio where wires capable of transmitting audio signals from one room to another connect various rooms, it may be implemented in a different way. This does not automatically make the pattern mutate into a new version. If the pattern is sufficiently abstract, it should still be valid across varying implementations.

As a general rule, the higher the level of abstraction of a pattern is, the more it can be repurposed. The more specialized a pattern is, the less likely it is that it can be repurposed. For example, you could modify the pattern we just discussed to allow the entire sequence of workflow to happen over the Internet instead of in a recording studio. In fact, startups such as Mix2r, MixMatchMusic, and JamGlue§ have implemented such a pattern, whereby the producer and the artists use the Internet as a collaborative platform for creating audio productions. Bands can include their fans and friends in the creative process by first posting a set of bed tracks for a song along with information about what they are looking for in the project. Fans can download the bed tracks and then use their own hardware and software to record their instruments alongside the tracks from the band. Once they're finished, they can upload their tracks as contributions to the final song, and the band's producer can download those and include them in the mix. This process differs from the typical recording scenario, but it still follows the same general patterns.

Capturing patterns can be an iterative process. Finding patterns involves examining case after case, looking for commonalities amidst the variation. As patterns start to emerge, it becomes possible to capture details of those patterns using a common metamodel or template. In this book, we use an architectural pattern metamodel to express both the static and dynamic aspects of a specific pattern. The metamodel expresses the semantics for each part of the pattern template and sets expectations for the logic of the patterns so that readers can interpret them correctly. This template also

---

§ See *http://www.mix2r.fm*, *http://www.splicemusic.com*, and *http://www.gluejam.com*.

captures aspects of the pattern that range from the high-level business story down to specific low-level idioms, some of which may actually contain code samples.

After a core set of patterns has been captured, it becomes possible to describe a larger and more abstract reference model. While the reference model comes after the patterns, it provides a context for their use and makes it easier to tell the story of how they work. We used commonalities within the set of patterns expressed in Chapter 7 as the basis for designing a reference model (discussed in Chapter 4). That model was used as the basis for developing the Web 2.0 reference architecture discussed in Chapter 5.

A Brief Introduction to Models

A *model* is an abstract representation of a set of concepts or components of a process, system, or structure, generally developed to aid understanding and analysis of a class of things. Models also capture knowledge about the components and concepts and the relationships between them, yet models are different from both architectures and patterns. Most models are abstract, meaning they're independent of any implementation. Because they are abstract, models cannot be directly implemented: they lack a sufficient level of detail. Figure 1-2 illustrates some of the relationships between models, patterns, and architectures.

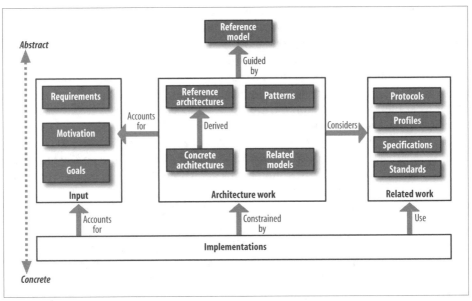

Figure 1-2. The use of a reference model to guide architecture projects (courtesy of OASIS SOA Reference Model Technical Committee)

As with architectural patterns, the best way to explain the concept of a model is with an example. For that, we'll return briefly to the architecture industry. In this industry, there is an implied model for all buildings. This model is stated as follows, with all the components in italic font:

> *Buildings* have *foundations* that mate the rest of the building to the terrain upon which the building may exist. A *floor* sits on top of the foundation and provides a platform in a three-dimensional existence where forces of gravity react in an aligned manner to pull objects toward the floor. *Walls* are connected to the floor and act to mark the perimeter of the building. Walls may optionally be used to subdivide the interior of a building into several smaller compartments. *Doorways* are portals in walls that let things pass from one side of a wall to another. A *roof* sits on top of the building to mark its uppermost perimeter and to protect the building from the top by providing a barrier.

The model captures and preserves the knowledge of what a building is in terms that are applicable to multiple types of buildings. It is relevant to both a house and a shopping mall, and even to a houseboat. The Web 2.0 model described in this book similarly captures key knowledge that is applicable to many types of Web 2.0 implementations.

Another type of model is a *metamodel*, which is a specialized model upon which other models can be built. Metamodels are often denoted as "models of models." The template for capturing Web 2.0 patterns in Chapter 6 can be considered a patterns metamodel.

The first generation of the Internet was largely based on a model commonly referred to as *client/server*, an abstraction that suggested common styles of interaction. The Web 2.0 model in Chapter 4 is abstract in terms of any specific implementation, yet it captures the knowledge of the major concepts present in multiple Web 2.0 implementations. It supports many full and partial definitions of Web 2.0, such as "a platform of connected devices." The model also supports the patterns for Web 2.0. It illustrates how the major components and concepts of Web 2.0 interact at a purely abstract level (i.e., not specific to any technology or real-world, concrete implementation).

How to Use Models and Patterns

Figure 1-2 showed how architectural models can be used during a conventional architectural process. Figure 1-3 shows the lineage of mining patterns from examples and then constructing models and architectures based upon those patterns.

Note that many types of people can do this sort of activity. Entrepreneurs regularly figure out how to solve problems based on certain models without ever really analyzing their processes. Inventors commonly reapply their knowledge to solve new problems and come up with unique ways to do so. You, the reader of this book, also have the ability to use this process map.

In the rest of this book, the term "model" will always mean "reference model." A *reference model* is an abstract model that actors use within an environment to understand the key concepts or artifacts within that environment. A reference model is not an architecture. It is a specialized type of model used when variations of the model may be possible. A reference model lets people with differing points of view or definitions

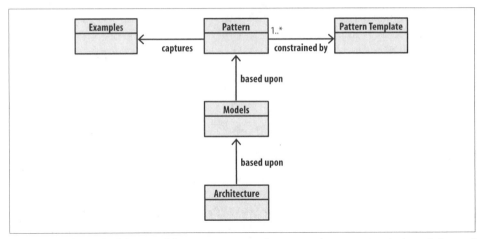

Figure 1-3. The methodology used for mining patterns from examples, capturing the knowledge, and then constructing models and architecture based on the commonalities in the patterns

use a model as a point of reference to describe their departures from that model. As there are likely to be various definitions of Web 2.0—after all, it would be extremely arrogant of any one group of people to presume that its definition was the universally accepted truth for such a contentious subject—the model in this book is really a reference model, and it can be used by those with differing opinions to explain their differences.

Reference models, like patterns, are not typically versioned. Models should capture knowledge so that they still hold even when the implementation details change. Software architects call this concept *durability*. Durability is one of the main design goals of the architecture described here and of its component models and patterns.

This point is especially important for entrepreneurs reading this book. A pattern used for tagging and sharing digital photographs could be reapplied, for example, in both an enterprise context (to let employees build their own communities of practice around sets of business data stored on the corporate network and navigated using hyperlinks) and by lone developers building new applications for personal use.

The Web 2.0 model is likely applicable both to the first rendition of the Internet and to what it is evolving into. The model lets you examine the developments of each of its component concepts, independent of the other concepts, to see where true innovations are being made. You could, for example, take the concept of "connectivity and reachability" and see what has evolved in the past 10 years. Examples might include the evolution of the web services family of technologies to include mechanisms for secure, reliable, and transacted messages, as well as the patterns of asynchronous communication between a component of an HTML web page loaded into a client browser and a server or servers. The latter represents an evolution from the old model of having to click the Refresh button and reload the entire page to update the information on a web page. The technology responsible is AJAX, a model for updating parts of a page instead of the page as a whole. Like many other models, AJAX depends on other technologies or architectural paradigms, such as Representational State Transfer (REST).[||]

As you go forward, bear in mind how patterns, models, and architectures relate to each other. The chapters that follow will delve more directly into the field of software architecture and the challenges it presents to those trying to document software systems and infrastructure. In Chapter 2, you'll start to put this knowledge into practice and apply it to the realm of Web 2.0.

[||] REST refers to a collection of network architecture principles and patterns that outline how resources are defined and addressed, as well as how they may interact with each other, based on the mechanisms defined by HTTP. Dr. Roy Fielding introduced the term in his 2000 doctoral dissertation (see *http://en.wikipedia.org/wiki/REST*).

CHAPTER 2

Different View of the Internet

"Trust I seek and I find in you
Every day for us, something new
Open mind for a different view
and nothing else matters."

—"Nothing Else Matters" by Metallica

Developing sets of patterns requires working from practice back up to theory. Individual case studies gathered together will show commonalities, making it possible to describe and refine patterns. Finding patterns involves looking over the recent past, sorting out which aspects of the work being reviewed are both useful and reusable, and developing a model to describe how those patterns fit together.

Best Practices for Forensic Architecture

In an ideal situation, software architecture is created in response to a documented set of requirements. *Forensic architecture* is the process of expressing the architecture for something after it's been built. Regardless of when the process is undertaken, software architects use a number of conventions and normative description languages and artifacts to express architecture. These typically include blueprints, patterns, models, diagrams, and text. Ideally, the sequence of events for creating an architecture involves the following steps, though there are many variations:

1. Identify a problem.
2. Document the problem.
3. Propose a solution.
4. Document specific requirements for the solution.
5. Propose an architecture to solve the problem.
6. Map requirements to solutions iteratively until all issues are resolved.
7. Build a final complete solution, and solve the problem.

A flowchart could capture this sequence as shown in Figure 2-1.

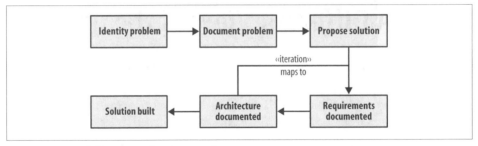

Figure 2-1. Rough flowchart of architectural process

In the real world, of course, there are usually some complications. Architecture processes can be vastly different, but these general guidelines apply to them all:

- Find some common ground early. Starting projects is easier if participants have a common alignment, understanding of, and agreement on a specific model or first order of logic.

- Create consensus, when possible, on what can be achieved before starting any architecture work.

- Work toward completeness. If something isn't documented in architecture, odds are good that it is not universally understood.

- Understand what a problem is before attempting to solve it.

- Avoid forces and constraints that may lead to decisions based on a preconceived notion of the solution. Politics often places pressure on the documenting of architecture.

- Minimize unnecessary dependencies among multiple components to help your architecture last. For software architecture in particular, being careful to avoid simple mappings between artifacts and current technologies can help the artifacts to survive long after the technologies have been forgotten.

- Define the rules and constraints for abstraction and what constitutes a normative part of the solution *before* creating a table of contents.

- Split large things into several smaller things when possible—and not just into components. Consider splitting knowledge into multiple sets of artifacts, at different levels of abstraction, to capture it for different audiences. For example, architects and modelers require different levels of detail than those writing code.

- Clearly define the audience for each artifact in advance.

- Avoid mixing together disparate views of architecture unless there is no alternative.

- Document the structure of a system as layers, to create a more understandable description than one large view that tries to incorporate multiple domains of knowledge.

- Never try to document a moving target with a static architecture specification. The task will be impossible to complete, and the results will be misaligned with the moving target.

That last bullet in particular makes Web 2.0 a difficult challenge for an architect to tackle. The first problem is that the Web is an evolving landscape populated by people and organizations with disparate views. Technologies come and go, while interaction patterns evolve and are linked to business models in new domains. Capturing Web 2.0 as a static architecture won't work. However, by documenting design and architecture patterns abstracted from technologies, we can still capture and preserve knowledge.

Internet Aspects

"Open mind for a different view," the key phrase from Metallica's hit song "Nothing Else Matters," should be the motto of forensic architects, as well as of many entrepreneurs. Those who dare to see things from a different point of view and have the courage to let go of their preconceived notions can truly gain wisdom and knowledge.

Before we stride into Web 2.0, it makes sense to examine its foundation, the Internet, from an architectural perspective and ask some architectural questions. The Internet is comprised of a series of interconnected devices, computers, and networks that interoperate via a set of protocols and standards governing their externally visible behavior. One could describe the Internet as a platform or large bus that allows multiple patterns of interaction. Figure 2-2 illustrates some of the principles and patterns of the Internet's design and history, including the way it fuses multiple disparate networks into one cohesive network.

The Internet embraces several common software architecture patterns, among them the Proxy pattern,[*] the Façade pattern,[†] and the Whole-Part pattern.[‡] Parts of the Internet make up the Internet as a whole when they are connected via a common set of protocols and technologies. There is no one specific Internet or multiple Internets; it is a vast, shifting network connecting devices dynamically.

The Internet is a distributed environment. Although some parts—even important parts—are vulnerable, there is no single central point where someone could attack it and bring it down. No one entity owns it or controls it. Instead, it acts more like a shared bus. A *bus*, loosely defined, is a common shared channel via which communications (data) can be routed to multiple registered nodes. The exact mechanisms for routing and protocols for determining the binding to nodes vary based on the type of bus, and the term can be used the same way in both software and hardware contexts.

---

[*] For more on the Proxy pattern, visit *http://en.wikipedia.org/wiki/Proxy_pattern*.

[†] For more on the Façade pattern, visit *http://en.wikipedia.org/wiki/Facade_pattern*.

[‡] For more on the Whole-Part pattern, visit *http://www.vico.org/pages/PatronsDisseny/Pattern%20Whole%20Part/index.html*.

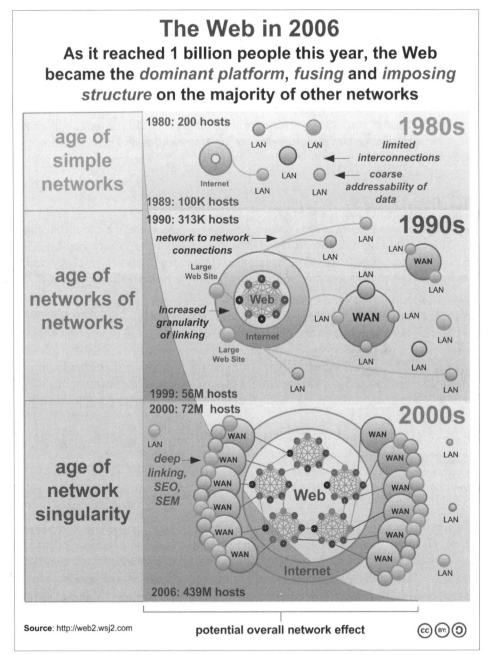

Figure 2-2. *How the Internet fuses together users, machines, and networks*

The Internet is, in fact, a bus-type environment; that is, components may be added or deleted without affecting the system's overall state or usability. The Internet doesn't require all devices to be connected simultaneously. Devices may connect, and then disconnect, change state, and reconnect to the Internet. It is true that enough components going offline might create bandwidth bottlenecks, but for the most part no one notices a new server, switch, or client browser being added or dropped.

Building on the concept of the bus, our architecture journey can now focus on specific changes that take place as devices and applications are added. Rather than being a wholesale, one-time change in the Internet, Web 2.0 is a slow evolution: a constant, gradual change taking place as older devices are retired from the bus and new applications are connected.

The Internet bus is based largely on open standards and protocols, and the Internet functions due to a common layer of understanding and a set number of protocols and standards that work together. Multiple standards and protocols may be at work in a single interaction and are concerned with many different tasks. Some of the most prominent of these include TCP/IP, HTTP, TLS/SSL, and FTP (workhorses for moving bit packets around) and HTML, CSS, and JavaScript (which control the presentation of information once it has reached its destination). Structured information is one of the major backbones of Web 2.0, whether it's created using microformats, XHTML, or XML. It is extremely important to note that Web 2.0, like its predecessor, will likely be built based mostly on open standards, maximizing the bus's accessibility to a wide range of users and products.

 Since we've brought up the topic of open standards, it would be prudent to share our definition. Open standards generally have the following characteristics:

- They're not controlled by any one private entity, and they can't be changed at the will of any one entity without an input process that facilitates consideration of the points of view and input of others.

- They're developed by organizations that are operating with an open and transparent process, allowing stakeholders to have a say in their development.

- They're not encumbered by any patents or other intellectual property claims that result in unfair distribution of the ability to implement them, whether for commercial or noncommercial purposes.

- They're designed to benefit the whole community of users rather than one specific subset of users for financial or other gains.

Basic Communications: TCP/IP

The Transmission Control Protocol (TCP) and Internet Protocol (IP), often grouped together as TCP/IP, are two of the core technology standards upon which the Internet relies. TCP/IP is a low-level protocol that ensures that signals can be moved from one place to another. IP moves packets of data from one point to another, with routers helping those packets find their way across networks. TCP builds reliable connections on top of IP, accepting that not all packets will complete their journeys and resending them as necessary. (A lighter-weight protocol known as the User Datagram Protocol, or UDP, provides more basic services on top of IP and lets applications manage their own error checking and corrections.)

The Hypertext Transfer Protocol (HTTP) works as a layer on top of TCP/IP, as can other protocols, such as the File Transfer Protocol (FTP). TCP/IP is the workhorse of the Internet, yet it doesn't care what its work accomplishes. In fact, it's largely agnostic to anything it may carry. This is by design, and it enforces a common architectural pattern of local state management. TCP/IP manages its own states and exceptions, but it doesn't get involved with the states of other processes or technologies running on it. An example of this is the HTTP code 404 Page Not Found error. When a node issues an HTTP GET request that results in this error, TCP/IP has no idea that the actual web page has not been found on the server; it just carries the request and the error message without needing to understand the details.

Though the foundation standards have remained stable, the payloads carried by these workhorses have changed. Many new payloads have migrated to the Internet or are starting to converge. Examples include telephony (Voice over IP, or VoIP), fax, audio, and video.

Conversations: HTTP and More

HTTP§ is a text-based messaging protocol that piggybacks on TCP/IP and handles the actions required for web browsers to interact with web resources. The HTTP specification defines eight core methods, the best known of which are GET and POST, commonly used to request information and submit information through forms. HEAD, almost an equivalent of a GET but returning only headers instead of the actual content, is very commonly used by software though largely invisible to users. Most of the methods are variations on the theme of sending a request object containing some bytes and receiving a response object, although the semantics of the different methods are well defined in the protocol and identify unique actions from an architect's point of view.

One key feature of HTTP is that it is a *stateless* protocol. There is nothing in the protocol itself that establishes connections between multiple requests. Each incoming HTTP request is treated uniquely and individually, and the web server itself doesn't need to know of any other previous requests that the same client may have made.

While the HTTP server doesn't need to know about previous requests, web-based applications often do need to know what has happened before to create a continuous experience for users. To support these needs, many browsers implement state-tracking mechanisms such as *cookies*, which websites commonly use, sometimes require, and occasionally abuse. A cookie is a small, persistent chunk of data that the server asks

§ See *http://www.w3.org/Protocols/*.

the web browser to cache locally and to pass back if the server requests it in the future. Usually just a unique identifier is stored on the user's browser, although information such as user preferences may also be kept in the cookie. Because it's not hard to examine the contents of cookies, the amount of information they hold should be kept as minimal as possible.

 HTTP does offer authentication mechanisms, which can provide a similar hook for keeping track of which user is making a given request.

Changes over the last decade have left the basic infrastructure of HTTP intact but made it possible to use it in new and transformative ways. It isn't always necessary to change the underpinnings of a system to be able to evolve it in unexpected directions.

Originally, when using the Web you had to reload or refresh an entire HTML page each time you wanted to get new information. Microsoft added the `XMLHTTPRequest` object to its Internet Explorer browser to change that, opening the way to more flexible approaches as more browsers integrated the feature. Called by scripts inside the browser, this simple method became the cornerstone of an asynchronous communication revolution called AJAX. AJAX still uses HTTP, but instead of having to refresh the entire page, it supports a pattern of incrementally updating only a small facet of an information set.

At about the same time, developers started exploring a range of possibilities that didn't necessarily involve web browsers. Called *web services*, these technologies use HTTP to share information across a wide variety of programs and environments. Some, such as SOAP, define an additional messaging layer—actually, many layers defined by a whole set of standards—while others take a much more minimalist approach. The most formal of these, REST,[||] relies on the GET, PUT, POST, and DELETE methods already present in HTTP to build a simple but powerful Create, Read, Update, and Delete (CRUD) interface. (You could implement REST without using HTTP, but in practice REST-based applications are usually built on HTTP.)

Security

As the Internet has grown up, many requirements for controlling access to information and functionality have manifested as a set of standards to address security concerns. Exposing more and more computing resources to build richer, more compelling interactions and applications means risking having these resources compromised. Security standards have therefore evolved in tandem with the Internet.

[||] See *http://en.wikipedia.org/wiki/Representational_State_Transfer*.

The Secure Sockets Layer, otherwise known as SSL, was developed by Netscape and subsequently approved by the Internet Engineering Task Force (IETF) as a standard for creating secure pipes upon which to transmit data as a layer via the Internet. The protocol utilizes a cryptographic system of two keys to encrypt and decrypt data. By convention, URLs that require an SSL connection start with *https://* instead of *http://*.

Transport Layer Security, or TLS, supersedes SSL and is an extension for SSL 3.0, a specific version of the SSL protocol. TLS is a dual-layered model wherein the first layer, the *record protocol*, piggybacks upon a reliable transport protocol and ensures that the connection is not eavesdropped upon by using a technique known as *symmetric data encryption*. The next layer, the *handshake protocol*, allows authentication between the server and client and the negotiation of an encryption algorithm and cryptographic keys before the application protocol transmits or receives any data. TLS is application-protocol-independent. Higher-level protocols can transparently layer on top of the TLS protocol.

There are also a number of recent standards focusing on how to secure web services in particular. The first, Web Services Security (WS-S), is an OASIS standard. A newer specification currently in the standardization process, called Web Services Secure Exchange (WS-SX), has additional functionality for using a security context rather than invoking various methods every time a message is received.

Content

While the technologies for transferring information across the Internet have evolved relatively slowly, technologies for describing content have sprouted rapidly since the inception of the Web. HTML, the original format for sharing information over the Web, remains the foundation for most content sharing, though it is now only one option among many. HTML itself has been fairly stable for about a decade, but the implementation of related technologies has advanced the state of the Web.

Text and data

HTML was the founding data format of the Web. For a time in the 1990s, its development raced forward in competitive sprints between Netscape and Microsoft, but most development calmed down with the advent of HTML 4 in 1998. For nearly a decade, work on HTML has focused primarily on cleaning up its syntax and modularizing it (XHTML). Recently there have been efforts to modernize the format (first XHTML 2 and now HTML 5), but in practice, nearly all web development is based on a 10-year-old specification of a 20-year-old technology. On the bright side, most web browsers in common use today support that specification completely.

HTML created an open format for sharing information between humans. Humans (or their tools) could use HTML to create documents that humans (through their browsers) could read. That worked well, unless you needed to send information from computer to computer. Instead of tags like `<b>` for **bold**, computers might prefer markup more like:

```
<name><given_name>Duane</given_name> <family_name>Nickull</family_name></name>
```

Those labels don't impart semantic meaning—for more on that, see the upcoming section "Semantics" on page 25—but they are useful hooks for programs and are reasonably intelligible to humans.

This kind of markup had been standardized since 1986 and is a key component of the background of HTML, but the Standard Generalized Markup Language (SGML) never really took off the way that HTML did. It was complex, difficult to master, and had a limited (and often expensive) toolset. To give the Web the power of SGML without the complication, a W3C Working Group set out to simplify SGML. In 1998, it produced the Extensible Markup Language (XML). While XML was originally meant to be a replacement for (or at least a supplement to) HTML as hypertext on the Web, it settled instead into a role of a format for exchanging data between programs and became a key component of web services.

Some of those programs do run in web browsers, of course. As noted earlier, AJAX is based on the `XMLHTTPRequest` object, which issues an HTTP call to a server to send or get (at least originally) XML. The AJAX program then processes the XML response and uses its content to update the web page. As it turned out, though, XML is actually overkill for many of these projects, and JavaScript Object Notation (JSON)—a creative reuse of technology already included in the web browser—has taken over its role in simple communications between programs running in browsers and other servers.

All that HTML still has lots of valuable data in it, though, and it can be very useful for programs to extract it. "Screen-scraping," in which programs pull down HTML and extract information based on the content or the markup, can work, but it's easier to find information whose creators want it to be found. *Microformats*[#] take advantage of the parts of HTML that were meant to allow extensibility, creating small standards for putting particular kinds of easily extracted information into HTML documents. Examples of microformats include hCard,[*] a simple, open, distributed format for representing people, companies, organizations, and places; hCalendar,[†] a simple, open, distributed calendaring and events format based on the RFC 2445 iCalendar standard; and XHTML Friends Network (XFN),[‡] a simple way to represent human relationships using hyperlinks.

The past decade has also seen the emergence of *syndication formats*, designed to let sites share information on information they've published in a form that's easy to extract

---

[#] See *http://microformats.org*.

[*] See *http://microformats.org/wiki/hcard*.

[†] See *http://microformats.org/wiki/hcalendar*.

[‡] See *http://www.gmpg.org/xfn/*.

and aggregate. News sites, weblogs, forums, and many other kinds of sites that update frequently often use these formats to create feeds describing their latest news. This makes it easier for readers to see what's new using software that checks all of their feeds automatically instead of having to visit every website, and it makes it much simpler to create sites whose content is gathered from other sites. There are several competing formats, including a number called RSS (but with different meanings for the acronym) and the more recent Atom format.

 Atom includes two pieces, the Atom Syndication Format and the Atom Publishing Protocol. The first is an XML-based data format, while the second is an HTTP-based protocol for editing and publishing resources that generally follows REST principles.

Presentation and scripting

Pure textual data gives the Web a solid foundation, but making it interesting, and supporting the level of interactivity required for Web 2.0 functionality, requires something more. Web browsers typically support two layers of additional functionality for making the textual data visually interesting and more interactive: styles and scripting.

A style, usually provided by Cascading Style Sheets (CSS), supplies the color, layout, fontography, and more for documents. Much of this used to be done in HTML directly, but separating the presentation information makes it much easier to create attractive and flexible styles for many documents at once. Changing a background color across a site shouldn't require visiting every page on the site and changing it there.

Scripting, usually provided by JavaScript, lets web developers create interfaces that respond more directly to user requests. Scripting can capture user interactions with a page and modify the HTML document or the stylesheet for the page in response. Dynamic HTML (DHTML) uses these techniques within the context of a single page, while AJAX (described earlier) adds the `XMLHTTPRequest` object to allow the scripts to communicate with a server to support many more complex interface possibilities.

Graphics

Graphics have been a part of the Web since most people noticed it. The Mosaic browser added the `IMG` tag in 1993, and pictures have been part of the Web ever since. Formats (JPEG, GIF, PNG, SVG) come and go, and a few new features (such as animation and transparency) have been introduced along the way, but graphics have mostly stayed within the same general parameters inside of web pages. Scripts can, of course, modify them and use them like everything else, making them interface components as well as content and decoration.

Multimedia

For many developers, the interactive capabilities of the early Web just weren't enough. Scripting made some interactivity possible, but it was slow, limited, and varied from browser to browser. Plug-ins—most notably Adobe's Flash—provided an alternative approach for supporting fast animation, more interactivity, and more control over features such as video and sound. (Plug-ins like QuickTime and RealPlayer supported particular audio and video formats, but Flash has remained more versatile.)

Although web browsers have evolved to support AJAX, even in ways that support functionality across multiple browsers, there's little sign that Flash is going away. It's even found new competition in Microsoft's Silverlight, which offers a similar experience built using Microsoft's development tools. Rich Internet Applications (RIAs) often include Flash, Silverlight, or similar plug-ins to create a more interactive experience than is easily done within the browser itself.

Semantics

The relation of semantics to the Web has been a hot—but difficult—topic of conversation for over a decade. Enthusiasts describe the Semantic Web as the next generation of the Internet, or even as "Web 3.0." Building semantics into the Web, however, has been a slow process.

Semantics involves the exploration of meanings. Semantics researchers often talk about definitions for declaring the semantics of a "thing." Although this approach seems simple, it's deeply complex. Definitions are intrinsically linked to the contexts in which the items or concepts in question are being examined or contemplated. A glass of water sitting on your dinner table means something slightly different from what it would if it were approaching your car's windshield at 100 mph as you drove on an expressway.

Another problem concerns the grounding of semantics in the real world. English dictionaries are really just large sets of circular references—each term is defined in terms of other words within the dictionary, those words are defined by others, and so on. So what makes something semantically meaningful? It needs to be grounded by *reference*.

The concept of semantic reference is easy to demonstrate with an example. Imagine you're at an Indian restaurant and you have to explain the semantics of "spicy" to someone who is from a distant galaxy. The conversation would be difficult (for simplicity's sake, just assume that the alien is fluent in English, except for the fact that he doesn't know the definition of "spicy"):

> *Alien*: Can I have some of that curry to eat?
> *You*: Yes, but be careful, it's spicy.
> *Alien*: What is "spicy"?
> *You*: It is sort of like hot, but not from heat. It will burn you, but not like a hot thing.
> *Alien* (looking very puzzled): I am not sure that I understand.
> *You*: It's damn S-P-I-C-Y! Just taste it!!

Without some form of grounding (in this case, experiencing a spicy dish burning your tongue), semantics are difficult to convey.

Applications—even web applications—cannot taste spicy food (trust us; we tried once at a party). Some people have simply stated that we need to use semantic tagging with a common, agreed-upon taxonomy, but that approach has been discredited. Although large, top-down frameworks have struggled for years trying to develop cognitive capabilities for applications, Web 2.0 applications often generate *folksonomies*, which seem to arise from nowhere (technically, from users providing tagging without much coordination) and become useful standards. Although many scientists still struggle with this bottom-up approach to semantics, few who have used tag clouds can argue that this pattern provides no value. The value of folksonomies to the ontological community has been the subject of discussion in various semantic circles, including most recently the Ontology Forum. (An *ontology* is a shared conceptualization of a domain and, by definition, states some rules and logic that capture the lexicon of that domain.) The inclusion of folksonomies in the 2007 Ontology Summit[§] illustrates that formal semantics research is interested in understanding the intrinsic value that folksonomies bring.

There is a distinct possibility that the Tag Cloud pattern (which we discuss as part of the Collaborative Tagging pattern in Chapter 7) represents a learning pattern similar to that which living organisms use to link a written token, such as a word, to a concept. Another pattern documented in Chapter 7, the Semantic Web Grounding pattern, is an advancement in the field of semantic applications. Could Web 2.0 be the best chance that humanity has at artificial intelligence? Although not quantifiable, the prospect is hard to ignore.

On a grand scale, semantics represents a far more contentious issue than this book can capture. XML encouraged some people to think that all you have to do is define some elements, and all the content in the world can be "tagged" in a way we can all understand. It doesn't work that way, though, because potential readers need to know an awful lot about the tags. Nevertheless, XML by itself does let people make references, and there are some newer approaches in semantics research that might one day have a huge impact on the Web. Some current technologies, such as the Ontology Web Language (OWL) and the Resource Description Framework (RDF), can be expressed in XML to make semantic declarations. Via the use of unique structured attributes, elements can also be linked to concepts within ontologies. XML's versatility will likely ensure that it plays a supporting role in the evolution of the Internet, and it has already brought about many changes in the Internet in the past decade.

§ See *http://ontolog.cim3.net/forum/ontology-summit/2007-03/msg00028.html*.

In the next chapter, we will apply the knowledge outlined in this chapter and dissect some of the examples of Web 1.0 and Web 2.0 that were illustrated in Figure 1-1. By dissecting these examples, we can start to inspect the patterns behind them and create a working knowledge base of some key differences between the Internet of the 1990s and Web 2.0.

CHAPTER 3

Dissecting Web 2.0 Examples

*"Web 1.0 was about connecting computers and making
technology more efficient for computers. Web 2.0 is
about connecting people and making technology
efficient for people."*

—Dan Zambonini

So, what actually changed between the emergence of Web 1.0 and Web 2.0? In this
chapter, we'll compare Web 1.0 companies and technologies with Web 2.0 companies
and technologies to begin developing the design patterns that distinguish them. We
use the term "Web 1.0" to refer to the Web as it was understood in the period of around
1995–2000, though obviously it's not a simple matter of dates. To help us get started,
Figure 3-1 shows again the list of Web 1.0 and Web 2.0 examples that Tim O'Reilly
and others compiled during an initial brainstorming session to get a "feel" for what
Web 2.0 was.

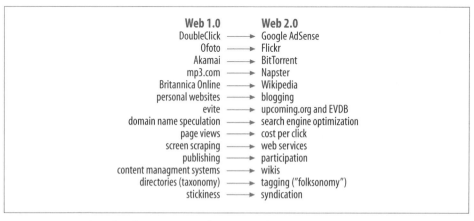

Figure 3-1. Tim's list of Web 1.0 versus Web 2.0 examples

It's important to note that some of the Web 1.0 companies included in Figure 3-1 have evolved substantially since Tim made his original comparison. For the latest information, definitely visit each company's website. Tim's choosing them as examples actually speaks to their success in that earlier age.

Although several of the companies we use as examples in this chapter are large enterprises or corporations, the patterns themselves don't apply only to enterprises. In fact, the value of patterns is that you can remove them from an enterprise context and reuse them in other applications. For example, Service-Oriented Architecture (SOA) is a pattern of exposing capabilities to potential end users. Whether the SOA pattern is used by online gamers to access the states of each other's joysticks or by large enterprises to reach into their customer relationship management (CRM) systems and provide users of their websites with rich interactive experiences, the core pattern is the same when abstracted to a high enough level. In both cases, a service offers some functionality or capability that another entity consumes.

DoubleClick and Google AdSense

Before we compare these two companies, we must point out that DoubleClick has vastly enhanced its platform since it was formed; so much so, in fact, that Google acquired DoubleClick in 2007 to further broaden its media advertising ambitions.[*] Therefore, instead of specifically illustrating DoubleClick's original ad model, we'll illustrate the generic pattern of banner ad impression sales that many online advertising companies used in the late 1990s.

Applicable Web 2.0 Patterns

Watch for illustrations of the following patterns in this discussion:

- Software as a Service (SaaS)
- Mashup
- Rich User Experience
- Semantic Web Grounding
- Asynchronous Particle Update

You can find more information on these patterns in Chapter 7.

---

[*] See *http://www.doubleclick.com/us/about_doubleclick/press_releases/default.asp?p=572*.

Advertising in Context

Banner ad placement originally operated on a simplistic model whereby advertisers purchased banner ads in lots (typically of 1,000 or more), and the banners were then placed on websites. The placement of these banner ads was often billed based solely on impressions, regardless of whether anyone actually clicked on the banners. This online advertising model clearly had room for improvement.

Initially, one of the main issues facing advertisers was the lack of any guarantee that the ads were effective; however, this problem was mitigated by the use of tracking software and new business models that charged based on the number of click-throughs. Another issue concerned the fact that some larger companies offering such services asked webmasters to place code in their sites and then served up ads whenever someone issued a request for a page containing that code. It was therefore quite possible that ads aimed at golfers, for example, might appear on fishing or other websites not concerned with golf. The placement pattern looked a lot like Figure 3-2.

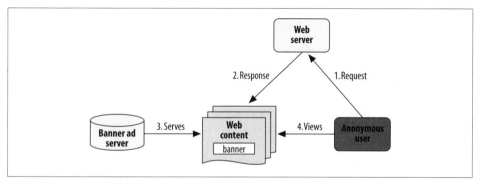

Figure 3-2. Basic pattern of banner ad placement

In contrast, Google AdSense is a paid ad service that serves contextually specific ads on web pages and tracks the number of clicks on each ad by visitors to those pages. This form of ad delivery uses a simple yet effective pattern of *contextual targeting*. Rather than just advertising blindly, AdSense attempts to quantify the context of a user's experience based on a keyword score within the web pages containing the ads. AdSense then cross-references the keywords with a list of potential target ads that might be of interest to the user of that web resource. As a result, visitors to a web page on golfing will typically see golf-related advertisements rather than completely random content. AdSense also lets web page owners filter out competitors' ads. For example, a golf club manufacturer could block competing companies' ads from being displayed on its website. This is a highly useful pattern for preventing competitors from targeting a website owner's customers. Figure 3-3 shows an example of this pattern.

Also attracting website owners to AdSense is the fact that ad revenues are split between Google and the website owner. Other banner ad companies also use this revenue model,

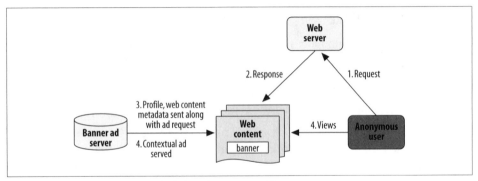

Figure 3-3. Contextual serving of ads based on user profile patterns

but AdSense users have a better chance of increasing their revenues because the ads on their sites are contextually specialized for their audiences, so users are more likely to click on them. Given the fact that net revenue from a website must be calculated once the costs of hosting are subtracted, it makes more business sense to go with a contextual pattern such as that offered by AdSense than with a non-contextual pattern.

A Peek at the Future of Online Advertising

Serving contextually specific information based on a single site visit is only one aspect of how online advertising is changing. With the evolution of the Internet and some underlying technologies, the science of targeted advertising is reaching new heights. Dr. Usama Fayyad, chief data officer and senior vice president of Research & Strategic Data Solutions at Yahoo!, stated in the March 2007 issue of *Business 2.0* magazine, "I know more about your intent than any 1,000 keywords you could type."[†] He knows this because of his Yahoo! research into the click-stream consciousness of web users. Dr. Fayyad is an actual rocket scientist who worked at NASA's Jet Propulsion Laboratory before moving to Yahoo! to manage the roughly 12 terabytes of user data—more than the entire content of the Library of Congress—that Yahoo! collects every day.

Yahoo! tracks user behavior with a multitude of technologies, including cookies, user account activity, bounce rates, and searches. The major search engine vendors have acquired the ability to build comprehensive user profiles based not just on contextual information from a single web page, but on many aspects of a user's behavior. For instance, Yahoo! and Google have created services that consumers can use to help them build successful businesses and/or websites. Along those lines, Yahoo!'s acquisition of Overture let people target search terms based on available inventory. Overture's tools can tell an advertiser how many people search for a specific term in a given month, as well as suggesting similar terms.

---

† See *http://money.cnn.com/magazines/business2/business2_archive/2007/03/01/8401043/index.htm*.

Another trend in Web 2.0 advertising is the move away from traditional graphic banner ads and toward text and video media. Bandwidth-light text has an advantage thanks in part to the increasing use of cell phones as people's primary devices for connecting to the Internet. Jupiter Research reported a trend of growth in all three categories (text, graphical banners, and video), implying either that there are more advertisers or that advertisers are continuing to pull financial resources away from traditional media such as television, magazines, and newspapers.[‡] This phenomenon must be somewhat scary to the incumbent media giants, especially when coupled with the recent history of small upstart Internet companies becoming the largest media sources within just a few years (YouTube and MySpace are good examples).

A third trend concerns the delivery of ever more targeted content. Engaging users in a context in which they're open to an ad's content requires walking a narrow line. Many bloggers make a few dollars a month on Google AdWords, but some deliver a more immersive experience, even using text ads within RSS feeds and carrying ads into their readers' aggregators. This can be effective, but if consumers are bombarded with ads, the entire mechanism starts to void itself out, as the human mind starts to filter out too-frequent advertisements.

ENTREPRENEUR ALERT

Contextually specific targeting is continually creating new opportunities. Instead of the traditional model of using websites as targets to deliver context-specific ads, imagine a plug-in to a calendar application that delivers relevant and appealing ads. For example, if you entered "travel to Spain" in a web-based calendar-planner application, the keywords used for the entry ("travel" and "Spain") could be registered against an index of ads that might be relevant. Some examples might be ads for Spanish translation books or other media to help you learn the language, or ads for tour guides, clothes that might be fitting for the region, travel insurance, and so on.

Online travel agencies already invoke this upsell pattern when you book airline tickets on their sites; however, the concept/pattern could be repurposed. iTunes uses a similar profiling feature to contextually deliver ads to your screen. As devices like the iPhone become GPS-aware, applications can deliver much more useful targeted content.

The ideas are there; hopefully some of you will figure out a way to capitalize on them.

Web 2.0 hasn't done much about the pressing question of how society will continue to react to ads that are often perceived as intrusive and unwelcome. We're referring to one of the most hated words since the dawn of the Internet: *spam*.

Email spam is probably the most despised form of advertising on the Web. Despite numerous mechanisms (such as spam filters and legislation) to control it, spam is still rampant. Like spam, banner ads also permeate many corners of the Internet and are

[‡] See *http://www.jupiterresearch.com/bin/item.pl/research:concept/87/id=99415/*.

common on many web pages. Do banner ads drive people away or do they provide value? Users have expressed time and again that sites that are uncluttered with commercial messages are more attractive. Google was widely heralded as setting a new model for search engines with a simple, noncommercial interface, although web historians could point out that Alta Vista was just as clean in its lack of commercialism. Consumers and users flocked to Google.com when it launched: it provided information they wanted without bombarding them with advertising. Similar models have evolved from companies such as Flickr (discussed in the next section), although the old-world ways of commercial ads still permeate much of the Internet landscape (even to pervasive levels within newer presences such as YouTube and MySpace).

Some have even organized communities to fight advertising. The most notable is Adbusters, an organization based in Vancouver, Canada. Adbusters is a global network of artists, activists, writers, pranksters, students, educators, and entrepreneurs who want a new social activism movement piggybacked on the information age. Their goal is simple: anarchy. Their aim is to topple existing power structures and forge a major shift in the way we'll live in the 21st century. In a similar vein, Canadian film producer Jill Sharpe released a documentary called *Culture Jam*,[§] a stab back at our mainstream media and advertising agencies. "Culture jamming" is a form of public activism that is generally in opposition to commercialism.[‖]

Despite these challenges, Google AdSense delivers a service that many people use and serves ad content that can be mashed into most websites. Google has provided many other value ad services that make it easy for anyone to become an advertiser and get some value for her budget. Google's stock price continues to rise as a reflection of its perceived strength and dominant position in the new advertising industry.

Ofoto and Flickr

Ofoto began life as an online photography service based in Berkeley, California. The service provided three basic features:

- It let people upload JPEG images so that others could view them by simply visiting the website.
- It let people create photo albums and share them online with friends.
- It enabled users to purchase prints online. This feature was supposed to be the foundation for Ofoto's business model, which was based on the premise that people would want traditional, printed photographs.

Ofoto later added a 35mm online film processing service and an online frame store, as well as some other services, but its core pattern still embraced a core model of static

[§] See *http://www.culturejamthefilm.com*.

[‖] See *http://en.wikipedia.org/wiki/Culture_jamming*.

publishing. In May 2001, Eastman Kodak purchased Ofoto, and the Ofoto Web Service was rebranded in 2005 as the Kodak EasyShare Gallery.

Flickr is another photo-sharing platform, but it was built with the online community in mind, rather than the idea of selling prints. Flickr made it simple for people to tag or comment on each other's images, and for developers to incorporate Flickr into their own applications. Flickr is properly a community platform and is justifiably seen as one of the exemplars of the Web 2.0 movement. The site's design and even the dropped *e* in the company name are now firmly established in Web 2.0's vernacular.

Applicable Web 2.0 Patterns

This comparison involves the following patterns:

- Software as a Service (SaaS)
- Participation-Collaboration
- Mashup
- Rich User Experience
- The Synchronized Web
- Collaborative Tagging
- Declarative Living and Tag Gardening
- Persistent Rights Management

You can find more information on these patterns in Chapter 7.

Collaboration and Tagging

Flickr is often used as an information source for other Web 2.0 platforms or mechanisms. It offers simple application programming interfaces (APIs) for accessing its content, enabling third parties to present images in new contexts and to access and use Flickr's services in their own mashups or other applications. Bloggers commonly use it as an online photo repository that they can easily connect to their own sites, but the APIs offer much more opportunity than that. Programmers can create applications that can perform almost any function available on the Flickr website. The list of possible operations is vast and covers most of the normal graphical user interface's capabilities.

 Flickr also lets developers choose which tools they want to use to access its services. It supports a REST-like interface, the XML Remote Procedure Call (XML-RPC), and SOAP (and responses in all three of those), plus JSON and PHP. For more, see *http://www.flickr.com/services/api/*.

Developers can easily repurpose Flickr's core content in mashups, thanks to its open architecture and collaborative nature. A mashup combines information or computing resources from multiple services into a single new application. Often, in the resulting view two or more applications appear to be working together. A classic example of a mashup would be to overlay Google Maps with Craigslist housing/rental listings or listings of items for sale in the displayed region.

Flickr's API and support for mashups are part of a larger goal: encouraging collaboration on the site, drawing in more users who can then make each others' content more valuable. Flickr's value lies partly in its large catalog of photos, but also in the metadata users provide to help themselves navigate that huge collection.

When owners originally upload their digital assets to Flickr, they can use keyword tags to categorize their work. In theory, they do this to make it easier to search for and locate digital photos. However, having users tag their photos themselves only starts to solve search problems. A single view of keywords won't work reliably, because people think independently and are likely to assign different keywords to the same images. Allowing other people to provide their own tags builds a much richer and more useful indexing system, often called a folksonomy.

A folksonomy (as opposed to a top-down taxonomy) is built over time via contributions by multiple humans or agents interacting with a resource. Those humans or agents apply tags—natural-language words or phrases—that they feel accurately label what the resource represents. The tags are then available for others to view, sharing clues about the resource. The theory behind folksonomies is that because they include a large number of perspectives, the resulting set of tags will align with most people's views of the resources in question.# The tags may even be in disparate languages, making them globally useful.

Consider an example. Say you upload a photo of an automobile and tag it as such. Even though a human would understand that someone looking for "automobile" might find photos tagged with "car" to be relevant, if the system used only a simple form of text matching someone searching for "vehicle," "car," or "transportation" might not find your image. This is because a comparison of the string of characters in "automobile" and a search string such as "car" won't produce a positive match. By letting others add their own tags to resources, Flickr increases the number of tags for each photo and thereby increases the likelihood that searchers will find what they're looking for. In addition to tagging your "automobile" photo with related words such as "vehicle," "car," or "transportation," viewers might also use tags that are tangentially relevant (perhaps you thought the automobile was the core subject of the photo, but someone else might notice the nice "sunset" in the background and use that tag).

With this in mind, how would you tag the photo in Figure 3-4?

\# Flickr's tagging is effective, but it represents only one style of folksonomy: a narrow folksonomy. For more information on different styles of folksonomy, see *http://www.personalinfocloud.com/2005/02/explaining _and_.html*.

Figure 3-4. How would you tag this photo?

We might tag the photo in Figure 3-4 with the following keywords: "mountain," "bike," "Duane," "Nickull," "1996," "dual," and "slalom." With Flickr, others can tag the photo with additional meaningful keywords, such as "cycling," "competition," "race," "bicycle," and "off-road," making subsequent searches more fruitful. Semantic tagging may require more thought, but as a general rule, the more minds there are adding more tags, the better the folksonomy will turn out.

Flickr has also built an interface that lets people visiting the site see the most popular tags. This is implemented as a *tag cloud*, an example of which appears in Figure 3-5.

07 africa amsterdam animals architecture art asia august australia baby barcelona beach berlin birthday black blackandwhite blue boston bw california cameraphone camping canada canon car cat chicago china christmas church city clouds color concert day de dog england europe fall family festival film florida flower flowers food football france friends fun garden geotagged germany girl graffiti greece green halloween hawaii hiking holiday home honeymoon house india ireland island italy japan july june kids la lake landscape light live london macro may me mexico mountain mountains museum music nature new newyork newyorkcity newzealand night nikon nyc ocean paris park party people photos portrait red river roadtrip rock rome san sanfrancisco scotland sea seattle show sky snow spain spring street summer sun sunset sydney taiwan texas thailand tokyo toronto tour travel tree trees trip uk urban usa vacation vancouver washington water wedding white winter yellow york zoo

Figure 3-5. Flickr tag cloud, from http://www.flickr.com/photos/tags/

The tag cloud illustrates the value of a bidirectional visibility relationship between resources and tags. If you're viewing a resource, you can find the tags with which the resource has been tagged. The more times a tag has been applied to a resource, the larger it appears in the tag cloud. You can also click on a tag to see what other assets are tagged with the same term.

ENTREPRENEUR ALERT

Tag clouds are just a visualization of what people are thinking about. Analyzing tags to see what new trends are emerging offers opportunities to find trends ahead of everyone else, giving you a head start in creating sites that are relevant to those trends and developing an audience.

There are some rudimentary tie-ins today, but figuring out a way to feed tag information into major search engines in real time could also lead to much more intuitive searches based on an up-to-date index. Technorati and Delicious led the way in implementing a pattern of using popular tags to find resources via their own websites; however, there are many other opportunities for using the Collaborative Tagging pattern on content other than blogs.

Another advancement Flickr offers is the ability to categorize photos into *sets*, or groups of photos that fall under the same metadata categories or headings. Flickr's sets represent a form of categorical metadata rather than a physical hierarchy. Sets can contain an infinite number of photos and may exist in the absence of any photos. Photos can exist independently of any sets; they don't have to be members of a set yet can be members of any number of sets. These sets demonstrate capabilities far beyond those of traditional photo albums, given that each digital photo can belong to multiple sets, one set, or no sets. In the physical world, this can't happen without making multiple copies of the photos.

Akamai and BitTorrent

Both Akamai and BitTorrent address the challenge of distributing large volumes of information across huge networks, striving to minimize bandwidth consumption and delays that users might notice. Their approaches to solving these problems, however, are very different.

Applicable Web 2.0 Patterns

This comparison discusses the following patterns:

- Service-Oriented Architecture
- Software as a Service
- Participation-Collaboration
- The Synchronized Web

You can find more information on these patterns in Chapter 7.

Alternate Solutions to Bandwidth

Akamai and BitTorrent both avoid the issue of a single host trying to supply bandwidth-intensive content to a potentially global audience. A single server starts to slow down as it reaches its maximum capability, and the network in the immediate vicinity of the host server is affected because it's handling a higher amount of traffic.

Again, the incumbent in this case (Akamai) has significantly changed its mechanics and infrastructure since the date of the original brainstorming session when the comparison of Web 1.0 and Web 2.0 was made (as depicted in Figure 3-1). Accordingly, understanding the patterns and advantages of each system is a good idea for budding Web 2.0 entrepreneurs. You shouldn't view Akamai as antiquated. It is performing tremendously well financially, far outstripping many of the Web 2.0 companies mentioned in this book. It's been one of NASDAQ's top-performing stocks, reporting 47% growth and revenues of $636 million in 2007. With 26,000 servers, Akamai is also a huge Internet infrastructure asset.

Akamai's original approach was to sell customers a distributed content-caching service. Its aim was simply to resolve bandwidth issues, and it solved that problem very well. If a customer like CNN News decided to host a video of a newscast, the content on the CNN server would be pulled through the Akamai network. The centrally located CNN server bank would modify the URIs of the video and other bandwidth-intensive content by morphing them to URLs of resources that were easier for the client making the request to access, often because they were hosted in physically closer locations. The client's browser would load the HTML template, which would tell it to hit the Akamai network for the additional resources it required to complete the content-rendering process. At the time of this writing, end users do not see any indication of Akamai.com being used (although streaming videos do require modification of URLs).

Figure 3-6 shows Akamai's core architecture (as analyzed when used in Figure 3-1).

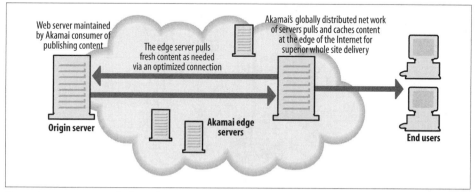

Figure 3-6. Overview of Akamai core pattern (courtesy of Akamai)

Pulling richer media (the larger files) from a system closer to the end user improves the user experience because it results in faster-loading content and streams that are more reliable and less susceptible to changes in routing or bandwidth capabilities between the source and target. Note that the Akamai EdgeComputing infrastructure is federated worldwide and users can pull files as required. Although Akamai is best known for handling HTML, graphics, and video content, it also offers accelerators for business applications such as WebSphere and SAP and has a new suite to accelerate AJAX applications.

BitTorrent is also a technology for distributing large amounts of data widely, without the original distributor incurring all the costs associated with hardware, hosting, and bandwidth resources. However, as illustrated in Figure 3-7, it uses a peer-to-peer (P2P) architecture quite different from Akamai's. Instead of the distributor alone servicing each recipient, in BitTorrent the recipients also supply data to newer recipients, significantly reducing the cost and burden on any one source, providing redundancy against system problems, and reducing dependence on the original distributor. This encompasses the concept of a "web of participation," often touted as one of the key changes in Web 2.0.

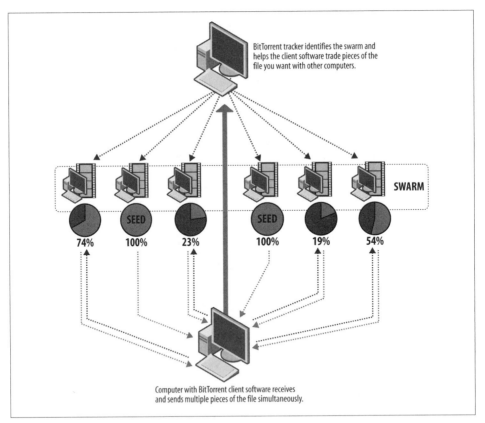

Figure 3-7. BitTorrent's pattern of P2P distribution

BitTorrent enables this pattern by getting its users to download and install a client application that acts as a peer node to regulate upstream and downstream caching of content. The viral-like propagation of files provides newer clients with several places from which they can retrieve files, making their download experiences smoother and faster than if they all downloaded from a single web server. Each person participates in such a way that the costs of keeping the network up and running are shared, mitigating bottlenecks in network traffic. It's a classic architecture of participation and so qualifies for Web 2.0 status, even if BitTorrent is not strictly a "web app."

The BitTorrent protocol is open to anyone who wants to implement it. Using the protocol, each connected peer should be able to prepare, request, and transmit files over the network. To use the BitTorrent protocol to share a file, the owner of the file must first create a "torrent" file. The usual convention is to append *.torrent* to the end of the filename. Every **.torrent* file must specify the URL of the tracker via an "announce" element. The file also contains an "info" section that contains a (suggested) name for the file, its length, and its metadata. BitTorrent clients use the Secure Hashing Algorithm-1 (SHA-1) to make declarations that let any client detect whether the file is intact and complete.

Decentralization has always been a hallmark of the Internet, appearing in many different guises that come (and sometimes go) in waves. Architecturally, this pattern represents a great way to guard against points of failure or slowdowns, as it is both self-scaling and self-healing.[*] A very elegant architectural trait of peer to peer in particular is that the more people there are interested in a file, the more it will propagate, resulting in more copies being available for download to help meet the demand.

MP3.com and Napster

By the time the first Web 2.0 conversations started, the first incarnations of MP3.com and Napster were both effectively history. Neither of them was particularly well liked by the music industry, for reasons that feed into Web 2.0 but aren't critical to the comparison between them. Their business stories share a common thread of major shift in the way music is distributed, but the way they went about actually transferring music files was very different, mirroring the Akamai/BitTorrent story in many ways.

Applicable Web 2.0 Patterns

Some of the technical patterns illustrated by this comparison are:

---

[*] Cloud computing, in which developers trust their programs to run as services on others' hardware, may seem like a return to centralization ("All those programs run on Amazon S3 and EC2...."). The story is more complicated than that, however, as cloud computing providers have the opportunity to give their customers the illusion of centralization and the easy configuration that comes with it, while supporting a decentralized infrastructure underneath.

- Service-Oriented Architecture
- Software as a Service
- Participation-Collaboration
- The Synchronized Web
- Collaborative Tagging
- Declarative Living and Tag Gardening
- Persistent Rights Management

You can find more information on these patterns in Chapter 7.

Shifting Patterns and Costs of Music Distribution

The music industry has historically been composed of three main groups: those who create music (writing, recording, or producing it); those who consume it; and those who are part of the conventional recording and music distribution industry, who sit in the middle (see Figure 3-8).

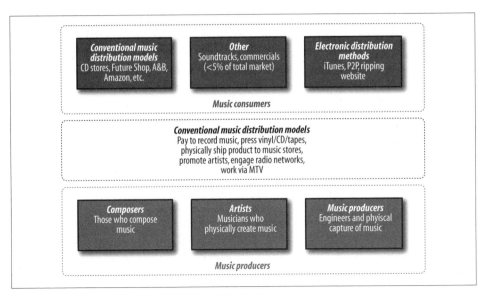

Figure 3-8. Conventional music industry model

Historically, music publishing and distribution has been done via physical media, from 78s to CDs. If you abstract the pattern of this entire process, you can easily see that the storage of music on physical media is grossly inefficient (see Figure 3-9).

Figure 3-10 contains two "Digital Signal" points in the sequence. The persistence to some form of physical storage medium is unnecessary for people who are capable of working directly with the digital signal. If you're providing a digital signal at the source,

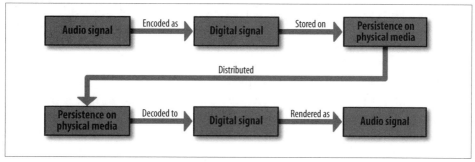

Figure 3-9. Distribution pattern for audio content

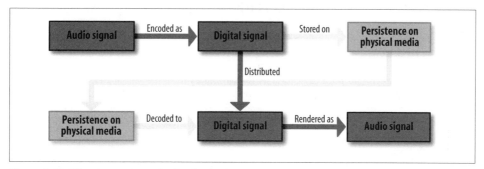

Figure 3-10. The electronic music distribution pattern

the signal can travel from the source to its ultimate target in this digital form, and the media is consumed as a digital signal, why would it make sense to use a non-digital storage medium (such as CD, vinyl, or tape) as an intermediate step? The shift to digital MP3 files has made the middle steps unnecessary. Figure 3-10 depicts a simpler model that has many advantages, except to those whose business models depend on physical distribution.

For instance, this new pattern is better for the environment, because it does not involve turning petroleum products into records and CDs, or transporting physical goods thousands of miles. It satisfies people's cravings for instant gratification, and it lets consumers store the music on physical media if they want, by burning CDs or recording digital audio tapes.

The old model also had one massive stumbling block: it arguably suppressed a large percentage of artists. For a conventional record company to sign a new artist, it must make a substantial investment in that artist. This covers costs associated with such things as recording the music, building the die for pressing it into physical media, and printing CD case covers, as well as the costs associated with manufacturing and distributing the media. The initial costs are substantial: even an artist who perhaps produces only 250,000 CDs may cost a record company $500,000 to sign initially. This doesn't include the costs of promoting the artist or making music videos. Estimates vary significantly, but it's our opinion that as a result, the conventional industry signs only one out of every 10,000 artists or so. If a higher percentage were signed, it might dilute each artist's visibility and ability to perform. After all, there are only so many venues and only so many people willing to go to live shows.

An industry size issue compounds this problem. If the global market were flooded with product, each artist could expect to capture a certain portion of that market. For argument's sake, let's assume that each artist garners 1,000 CD sales on average. Increasing the total number of artists would cause each artist's share of the market to decrease. For the companies managing the physical inventory, it's counterproductive to have too much product available in the marketplace. As more products came to market, the dilution factor would impact sales of existing music to the point where it might jeopardize the record company's ability to recoup its initial investment in each artist.

 Love's Manifesto, a speech given by Courtney Love during a music conference, illuminates several of the problems inherent in the music industry today and is a brilliant exposé of what is wrong with the industry as a *whole* (pun intended) and the realities faced by artists. You can read the speech online at *http://www.indie-music.com/modules.php?name=News&file=article&sid=820.*

Producers and online distributors of digital music benefit from two major cost reductions. In addition to not having to deal with physical inventory and all its costs, they also offload the cost of recording music onto the artists, minimizing some of the risk associated with distributing the work of previously unsigned bands. These companies often adopt a more "hands off" approach. Unlike conventional record companies, online MP3 retailers can easily acquire huge libraries of thousands of new, previously unsigned artists. They don't need to censor whose music they can publish based on their perceptions of the marketplace, because adding tracks to their labels poses minimal risk. (They do still face some of the same legal issues as their conventional predecessors, though—notably, those associated with copyright.)

This approach also has significant benefits for many artists. Instead of having to convince a record company that they'll sell enough music to make the initial outlay worthwhile, new independent artists can go directly to the market and build their own followings, demonstrating to record companies why they're worth signing. AFI, for example, was the first MySpace band to receive more than 500,000 listens in one day. Self-promotion and building up their own followings allows clever artists to avoid record companies while still achieving some success.

In this model, artists become responsible for creating their own music. Once they have content, they may publish their music via companies such as Napster and MP3.com. Imagine a fictional company called OurCo. OurCo can assimilate the best of both the

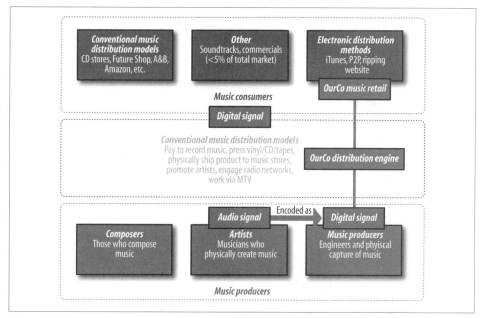

Figure 3-11. The best of the old and the new distribution models

old and the new distribution models and act as a private label distribution engine, as depicted in Figure 3-11.

ENTREPRENEUR ALERT

Entrepreneurs will note that Internet distribution of other file types is already happening. The YouTube revolution and the distribution of several other formats (such as photos, audio, telephony, television signals, and independent news reports) attest to the fact that this pattern is valuable and important for businesspeople to understand.

So where are the next revolutions going to occur? If you look at the patterns and workflow of creating and distributing audio and video files, you'll notice that they could also be applied to other content distributed via the Internet.

Music creation has conventionally been done in a recording studio. The workflow looks like that shown in Figure 3-12.

This workflow doesn't have to happen synchronously. Several new Internet startups have developed online portals that let musicians lay down individual audio tracks, and then upload them and have other artists add their own tracks. Companies such as Mix2r, MixMatchMusic, and Gluejam facilitate this sort of online music creation. Other startups looking to facilitate the same sort of workflow for video production include Jeremy Allaire's new venture, Brightcove.

Whenever an electronic signal is involved in a pattern, determine what advantages can be wrought from allowing the electronic signal to be distributed over the Internet.

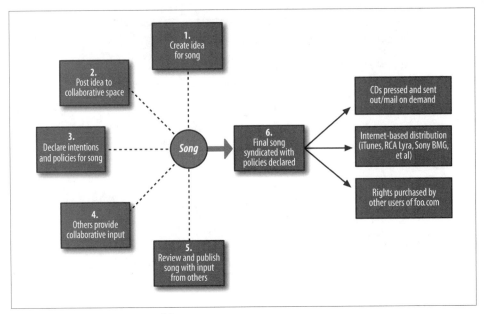

Figure 3-12. Music creation workflow

MP3.com and Napster Infrastructures

When analyzing P2P infrastructures, we must recognize the sophistication of the current file-sharing infrastructures. The concepts of a web of participation and collaboration form the backbone of how resources flow and stream in Web 2.0. Napster is a prime example of how P2P networks can become popular in a short time and—in stark contrast to MP3.com—can embrace the concepts of participation and collaboration among users.

MP3.com, started because its founder realized that many people were searching for "mp3," was originally launched as a website where members could share their MP3 files with each other.

 The original MP3.com ceased to operate at the end of 2003. CNET now operates the domain name, supplying artist information and other metadata regarding audio files.

The first iteration of MP3.com featured charts defined by genre and geographical area, as well as statistical data for artists indicating which of their songs were more popular. Artists could subscribe to a free account, a Gold account, or a Platinum account, each providing additional features and stats. Though there was no charge for downloading music from MP3.com, people did have to sign up with an email address, and online advertisements were commonplace across the site. Although MP3.com hosted songs from known artists, the vast majority of the playlist comprised songs by unsigned or independent musicians and producers. Eventually MP3.com launched "Pay for Play," which was a major upset to the established music industry. The idea was that each artist would receive payments based on the number of listens or downloads from the MP3.com site.

The original technical model that MP3.com employed was a typical client/server pattern using a set of centralized servers, as shown in Figure 3-13.

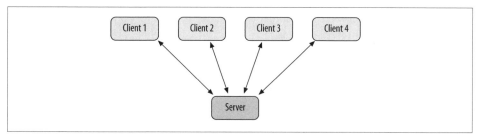

Figure 3-13. Typical client/server architecture model

MP3.com engineers eventually changed to a new model (perhaps due to scalability issues) that used a set of federated servers acting as proxies for the main server. This variation of the original architectural pattern—depicted in Figure 3-14 using load balancing and clusters of servers—was a great way to distribute resources and balance loads, but it still burdened MP3.com with the expense of hosting files. (Note that in a P2P system, clients are referred to as "nodes," as they are no longer mere receivers of content: each node in a P2P network is capable of acting as both client and server.)

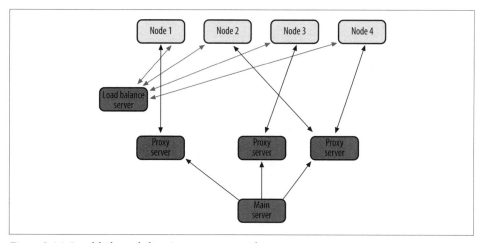

Figure 3-14. Load-balanced client/server pattern with proxies

In Figure 3-14, all nodes first communicate with the load balancing server to find out where to resolve or retrieve the resources they require. The load balancing server replies with the information based on its knowledge of which proxies are in a position to serve the requested resources. Based on that information, each node makes a direct request to the appropriate node. This pattern is common in many web architectures today.

Napster took a different path. Rather than maintaining the overhead of a direct client/server infrastructure, Napster revolutionized the industry by introducing the concept of a shared, decentralized P2P architecture. It worked quite differently from the typical client/server model but was very similar conceptually to the BitTorrent model. One key central component remained: keeping lists of all of the peers for easy searching. This component not only created scalability issues, but also exposed the company to the legal liability that ultimately did it in.

Napster also introduced a pattern of "Opting Out, Not Opting In." As soon as you downloaded and installed the Napster client software, you became, by default, part of a massive P2P network of music file sharers. Unless you specifically opted out, you remained part of the network. This allowed Napster to grow at an exponential rate. It also landed several Napster users in legal trouble, as they did not fully understand the consequences of installing the software.

P2P architectures can generally be classified into two main types. The first is a pure P2P architecture where each node acts as a client and a server. There is no central server or DNS-type node to coordinate traffic, and all traffic is routed based on each node's knowledge of other nodes and the protocols used. BitTorrent, for example, can operate in this mode. This type of network architecture (also referred to as an *ad hoc architecture*) works when nodes are configured to act as both servers and clients. It is similar conceptually to how mobile radios work, except that it uses a point-to-point cast rather than a broadcast communication protocol. Figure 3-15 depicts this type of network.

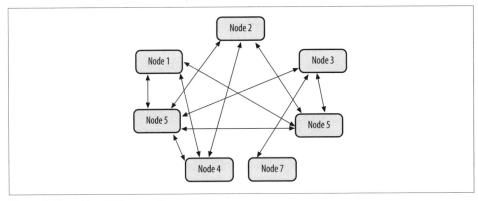

Figure 3-15. Ad hoc P2P network

In this pure-play P2P network, no central authority determines or orchestrates the actions of the other nodes. By comparison, a centrally orchestrated P2P network includes a central authority that takes care of orchestration and essentially acts as a traffic cop, as shown in Figure 3-16.

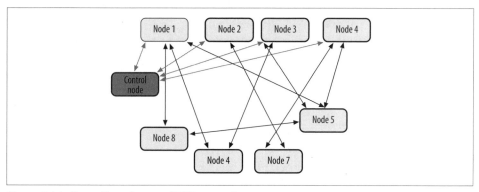

Figure 3-16. Centrally orchestrated P2P network

The control node in Figure 3-16 keeps track of the status and libraries of each peer node to help orchestrate where other nodes can find the information they seek. Peers themselves store the information and can act as both clients and servers. Each node is responsible for updating the central authority regarding its status and resources.

Napster itself was a sort of hybrid P2P system, allowing direct P2P traffic and maintaining some control over resources to facilitate resource location. Figure 3-17 shows the classic Napster architecture.

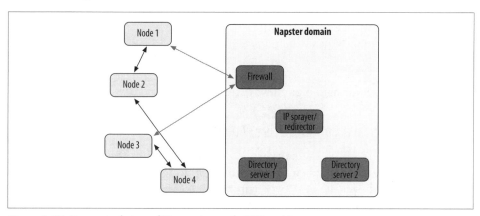

Figure 3-17. Conceptual view of Napster's mostly P2P architecture

Napster central directories tracked the titles of content in each P2P node. When users signed up for and downloaded Napster, they ended up with the P2P node software running on their own machines. This software pushed information to the Napster domain. Each node searching for content first communicated with the IP Sprayer/Redirector via the Napster domain. The IP Sprayer/Redirector maintained knowledge of the state of the entire network via the directory servers and redirected nodes to nodes that were able to fulfill its requests. Napster, and other companies such as LimeWire, are based on hybrid P2P patterns because they also allow direct node-to-node ad hoc connections for some types of communication.

Both Napster and MP3.com, despite now being defunct, revolutionized the music industry. MySpace.com has since added a new dimension into the mix: social networking. Social networking layered on top of the music distribution model continues to evolve, creating new opportunities for musicians and fans.

Britannica Online and Wikipedia

A disruptive technology can do more than cost a business money. Sometimes the disruption extends so deep that the virtues of the business's past become problems, and techniques that would previously have been vices suddenly become virtues. The emergence of Wikipedia and its overshadowing of the Encyclopedia Britannica is one case where the rules changed decisively in favor of an upstart challenger.

Applicable Web 2.0 Patterns

The collaborative encyclopedia approach ushered in by Wikipedia capitalizes on several Web 2.0 patterns:

- Software as a Service
- Participation-Collaboration
- Rich User Experience
- The Synchronized Web
- Collaborative Tagging

You can find more information on these patterns in Chapter 7.

From a Scholarly to a Collaborative Model

The Encyclopedia Britannica was originally published in 1768 as a three-volume set, emerging from the intellectual churn of Edinburgh. It grew quickly, reaching 21 volumes by 1801, and over the next two centuries, it solidified its reputation as a comprehensive reference to the world. Producing the printed tomes was a complex and expensive enterprise, requiring editors to judge how long to leave an edition in print, how much to change between editions, what new material to cover, and who should cover it.

The possibility of an electronic edition was in many ways a relief at first. The Encyclopedia Britannica took huge strides during the computer revolution to survive a changing world. In the mid-1990s, the static book publisher tried bundling an Encyclopedia

Britannica CD with some PCs. That experiment was short-lived, as it soon became obvious that any publishing effort in the new digital age had to be dynamic. The company then migrated its entire encyclopedia set to the Web, where it was free of many of the edition-by-edition obstacles to updating that had limited its print and CD editions.

Although this was a daring move, and Britannica continues to sell its content online, the model behind the encyclopedia's creation now faced a major challenge from newcomer Wikipedia. Whereas Encyclopedia Britannica had relied upon experts and editors to create its entries, Wikipedia threw the doors open to anyone who wanted to contribute. While it seemed obvious to many that an encyclopedia created by volunteers—many of them non-experts, many of them anonymous, and some of them actually out to cause trouble—just had to be a terrible idea, Wikipedia has thrived nonetheless. Even Wikipedia's founders didn't quite know what they were getting into—Wikipedia was originally supposed to feed into a much more formal, peer-reviewed Nupedia.

In Wikipedia, rather than one authority (typically a committee of scholars) centrally defining all subjects and content, people all over the world who are interested in a certain topic can collaborate asynchronously to create a living, breathing work. Wikipedia combines the collaborative aspects of wiki sites (websites that let visitors add, remove, edit, and change content) with the presentation of authoritative content built on rich hyperlinks between subjects to facilitate ultra-fast cross-references of facts and claims.

Wikipedia does have editors, but everyone is welcome to edit. Volunteers emerge over time, editing and re-editing articles that interest them. Consistency and quality improve as more people participate, though the content isn't always perfect when first published. Anonymous visitors often make edits to correct typos or other minor errors. Defending the site against vandals (or just people with agendas) can be a challenge, especially on controversial topics, but so far the site seems to have held up. Wikipedia's openness allows it to cover nearly anything, which has created some complications as editors deleted pages they didn't consider worthy of inclusion. It's always a conversation.

The shift from a top-down editorial approach to a bottom-up approach is a painful reversal for people who expect only expert advice when they look up something—and perhaps an even harder reversal for people who've built their careers on being experts or editors. Businesses facing this kind of competition need to study whether their business models are sustainable, and whether it is possible to incorporate the bottom-up approach into their own work.

Personal Websites and Blogs

The term *blog* is short for *weblog*, a personal log (or diary) that is published on the Internet. In many cases, blogs are what personal websites were initially meant to be. Many early website gurus preached the idea that online content should always be fresh and new to keep traffic coming back. That concept holds just as true now as it did then—the content has just shifted form.

Applicable Web 2.0 Patterns

Many blogs embrace a variety of the core patterns discussed in Chapter 7, such as:

- Participation-Collaboration
- Collaborative Tagging
- Declarative Living and Tag Gardening
- Software as a Service
- Asynchronous Particle Update (the pattern behind AJAX)
- The Synchronized Web
- Structured Information (Microformats)

Shifting to Blogs and Beyond

Static personal websites were, like most websites, intended to be sources of information about specific subjects. The goal of a website was to pass information from its steward to its consumers. Some consumers might visit certain websites (personal or otherwise) only once to retrieve the information they sought; however, certain groups of users might wish to visit again to receive updated information.

In some ways, active blogs are simply personal websites that are regularly updated, though most blog platforms support features that illustrate different patterns of use. Because there are no hard rules for how frequently either a blog or a personal website should be updated, nor is it possible to classify either in a general sense, it is probably not possible to identify clear differences as patterns. However, here are a few key points that differentiate blogs:

- Blogs are built from posts—often short posts—which are usually displayed in reverse chronological order (newest first) on an organizing front page. Many blogs also support some kind of archive for older posts.
- Personal websites and blogs are both published in HTML. Blog publishing, however, usually uses a slightly different model from traditional HTML website publishing. Most blog platforms don't require authors to write HTML, letting them simply enter text for the blog in an online form. Blog hosting generally allows users to know less about their infrastructure than classic HTML publishing. Blogs' ease

of use makes them attractive to Internet users who want a web presence but have not yet bothered to learn about HTML, scripts, HTTP, FTP, and other technologies.

- Blogs often include some aspects of social networking. Mechanisms such as a *blogroll* (a list of other blogs to which the blog owner wishes to link from his blog) create mini-communities of like-minded individuals. A blogroll is a great example of the Declarative Living pattern documented in Chapter 7. Comment threads can also help create small communities around websites.

- Blogs support mechanisms for publishing information that can be retrieved via multiple patterns (like Search and Retrieve, Push, or Direct Request). Instead of readers having to request the page via HTTP GETs, they can subscribe to feeds (including Atom and RSS) to receive new posts in a different form and on a schedule more convenient to them.

Standard blog software (e.g., Blogger or WordPress) has evolved well beyond simple tools for presenting posts. The software allows readers to add their own content, tag content, create blogrolls, and host discussion forums. Some blog management software lets readers register to receive notifications when there are updates to various sections of a blog. The syndication functionality of RSS (or Atom) has become a core element of many blogs. Many blogs are updated on a daily basis, yet readers might not want to have to reload the blog page over and over until a new post is made (most blog authors do not post exact schedules listing the times their blogs are updated). It is much more efficient if the reader can register interest and then receive a notification whenever new content is published. RSS also describes the content so that readers can decide whether they want to view the actual blog.

Blogs are also moving away from pure text and graphics. All kinds of blog mutations are cropping up, including mobile blogs (known as *moblogs*), video blogs, and even group blogs.

Developers are adding tools that emphasize patterns of social interactions surrounding blogs. MyBlogLog.com has software that uses an AJAX widget to place the details of readers of a blog on the blog page itself so that you can see who else has been reading a specific blog. Figure 3-18 shows the latest readers of the Technoracle blog at the time of this writing.[†]

Most blog software also offers the ability to socially network with like-minded bloggers by adding them to your blogroll. Having your blog appear on other people's blogrolls helps to elevate your blog's status in search engines, as well as in blog directories such as Technorati that track blog popularity. It also makes a statement about your personality and your stance on a variety of subjects. Figure 3-19 shows an example of a blogroll.

[†] See *http://technoracle.blogspot.com*.

Figure 3-18. Screenshot of MyBlogLog.com blog widget

A blogroll is a good example of the Declarative Living and Tag Gardening pattern, as the list of fellow bloggers in some ways tags the person who posts it. By making a statement regarding whose blogs they encourage their readers to read, blog owners are declaring something about themselves. Blog readers can learn more about blog writers by looking at who they have on their blogrolls. For example, in Figure 3-19, knowing that John Lydon is in fact Johnny Rotten, the singer for the Sex Pistols, may imply to a reader that the owner of Technoracle has a somewhat disruptive personality and will try to speak the truth, even if it's unpopular.

Blogs lowered the technical barrier for getting a personal presence on the Internet, making it much easier for many more people to join the conversation. Blogs have also changed the patterns of dissemination of information. Rather than simply reading a news story on a particular topic, interested readers can also find related blogs and find out what the average person thinks about that topic. Blogs represent a new kind of media and offer an alternative source for people who want more than news headlines.

More recently, blogs have evolved beyond their basic form. Blogs have become one of many components in social networking systems like MySpace and Facebook: one component in pages people use to connect with others, not merely to present their own ideas. Going in a different direction, Twitter has stripped blogging down to a 140-character minimalist approach, encouraging people to post tiny bits of information on a regular basis and providing tools for following people's feeds.

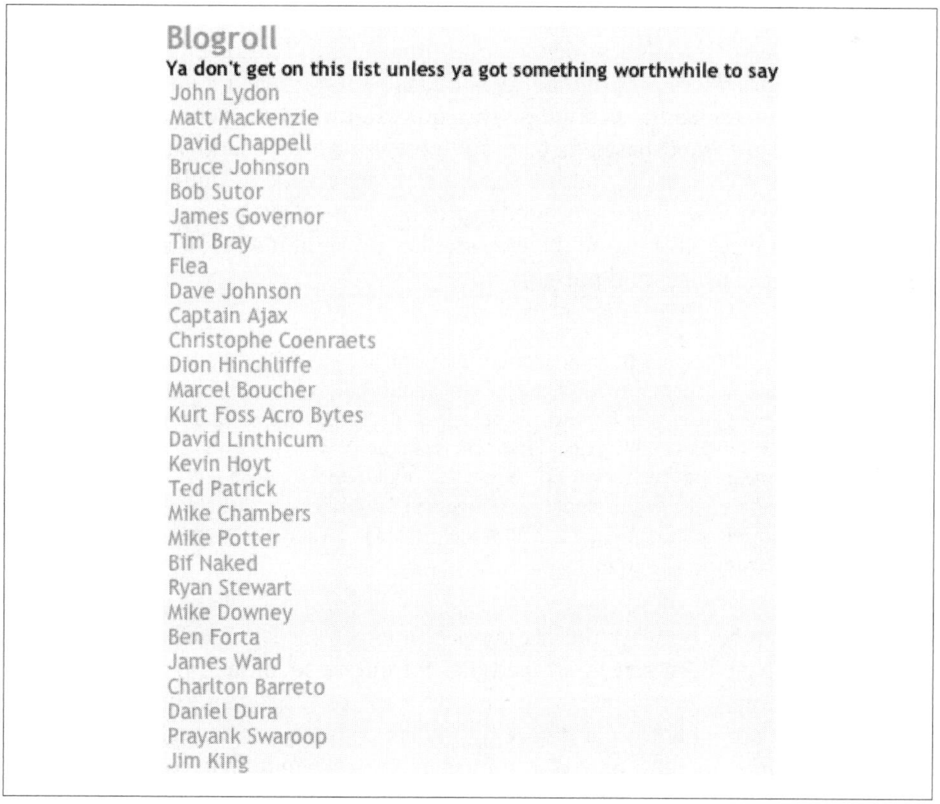

Blogroll

Ya don't get on this list unless ya got something worthwhile to say

John Lydon
Matt Mackenzie
David Chappell
Bruce Johnson
Bob Sutor
James Governor
Tim Bray
Flea
Dave Johnson
Captain Ajax
Christophe Coenraets
Dion Hinchliffe
Marcel Boucher
Kurt Foss Acro Bytes
David Linthicum
Kevin Hoyt
Ted Patrick
Mike Chambers
Mike Potter
Bif Naked
Ryan Stewart
Mike Downey
Ben Forta
James Ward
Charlton Barreto
Daniel Dura
Prayank Swaroop
Jim King

Figure 3-19. Example of a blogroll from Technoracle.blogspot.com

Screen Scraping and Web Services

Even in the early days of the Web, developers looked for ways to combine information from multiple sites. Back then, this meant *screen scraping*—writing code to dig through loosely structured HTML and extract the vital pieces—which was often a troublesome process. As Web 2.0 emerged, more and more of that information became available through web services, which presented it in a much more structured and more readily usable form.

Applicable Web 2.0 Patterns

These two types of content grabbing illustrate the following patterns:

- Service-Oriented Architecture
- Collaborative Tagging

You can find more information on these patterns in Chapter 7.

Intent and Interaction

In the earliest days of the Web, screen scraping often meant capturing information from the text-based interfaces of terminal applications to repurpose them for use in web applications, but the same technology was quickly turned to websites themselves. HTML is, after all, a text-based format, if a loosely (or even chaotically, sometimes) structured one. Web services, on the other hand, are protocols and standards from various standards bodies that can be used to programmatically allow access to resources in a predictable way. XML made the web services revolution when it made it easy to create structured, labeled, and portable data.

 There is no specific standardized definition of *web services* that explains the exact set of protocols and specifications that make up the stack, but there is a set that is generally accepted. It's important to examine the web services architecture document from the W3C to get a feel for what is meant by "web services." When this book refers to "web services," it doesn't specifically mean SOAP over HTTP, although this is one popular implementation. RESTful services available via the Web are just as relevant.

One major difference between the two types of interactions is intent. Most owners of resources that have been screen-scraped did not intend to allow their content to be repurposed. Many were, of course, probably open to others using their resources; otherwise, they probably wouldn't have posted the content on the Internet. However, designing resources for automated consumption, rather than human consumption, requires planning ahead and implementing a different, or even parallel, infrastructure.

A classic example of the shift from screen scraping to services is Amazon.com. Amazon provides a tremendous amount of information about books in a reasonably structured (though sometimes changing) HTML format. It even contains a key piece of information, the Amazon sales rank, that isn't available anywhere else. As a result, many developers have written programs that scrape the Amazon site.

Rather than fighting this trend, Amazon realized that it had an opportunity. Its network of Amazon Associates (people and companies that help Amazon sell goods in exchange for a commission) could use the information that others were scraping from the site. Amazon set out to build services to make it easier for its associates to get to this information—the beginning of a process that has led Amazon to offer a variety of web services that go far beyond its product information.

Most web services work falls under the Service-Oriented Architecture (SOA) pattern described in Chapter 7. SOA itself doesn't depend on the web services family of technologies and standards, nor is it limited to the enterprise realm where SOA is most ubiquitous. Web services are built on a set of standards and technologies that support programmatic sharing of information. These usually include XML as a foundation, though JSON has proven popular lately for lightweight sharing. Many web services are built using SOAP and the Web Services Description Language (WSDL), though others take a RESTful approach. Additional useful specifications include the SOAP processing model,[‡] the XML Infoset[§] (the abstract model behind XML), and the OASIS Reference Model for SOA (the abstract model behind services deployed across multiple domains of ownership).

While web services and SOA are often thought of as technologies used inside of enterprises, rather than publicly on the Internet, the reality is that there is a wide spectrum of uses in both public and private environments. Open public services are typically simpler, while services used internally or for more specific purposes than information broadcast and consumption often support a richer set of capabilities. Web services now include protocol support for expressing policies, reliable messaging features, secure messaging, a security context, domains of trust, and several other key features. Web services have also spawned an industry for protocols and architectural models that make use of services such as Business Process Management (BPM), composite services, and service aggregation. The broader variety of web services standards has been documented in many other books, including *Web Services Architecture and Its Specifications* by Luis Felipe Cabrera and Chris Kurt (Microsoft Press).

Content Management Systems and Wikis

As the Web evolved from the playground of hobbyists to the domain commercial users, the difficulty of maintaining sites capable of displaying massive amounts of information escalated rapidly. Content management systems (CMSs) such as Vignette leaped into the gap to help companies manage their sites. While CMSs remain a common component of websites today, the model they use is often one of outward publication: a specific author or organization creates content, and that content is then published to readers (who may be able comment on it). Wikis take a different approach, using the same system to both create and publish information and thereby allowing readers to become writers and editors.

Applicable Web 2.0 Patterns

The patterns illustrated in this discussion focus on collaboration:

- Participation-Collaboration
- Collaborative Tagging

You can find more information on these patterns in Chapter 7.

[‡] See *http://www.w3.org/TR/soap12-part1/#msgexchngmdl*.

[§] See *http://www.w3.org/TR/xml-infoset/*.

Participation and Relevance

Publishing is often a unilateral action whereby content is made available and further modifications to the content are minimal. Those who consume the content participate only as readers.

Wikis may look like ordinary websites presenting content, but the presence of an edit button indicates a fundamental change. Users can modify the content by providing comments (much like blog comments), use the content to create new works based on the content (mashups), and, in some cases, create specialized versions of the original content. Their participation gives the content wider relevancy, because collective intelligence generally provides a more balanced result than the input of one or two minds.

The phrases "web of participation" and "harnessing collective intelligence" are often used to explain Web 2.0. Imagine you owned a software company and you had user manuals for your software. If you employed a static publishing methodology, you would write the manuals and publish them based on a series of presumptions about, for example, the level of technical knowledge of your users and their semantic interpretations of certain terms (i.e., you assume they will interpret the terms the same way you did when you wrote the manuals).

A different way to publish the help manuals would be to use some form of website—not necessarily a wiki, but something enabling feedback—that lets people make posts on subjects pertaining to your software in your online user manuals. Trusting users to apply their intelligence and participate in creating a better set of software manuals can be a very useful way to build manuals full of information and other text you might never have written yourself. The collective knowledge of your experienced software users can be instrumental in helping new users of your software. For an example of this pattern in use, visit *http://livedocs.adobe.com* and see how Adobe Systems trusts its users to contribute to published software manuals.

Directories (Taxonomy) and Tagging (Folksonomy)

Directories are built by small groups of experts to help people find information they want. Tagging lets people create their own classifications.

Applicable Web 2.0 Patterns

The following patterns are illustrated in this discussion:

- Participation-Collaboration
- Collaborative Tagging
- Declarative Living and Tag Gardening
- Semantic Web Grounding
- Rich User Experience

You can find more information on these patterns in Chapter 7.

Supporting Dynamic Information Publishing and Finding

Directory structures create hierarchies of resource descriptions to help users navigate to the information they seek. The terms used to divide the hierarchy create a taxonomy of subjects (metadata keywords) that searchers can use as guideposts to find what they're looking for. Library card catalogs are the classic example, though taxonomies come in many forms. Within a book, tables of contents and especially indexes often describe taxonomies.

Navigation mechanisms within websites also often describe taxonomies, with layers of menus and links in the place of tables of contents and a full-text search option in place of an index. These resources can help users within a site, but users' larger problem on the Web has often been one of finding the site they want to visit. As the number of sites grew exponentially in the early days of the Web, the availability of an incredible amount of information was often obscured by the difficulty of finding what you wanted. The scramble for domain names turned into a gold rush and advertisers rushed to include websites in their contact information—but many people arrived on the Web looking for information on a particular subject, not a particular advertiser.

The answer, at least at the beginning, was directories. Directory creators developed taxonomic classification systems for websites, helping users find their way to roughly the right place. Online directories usually started with a classification system with around 8 to 12 top-level subjects. Each subject was further classified until the directory browser got to a level where most of the content was very specialized. The Yahoo! directory was probably the most used directory in the late 1990s, looking much like Figure 3-20. (You can still find it at *http://dir.yahoo.com.*)

Each category, of course, has further subcategories. Clicking on "Regional," for example, provided users with the screen in Figure 3-21.

Similarly, clicking on "Countries" in the subcategory listing shown in Figure 3-21 yielded an alphabetical list of countries, which could be further decomposed into province/state, city, community, and so on, until you reached a very small subset of specific results.

Directories have numerous problems. First and foremost, it is very difficult for a small group—even a small group of directory specialists—to develop terms and structures that readers will consistently understand. Additionally, there is the challenge of placing information in the directory. When web resource owners add pages to the Yahoo! directory, they navigate to the nodes where they think the pages belong and then add their resources from there. However, other people won't necessarily go to the same place when looking for that content.

Figure 3-20. The Yahoo! directory

- **U.S. States** (1618010) NEW!
- **Regions** (10211) NEW!
- **Countries** (758572) NEW!

Figure 3-21. Subcategories under the Regional category

Say, for example, you had a rental car company based in Vancouver, British Columbia, Canada. Would you navigate to the node under Regional→Countries→Canada→Provinces→British Columbia→Cities→Vancouver, and then add your content? Or would you instead add it under Recreation & Sports→Travel→Transportation→Commuting, or perhaps Business & Economy→Shopping and Services→Automotive→Rentals? Taxonomists have solved this problem by creating *polyhierarchies*, where an item can be classified under more than one node in the tree. However, many Internet directories are still implemented as *monohierarchies*, where only one node can be used to classify any specific object. While polyhierarchies are more flexible, they can also be confusing to implement.

Another problem concerns terminology. Although terms such as "vehicles for hire" and "automobiles for lease" are equally relevant regarding your rental car company, users searching for these terms will not be led to your website. Adding non-English-speaking users to the mix presents a whole new crop of problems. Taxonomists can solve these problems too, using synonyms and other tools. It just requires an ever-greater investment in taxonomy development and infrastructure.

Hierarchical taxonomies are far from the only approach to helping users find data, however. More and more users simply perform searches. Searches work well for textual content but often turn up false matches and don't apply easily to pictures and multimedia. As was demonstrated in our earlier discussion of Flickr, tagging offers a much more flexible approach—one that grows along with a library of content.

Sites such as Slashdot.org have implemented this type of functionality to let readers place semantic tags alongside content. Figure 3-22 shows an example of the tagging beta on a typical Slashdot.org web page. The tags appear just below the article.

Figure 3-22. Screenshot from Slashdot.org showing user tags (the tags appear in the oval)

The most effective tagging systems are those created by lots of people who want to make it easier for themselves (rather than others) to find information. This might seem counterintuitive, but if a large number of people apply their own terms to a few items, reinforcing classification patterns emerge more rapidly than they do if a few people try to categorize a large number of items in the hopes of helping other people find them. For those who want to extract and build on folksonomies selfish tagging can be tremendously useful, because people are often willing to share their knowledge about things in return for an immediate search benefit to them.

Delicious, which acts as a gigantic bookmark store, expects its users to create tags for their own searching convenience. As items prove popular, the number of tags for those items grows and they become easier to find. It may also be useful for the content creators to provide an initial set of tags that operate primarily as seed tags—that is, a way of encouraging other users to add their own tags.

More Hints for Defining Web 2.0

Tim's examples illustrate the foundations of Web 2.0, but that isn't the end of the conversation. Another way to look at these concepts is through a *meme* (pronounced "meem") *map*. A meme map is an abstract artifact for showing concepts and their relationships. These maps are, by convention, ambiguous. For example, if two concepts are connected via a line, you can't readily determine what type of relationship exists between them in tightly defined ontological terms. Figure 3-23 depicts the meme map for Web 2.0, as shown on the O'Reilly Radar website (*http://radar.oreilly.com/*).

This map shows a lot of concepts and suggests that there are "aspects" and "patterns" of Web 2.0, but it doesn't offer a single definition of Web 2.0. The logic captured in the meme map is less than absolute, yet it declares some of the core concepts inherent in Web 2.0. This meme map, along with the Web 2.0 examples discussed earlier in the chapter, was part of the conversation that yielded the patterns outlined in Chapter 7. Concepts such as "Trust your users" are primary tenets of the Participation-Collaboration and Collaborative Tagging patterns. "Software that gets better the more people use it" is a key property of the Collaborative Tagging pattern (a.k.a. folksonomy). "Software above the level of a single device" is also represented with the Software as a Service and Mashup patterns.

Reductionism

Figure 3-24 shows a reductionist view of Web 2.0. *Reductionism* holds that complex things can always be reduced to simpler, more fundamental things, and that the whole is nothing more than the sum of those simpler parts. The Web 2.0 meme map, by contrast, is a largely holistic analysis. *Holism*, the opposite of reductionism, says that the properties of any given system cannot be described as the mere sum of its parts.

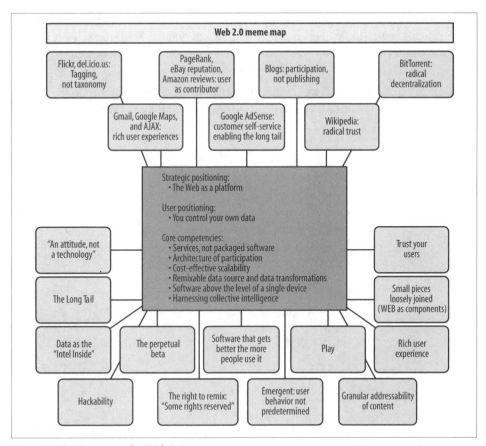

Figure 3-23. Meme map for Web 2.0

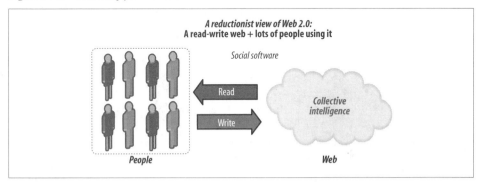

Figure 3-24. Reductionist view of Web 2.0

In a small but important way, this division captures an essential aspect of the debates that surround Web 2.0 and the next generation of the Web in general: there is one set of thinkers who are attempting to explain what's happening on the Web by exploring the fundamental precepts, and another set who seek to explain in terms of the things we're actually seeing happen on the Web (online software as a service, self-organizing communities, Wikipedia, BitTorrent, Salesforce, Amazon Web Services, etc.). Neither view is complete, of course, though combining them could help.

In the next part of the book, we'll delve deeper into detail, some of it more technical, and try to distill core patterns that will be applicable in a range of scenarios.

CHAPTER 4

Modeling Web 2.0

*"The Internet is a platform spanning all
connected devices."*

—Tim O'Reilly, 2005

Now that we've explored some real-world examples of Web 2.0, it's time to move up a level of abstraction to a model, so we can figure out what's changed in the broader story. A model captures knowledge about a real-world system in a representative form or pattern. Models also act as points of reference and as sources of insight into the subtler aspects of real-world things. By breaking the whole down into its component parts, we can conduct a more granular examination of those components.

Examining a model in this manner is similar to watching track-and-field high jumpers to learn their secrets: although it might be useful to watch real-time footage of the jumps as a whole, it is often more insightful to watch slow-motion replays of each part of the jump process, focusing closely on the various components to understand the subtle things that are going on at each stage.

A New Client/Server Model for Web 2.0

Web 2.0 patterns of interaction are more elaborate than the simple request/response interaction patterns facilitated by the client/server model of the original Web. Common Web 2.0 practices require that interactions reach deeper and into more capabilities than the web applications of the past. Fortunately, one of the Web 2.0 patterns—Service-Oriented Architecture (SOA)—allows capabilities to be exposed and consumed via services across disparate domains of ownership, making it much easier for the other patterns to operate.

The evolution of the old client/server model into a five-tier model for Web 2.0, as shown in Figure 4-1, can be extended over time as new patterns and functionality are introduced into the equation. The Synchronized Web pattern, for example, requires that concepts such as connectivity and reachability be more carefully thought out in the core architecture, and these concepts need to be expanded to cover consistent models

Figure 4-1. A model for Web 2.0

for objects, state, events, and more. The connectivity/reachability layer has to account for both online and offline states as well as the interactions between multiple agents or actors within a system's architecture.

> Remember, Figure 4-1 is not an architecture; it's an *abstract model*. The model's purpose is to capture a shared conceptualization of the Internet as a platform for engaging people, processes, and applications. Readers should likewise not consider this the single authoritative model for Web 2.0. It is simply "a" model, and other models may be equally applicable.

This model reflects how Web 2.0 connects capabilities and users, recognizing several key evolutions beyond the simple client/server approach used in earlier web development. It may be reflected in implementations in a variety of environments. One implementation might be an enterprise sharing corporate information with its customers. A different implementation could apply the model to a peer-to-peer network. It could also be applied beyond the Internet itself. For example, software developers could use this model to expose the functionality encapsulated in a single class to other software components via a defined interface throughout the specific environment (connectivity/reachability) in which the interface exists.

The Internet is a platform used to connect devices (increasingly via "services"), but Web 2.0 is much more. As more and more types of devices are coupled to the Internet, the services have to be more carefully thought out in terms of their architecture, implementation, and descriptions. The client tier typically expressed in client/server models has been split in this model to emphasize three specific aspects of the client: the *applications*, the *runtimes*, and the *users* that are the ultimate targets of most interaction patterns. Because Web 2.0 is largely about humans as part of the machine, the model must reflect their existence. Many Web 2.0 success stories, such as Facebook, eBay, MySpace, and YouTube, involve a lot of human-generated content.

This model also acknowledges that the edge isn't where it used to be. In recent years, we've seen refrigerators that connect to the Internet, personal digital assistants (PDAs) used to encrypt email, musicians around the world jamming with each other by plugging their guitars into their online computers, cars using the Global Positioning System (GPS) to query search services to find facilities in a specific locale, and more.

In the following sections, we'll take a closer look at each layer in our Web 2.0 model.

Capabilities

The term *capability*, as used in this model, denotes any functionality that results in a real-world effect. That functionality does not necessarily have to reside in a computer; for example, a capability may involve a video game console detecting user input and turning it into a stream of bytes that provides another player with a gaming challenge. The model is not tied to any specific fixed implementation. Capabilities can be owned or provided by government departments, businesses of any size, or individuals with some backend functionality they wish to share with users (for example, the ability to share a text file with another person).

In a typical client/server architecture, during certain phases of communication a client assumes some of the roles of a server. Similarly, a user can be (or become) the provider of capabilities. Figure 4-2 shows a classic client/server interaction.

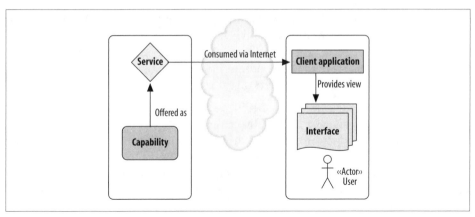

Figure 4-2. A basic service-consumer pattern

Figure 4-3 shows how all of that may change if the user is working with BitTorrent or similar P2P applications and protocols: the "client" in one transaction may subsequently become the provider of a capability that others consume.

Services

The services tier makes capabilities available for people and programs to consume via a common set of protocols and standards. Service consumers do not necessarily know *how* the services are being fulfilled, as the service boundaries may be opaque. Services have a data model that manifests itself as data (payloads) going in and coming out of

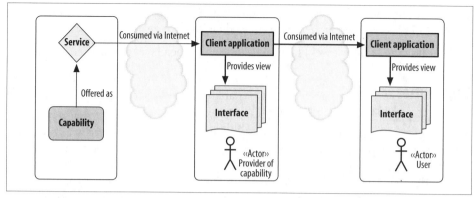

Figure 4-3. A service consumer acting as a service provider or "intermediary"

the service during its invocation life cycle. Even though the payloads themselves vary, the service pattern itself remains unchanged.

Many capabilities existed within modern enterprises before the Internet appeared, but this recently developed services layer is where many enterprises are starting to expose their core IT functionality. Each service provider, regardless of whether it is a corporate, government, or educational entity, follows a common pattern of using applications for some part of its core business functionality. During the first wave of the Web, much of this functionality remained largely unusable outside of an organization's firewall. The first company websites were generally nothing more than static advertisements serving up very basic information to consumers on the client side.

Only a few industry leaders in 1996 and 1997 were sophisticated enough to incorporate customer relationship management (CRM) or enterprise resource planning (ERP) systems, databases of product inventory or support for email, forms, and blogs in their web systems. Siebel Systems, now part of Oracle, was one of those leaders. Siebel started out with a mandate to design, develop, market, and support CRM applications. Other companies, such as Amazon.com and eBay, built their CRM infrastructures from the ground up on the Web.

The architectural model behind the services tier is generally referred to as Service-Oriented Architecture.[*] Although it is often considered an enterprise pattern, SOA is an essential concept for the Internet as a whole. SOA is a paradigm for organizing and using distributed capabilities that may be under the control of different ownership domains. The reference model for SOA emphasizes that entities have created capabilities to solve or support solutions to the problems they face in the course of their business. One entity's needs could be fulfilled by capabilities offered by someone else; or, in the world of distributed computing, one computer agent's requirements can be met by a computer agent belonging to a different entity.

---

[*] SOA is formally defined as an abstract model within the Organization for Advancement of Structured Information Systems (OASIS) Reference Model for Service-Oriented Architecture.

SOA accounts for the fact that these systems are distributed over disparate domains of ownership, which means that they require additional mechanisms (e.g., service descriptions in semantically meaningful dialects) in order to consume each other's services. There isn't a one-to-one correlation between needs and capabilities: the granularity of needs and capabilities varies from fundamental to complex, and any given need may require combining numerous capabilities, whereas any single capability may address more than one need. SOA is an architectural discipline that provides a powerful framework for identifying capabilities to address specific needs and matching up services and consumers.

Within SOA, if service interactions are to take place, visibility and reachability are key. *Visibility* refers to the capacity for those with needs and those with capabilities to see each other. This requirement can be met by using the standards and protocols common to the Internet. Service interactions are also facilitated by *service descriptions* that provide details about the service's functions and technical requirements, related constraints and policies, and mechanisms for access or response. For services to be invoked from different domains, these descriptions need to be written in (or transformed into) a form in which their syntax and *semantics* will be interpretable.

In the services tier itself, the concept of interaction is the key activity of using a capability. Service interactions are often mediated by the exchange of messages, though it's possible to have interactions that aren't based on messages; for example, a service could be invoked based on some event, such as a timeout event or a no-response event. Interactions with capabilities may proceed through a series of information exchanges and invoked actions. Interaction has many facets, but they're all grounded in a particular *execution context*, the set of technical and business elements that form a path between those with the capabilities and the ultimate users. An interaction is "an act" as opposed to "an object," and the result of an interaction is an effect (or a set/series of effects). The resultant effect(s) may be reported to other system actors in event messages capturing the knowledge of what has transpired or other details about the state of a specific invocation.

A real-world example can illustrate how similar mechanisms function in different environments. Starbucks provides a service (it exchanges food and beverages for money). Its service has visibility (you can see and enter the store) and a service description (a menu written in a language you can understand). There is a behavior model (you stand in one line and place your order, pay the cashier when your order is accepted, and then stand in another line to receive the goods you bought) and a data model (how you interact, exchange currency, and so on). In one execution context (say, in Canada), the signs may be displayed in both French and English, you'll pay with Canadian currency, and you'll probably need to keep the door closed to keep out the cold weather. In another execution context (perhaps at a Starbucks in a hotel near the equator), the prices may be in a different currency, you may order in a different language, and you may not have to actually exchange money; the charges may be billed to your hotel room. Although the service is the same at a higher level of abstraction, the business context varies. Consumers, therefore, must fully understand the legal and real-world effects of interacting with services in a specific execution context.

Architects also generally want to distinguish between *public* and *private* actions and realms of visibility. Private actions are inherently unknowable by other parties, yet may be triggered by publicly visible service interfaces. Public actions result in changes to the *state* that is shared between those involved in the current execution context and, possibly, others.

Support for private actions is one of the key characteristics of services. Such actions are handled with "managed transparency." A service performing private functions that consumers cannot see hides the implementation of the capability it's delivering from the service consumers or users. This opacity makes it possible to swap underlying technologies when necessary without affecting the consumer or user tier (those who consume the services). When implementing managed transparency, the service designers consider the minimal set of things consumers need to know regarding what lies beyond the service interface to make the service suit their needs. The declaration of what is behind a service is largely just a set of claims and cannot necessarily be monitored during runtime. Within reliable messaging frameworks such as the OASIS WS-RX[†] specification, service endpoints may "claim" that they've delivered a message payload to a final endpoint application, but there's no way for the service consumer to validate this; it must rely on the service's claims. That may seem like a problem, but the consumer being able to verify delivery would sidestep the service interface and possibly negate the benefits of SOA.

Another important concept of SOA from the OASIS standard is that of services having *real-world effects*. These effects are determined based on changes to shared state. The expected real-world effects of service invocation form an important part of deciding whether a particular capability matches the described needs. At the interaction stage, the description of the real-world effects shapes the expectations of those using the capability. Of course, you can't describe every effect of using a capability, and in fact a cornerstone of SOA is that you can use capabilities without having to know all the details of how they're implemented. A well-designed services tier might want to reflect a level of transparency that's adequate for the purposes at hand, but it should be no more transparent than is necessary to fulfill its tasks.

The evolution toward a services tier in the Web 2.0 model represents a fundamental shift in the way the Internet works. This new paradigm forms the basis for many of the interactions considered "Web 2.0." In the Mashup pattern, clients consume multiple services to facilitate their functionality. Software as a Service (SaaS) is a variation of the basic service packages in which functional units of computing are consumed via the service interface. Likewise, the rush to harness collective intelligence often involves making some capabilities available as services.

---

† See *http://www.oasis-open.org/committees/ws-rx/*.

Connectivity/Reachability

For interoperability on the wire to be possible, there must be some level of agreement on a set of protocols, standards, and technologies. The Internet became a visual tool usable by the average person when browsers that supported the Hypertext Transfer Protocol (HTTP) and Hypertext Markup Language (HTML) appeared. Browser development, making the Internet human-friendly, became a race. HTTP enabled data to be transmitted and HTML provided a foundation for declaring how data should be rendered visually and treated.

The Internet, like any network, has to have a common fabric for nodes to connect with each other. In the real world, we use roads, highways, sidewalks, and doors to reach one another. In cyberspace, protocols, standards, and technologies fulfill a major part of the infrastructure requirements. Additional mechanisms, such as the Domain Name System (DNS), specify how domain name servers can participate in a global federation to map domain names to physical IP addresses. From a user's standpoint, search engines have become increasingly important in terms of visibility and reachability. You can't use what you don't know about, and you can't use what you can't reach.

So, how have reachability and visibility on the Internet evolved? Several web services standards have evolved, along with standards to serialize and declare information. HTTP today is a boring yet stable old workhorse. Its core functionality, in addition to being the basic way for browsers and servers to communicate, is to provide a solid foundation on which to implement more complex patterns than the basic request/response cycle.

The real technical (r)evolution here has been the advancement of web services standards to facilitate a new type of connectivity between users and capabilities—the application-to-application realm. These standards include Asynchronous JavaScript and XML (AJAX), the Simple Object Access Protocol (SOAP), Message Transmission Optimization (MTOM), the use of SOAP over the Universal Datagram Package (UDP) , Web Services-Security (WS-S), Web Services Reliable Exchange (WS-RX), and many others.

It's not just data transmission that's changing—there's a lot more than HTML traversing the Web today. Many sites now offer RSS for syndication as well as Atom, and microformats make HTML at least somewhat machine-readable without requiring developers to go all the way to XML or RDF. Other sites have taken syndication to the extreme. For example, at *http://www.livejournal.com/syn/list.bml*, you can find a feed for just about any subject imaginable.

Each of these protocols and advancements has helped to spur the development of new user experiences in the web realm. Perhaps the single most common technology that most people equate with Web 2.0 is AJAX. Breaking away from the old pattern of complete web pages as single entities, AJAX lets developers build sites that can incrementally update a web page or other information view. Though AJAX builds on technologies such as JavaScript, the Document Object Model (DOM), and Cascading Style Sheets (CSS), as well as the `XMLHTTPRequest` object that had been lurking in browsers for years, the realization that these pieces could be combined to change the web-browsing experience was revolutionary. Developers were freed from the cage of pages, and users experienced improved interaction with resources without having to constantly move from page to page. AJAX shattered the previous model in which each page request was treated as being stateless, and no other requests were considered part of its context.

The emergence of AJAX signified a pivotal moment where the Web started to grow up and caused a revolution for users. However, web services also play an important role in the reachability and visibility concept of the model in Figure 4-1. Many businesses require more than *best effort* messages (messages not considered 100% reliable). *Reliable messaging* is a term used to denote messaging behavior whereby messages will reach their destinations 100% of the time, with externally auditable results, or failures will be reported to the appropriate parties. While failures may occur, reliable messaging ensures that every single message has a known disposition and outcome; in absolutely no instance can a sender be unsure of the status of a specific message or set of messages.

Although reliable messaging dates back to at least the mid-1980s with systems such as ISIS and ANSAware in the academic field, the first web-based protocols for reliable messaging evolved out of an OASIS and United Nations (UN/CEFACT) set of standards called Electronic Business XML (ebXML).‡ The characteristics of the message exchange patterns in ebXML were modeled on the older reliable messaging patterns of Electronic Data Interchange (EDI). EDI value-added networks played an important role in ensuring message delivery and kept audit trails that both sender and receiver could use to ensure *nonrepudiation* (not being able to deny having sent a message) and *recoverability* (being able to bring the state of a business process back to the last known agreed state should a network fail during transmission).

Although the ebXML effort itself failed to achieve significant adoption, much of the thinking that went into ebXML shaped the functionality of the web services standards that followed, like the OASIS Web Services Reliable Exchange (WS-RX) Technical Committee's work. The problem with basic reliable messaging is that it still concerns only individual messages. The WS-RX specification can create reliable messaging for groups of related messages and, in the process, can be implemented with a lower overhead than applying reliable messaging functionality to each message individually.

At a physical level, Internet connectivity may typically be achieved via CAT5 network cables and other high-speed fiber channels. As the Internet continues to evolve, however, more devices are being connected to it that use different physical means of signaling. We're already seeing Internet-connected digital billboards, large-screen outdoor monitors, smart phones, PDAs, electronic paper, digital cameras, automobiles, mobile audio devices, and more. Each new model of interaction may require a different mode of physical delivery.

---

‡ ebXML is described in more detail at *http://www.ebxml.org*.

Wireless communication is becoming by far the most popular connectivity option. Many devices rely on technologies such as Wi-Fi, Bluetooth, and other protocols to connect to the Internet. This evolution is important to understand from an architectural perspective, given that it's a strong driver for separating the actual Internet protocols (such as HTTP) from the underlying physical means of communication.

There are also some transport mechanisms that are not so obviously part of Web 2.0. We'll take a look at those in the next few subsections.

Paper as a transport mechanism

Some of the physical transport media mentioned in the last section challenge common perceptions of the Internet. For example, how can paper interact with the Internet?

Let's look at an example. A few years ago, Adobe developed a system for imprinting international trade documents with 2D barcodes. The barcode captures information from an electronic message and is then printed on a paper document. The entire message can then be reserialized as an electronic message by scanning the barcode and interpreting it into a stream of bytes.

Considering the Internet's ability to impact the quality of life on earth, hooking people who do not have electricity or computers into the Internet is a daunting but important task. The 2D barcode on paper represents one way of thinking outside the box.

ENTREPRENEUR ALERT

The concept of translating information from electronic to paper and back to electronic form has applicability beyond the realm of trade documents. For example, it could be repurposed for the financial industry (picture filling out an electronic form, printing and signing it, mailing or faxing it to its destination, and then reserializing it into an electronic format) and many other business models. Consider the kiosks at hotels that print maps for tourists. Someone could use the same technology to track referrals to local restaurants and businesses in exchange for fees from those businesses. The restaurants could then scan the barcodes on the printed maps to determine which kiosks best use their advertising dollars.

Similarly, by embedding a 2D barcode into each monthly transit pass, city planners could use the technology to track public transit usage patterns. If transit passes were made into smart cards, passengers could also use a technology such as Radio Frequency Identification (RFID) to capture information and special offers from ads in buses and subways, which would yield a new robust information mining capability for effective expenditure of advertising. RFID is a technology whereby very small chips can respond to queries and identify themselves when they pass specific scanning devices. The identification tokens can be mapped to useful business information, such as production dates of consumer goods; serial numbers of equipment; or profiles of specific people, devices, or other physical entities.

Ordinary bar codes printed on products also make it possible for users to gather more information about real-world products from wireless devices that take a picture of the bar code, send it to a service for processing, and thereby find out more about what the barcode identifies. The barcode wasn't meant as a deliberate "message" to the user or the service, but it can easily be hijacked for different applications.

USB storage as part of a network

The low cost of storage for digital content has opened new frontiers for permanently and temporarily connected devices. Most of us tend to think of the Internet as an "always connected" high-speed bit pipe, but this is not the only model. If a transmission moves from such a pipe to a person's computer and is transferred to a USB device that another system subsequently detaches and reads, it's still part of the data transmission. (The same was true of floppy disks and CDs in earlier years.) It isn't efficient or fast, but this is a pattern that has evolved in the physical layer of the Open Systems Interoperability (OSI) reference model stack during the Web 2.0 revolution.

 Jim Gray wrote an article about the so-called Sneakernet in 2007 that elaborated on why the economics of this concept were favorable to using network connections to transfer larger data packages, and Jeff Atwood further elaborated on the concept at *http://www.codinghorror.com/blog/archives/000783.html*.

Client Applications/Runtimes

The client tier of the old client/server model remains in the new Web 2.0 model with minimal changes, but some new issues are raised. First, the idea of SOA begs the question, "Why is everyone concentrating on the servers and not the clients for this new paradigm?" It's very important to mitigate the client-side connectivity considerations for online and offline tolerance to deliver a rich user experience. Many new client-tier application runtimes have evolved out of the realization that a hybrid approach, somewhere between a browser and a desktop application, might be an indispensable model for developers in the future. Developments such as Adobe Systems's Adobe Integrated Runtime (AIR)§ and Sun Microsystems's Java FX‖ have shown us that there is serious developer and vendor interest in exploring new models.

Figure 4-4 shows shifts on the part of both web-dependent and native applications to a new breed of client-tier applications that embody the best of both worlds. "RIA desktop apps" include traits from both old-school desktop applications and the latest web-delivered Web 2.0 applications, yet they also add some unique functionality. Typically, security models have kept applications delivered over the Internet from interacting with

§ See *http://labs.adobe.com/technologies/air/*.

‖ See *http://java.sun.com/javafx/*.

local system resources. The hybrid RIA ability to expand the basic security model to accomplish things such as reading and writing to local hard drives gives Web 2.0 developers an extended set of capabilities. AIR, formerly named "Apollo," was the first development platform to reach into this void, and Sun's Java FX and Google Gears soon followed.#

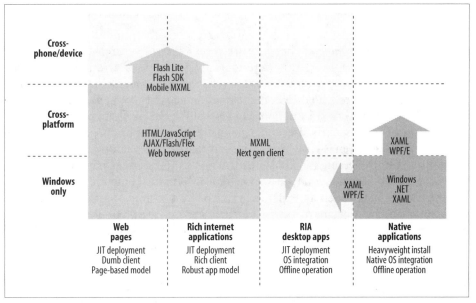

Figure 4-4. The landscape leading to hybrid online/offline development platforms

The patterns described in Chapter 7 raise additional questions about the functionality of clients. For example, the Mashup pattern describes a system whereby one client application can concurrently communicate with several services, aggregate the results, and provide a common view. The client may have both read and write access to data from different domains. Each service's policies must be respected, and, in some cases, different models for security are required within one application. Similarly, the Synchronized Web pattern discusses state alignment across multiple nodes, where you need to be aware that events transpiring in one browser event might affect the states of multiple other components of a system. We discuss some of the core concepts for consideration within the client tier in Chapter 5.

Users

Including the user as a core part of the model is one of the main factors that distinguishes Web 2.0 from previous revolutions in the technology space. The concept of a user, like

---

See *http://gears.google.com*.

the concept of an enterprise, is a stereotype that encompasses several different instantiations. A user can be an individual who is looking at a PDA screen, interacting with information via a telephone keypad, using a large IBM mainframe, using a GPS-aware smart device where data triggers events, or uploading video content to YouTube, among many other things. The user is the consumer of the interaction with the enterprise, and reciprocally, the provider of capabilities that the enterprise consumes. Users may also share the results of an interaction with other users, taking on the capabilities role in that exchange.

Users have become an integral part of the Internet's current generation. In most early interactions and exchanges, users were typically anonymous actors who triggered events that resulted in interaction requests. A person opening a web browser on a home computer visited sites to read their content but didn't exactly *participate* in them. Over time, websites made these interactions contextually specialized, taking advantage of knowing something about the user and making the user an important part of the overall model for Web 2.0. Even users who were just visiting provided information about their level of interest. Delivering a rich user experience requires understanding something about the user; otherwise, you're just anonymously sending content that will likely be too generic to deliver such an experience. Users are becoming part of the machine, although not in the way fans of a cyborg (cybernetic organism) population might have envisioned. Our collective interactions with computer processes are becoming part of our collective human experience. This phenomenon is blurring the lines between the real and cyber worlds.

Examining the concept of harnessing collective intelligence illustrates one of the most notable aspects of how important the user is to Web 2.0. Ellyssa Kroski's superbly researched and written article "The Hype and Hullabaloo of Web 2.0"[*] is a must-read, whether you're a die-hard aficionado or a battle-hardened detractor. Ellyssa provides some practical examples of harnessing collective intelligence, one of the linchpin techniques of successful Web 2.0 software. The article describes this as when the "critical mass of participation is reached within a site or system, allowing the participants to act as a filter for what is valuable."

This description is an understatement. The article gives some excellent examples of collective intelligence, but saying that harnessing collective intelligence allows web systems to be "better" is like saying that Moore's Law states how computers become faster over time. It wasn't for nothing that Einstein said that compound interest was the most powerful force in the universe. Harnessing collective intelligence has the same kinds of exponential effects.

---

[*] See *http://infotangle.blogsome.com/2006/01/13/the-hype-and-the-hullabaloo-of-web-20*.

The product that highly successful companies such as eBay, MySpace, YouTube, Flickr, and many others offer is in fact the aggregation of their users' contributions. So, too, is the blogosphere. The pattern of user-generated content (the Participation-Collaboration pattern) is potent and immensely powerful. Thus, mastering architectures of participation to create real value will be essential to success in the Web of the future.

Here is a list of five great ways to harness collective intelligence from your users:

Be the hub of a data source that is hard to recreate

Success in this context is often a matter of being the first entry with an above-average implementation. Runaway successes such as Wikipedia and eBay are almost entirely the sum of the content their users contribute. And far from being a market short on remaining space, lack of imagination is often the limiting factor for new players. Digg[†] (a social link popularity ranking site) and Delicious[‡] (a social bookmarking site) offer models for how to become a hub quickly. Don't wait until your technology is perfect; get a collective intelligence technique out there that creates a user base virtually on its own from the innate usefulness of its data, in a niche where users are seeking opportunities to share what they have.

Gather existing collective intelligence

This is the Google approach. There is an endless supply of existing information waiting out there on the Web to be analyzed, derived, and leveraged. You can be smart and use content that already exists instead of waiting for others to contribute it. For example, Google uses hyperlink analysis to determine the relevance of any given page and builds its own database of content that it then shares through its search engine. Not only does this approach completely avoid dependency on the ongoing kindness of strangers, but it also lets you start out with a large content base.

Trigger large-scale network effects

This is what Katrinalist[§] (a Web 2.0 effort to pool knowledge in the aftermath of Hurricane Katrina to locate missing people), CivicSpace[||] (an on-demand custom space for any social website), Mix2r[#] (a collaborative music-creation web space where people who have never physically met can add to and remix each other's music), and many others have done. It is arguably harder to do than either of the preceding two methods, but it can be great in the right circumstances. With 1.2 billion connected users on the Web,[*] the potential network effects are theoretically almost limitless. Smaller examples can be found in things such as the Million Dollar

---

[†] See *http://digg.com.*

[‡] See *http://del.icio.us.*

[§] See *http://www.katrinalist.net.*

[||] See *http://civicspacelabs.org.*

[#] See *http://www.mix2r.com.*

[*] See *http://www.internetworldstats.com/stats.htm.*

Pixel Page,[†] an attempt to raise $1 million by building web pages of 1,000 by 1,000 pixels and selling each of them for $1. Network effects can cut both ways and are not reliably repeatable, but when they happen, they can happen big.

Provide a folksonomy

Self-organization by your users can be a potent force to allow the content on your site or your social software to be used in a way that better befits your community. This is another example of the law of unintended uses, something Web 2.0 design patterns strongly encourage. Let users tag the data they contribute or find, and then make those tags available to others so they can discover and access resources in dynamically evolving categorization schemes. Use real-time feedback to display tag clouds of the most popular tags and data; you'll be amazed at how much better your software works. It worked for Flickr and Delicious, and it can work for you too. (And even if you don't provide an explicit tagging system, you may find that your users create one, like the *#subject* notation in Twitter.)

Create a reverse intelligence filter

As Ellyssa pointed out, the blogosphere is the greatest example of a reverse intelligence filter, and sites such as Memeorandum[‡] (a political spin reversal web page) have been using this to great effect. Hyperlinks, trackbacks, and other references can be counted and used to determine what's important, with or without further human intervention and editing. Combine them with temporal filters and other techniques, and you can easily create situation-awareness engines. It sounds similar to the method of seeking collective intelligence, but it's different in that you can use it with or without external data sources. Plus, the filter is aimed not at finding, but at eliding the irrelevant.

Time Magazine's Person of the Year: You (and Web 2.0)

Still not convinced of the importance of the user in the Web 2.0 model in Figure 4-1? Despite its being considered "so 10 minutes ago" in some corners of the Internet, *Time Magazine* selected Web 2.0—and in particular, those people who are directly shaping it—as its esteemed Person of the Year for 2006, just as Web 2.0 was gathering steam.

Specifically, in December 2006 *Time* singled out *you* in recognition of your achievement as the actual source of the exciting things happening on the Internet and in society today. Yes, you, reading this right now (at least, if you've been contributing to the Web in some way using today's increasingly ubiquitous tools and technologies, ranging from the basic blog or wiki to video-sharing platforms and social bookmarking sites).

The truth of the matter is that just about any interaction with the Web generates new content that someone else can use. The Web in this context is generally referred to as

[†] See *http://www.milliondollarhomepage.com/faq.php*.

[‡] See *http://www.memeorandum.com*.

the Database of Intentions. What this means is that if you're using the Web today, you've become an integral part of a new generation of openness, sharing, and community that some think may be recognized in hindsight as breaking down important cultural barriers and institutions, in a fashion similar to what happened in the 1960s. True, it may not seem like a revolution to those who see the Web growing bit by bit every day, but taken as a whole, there's now little doubt that the Web has become the most powerful, egalitarian, and knowledge-rich platform in human history. Rapid evolution appears to have accelerated into a sort of revolution.

Time's Person of the Year cover story appeared with the tagline "In 2006, the World Wide Web became a tool for bringing together the small contributions of millions of people and making them matter." This bestowal felt very different from *Time*'s 1982 honoring of the PC,§ which the magazine went so far as to call "Machine of the Year." After examining some of the world's problems, the cover story's lead author, Lev Grossman, wrote:

> But look at 2006 through a different lens and you'll see another story, one that isn't about conflict or great men. It's a story about community and collaboration on a scale never seen before. It's about the cosmic compendium of knowledge Wikipedia and the million-channel people's network YouTube and the online metropolis MySpace. It's about the many wresting power from the few and helping one another for nothing and how that will not only change the world, but also change the way the world changes.

The cynical among us will find some of Lev's analysis to be starry-eyed and excessively optimistic. However, calling out Web 2.0 by name, the Person of the Year cover story makes careful note that the mass participation we're witnessing on a grand scale on the Internet cuts both ways:

> Sure, it's a mistake to romanticize all this any more than is strictly necessary. Web 2.0 harnesses the stupidity of crowds as well as its wisdom. Some of the comments on YouTube make you weep for the future of humanity just for the spelling alone, never mind the obscenity and the naked hatred.

That lead story was just the beginning; *Time* prepared an extravaganza of supporting material and documentation in the form of 13 separate stories that ranged across the Web 2.0 terrain, covering subjects from online virtual worlds such as *Second Life*‖ to digital photography.

2006 was undoubtedly Web 2.0's opportunity to reach a wider audience, with the term making the covers of major publications such as *Newsweek* and *The Economist*. In the blogosphere, made up of the self-appointed contributors who are making some of this happen, the commentary on *Time*'s choice covered the spectrum. Jeff Jarvis, of the Buzz Machine blog fame, agreed with most of what the authors wrote, and just requested that they turn down the volume a bit. Nick Carr, of the Rough Type blog, was surprisingly easy on the article, though he'd long since posted his opinions of the Web 2.0

---

§ See *http://www.time.com/time/personoftheyear/archive/covers/1982.html*.

‖ See *http://secondlife.com*.

phenomenon. Infectious Greed's Paul Kedrosky accused the series of being a blatant cop-out, with more important issues elsewhere in the world deserving more attention.

The fact remains that the Web as it exists today—with sites such as MySpace and YouTube eagerly offering anyone who wants one a more or less permanent, scalable "channel" of his own on the Internet—makes it possible for anyone with great, or at least interesting, ideas to reach its billion-plus users. Never before in history has access to the largest audience of users in the world been, apart from the personal time it takes to contribute, essentially free.

The long-term effects of this connectedness will no doubt be as unpredictable as they will be significant, as the control over information and content becomes relentlessly decentralized. The Web is a system without an owner, a platform that's under no one's control, though anyone is free to build a new platform on top of it. Companies have had varying success doing just that, but the design patterns and business models for making the Web work best are at last beginning to be understood. Control is shifting to the edge of the Internet instead of the center, and it's not likely to shift direction without extremely potent motivation.

Collectively, this trend (the shift of control, the pervasive ability of anyone to trigger inflection points, and so on) is sometimes referred to as *social computing*, and its effects will be long in unfolding. As depicted in Figure 4-5, companies and organizations that continually hand over more nonessential control to their employees, customers, and suppliers will almost certainly be the big winners. Although the precise definition of Web 2.0 continues to evolve, its fundamental effect—the harnessing of collective intelligence—has the genuine potential to fundamentally remake our cultures, societies, and businesses, and even, as Grossman states in the *Time* series, to "change the way we change the world."

Whether or not you like the term Web 2.0, the Web is putting you in charge of just about anything you can imagine. We recently spoke to a major fashion industry CEO who said he eventually expects to have product lines that are designed entirely by user contribution, with the best of the resulting submissions being selected by the company's customers as what will be available that year. The consumers are becoming the producers. Turning over nonessential control can result in enormous gains in economic efficiency, as tens of thousands or even millions of customers' creative output is harnessed in a mutually beneficial way. Organizations that do not embrace the Web's natural communication-oriented strengths will fail when they enter into competition with those that do.

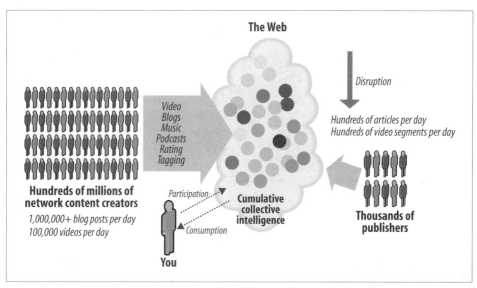

Figure 4-5. The You Era: Consumer-generated content swamping and disrupting traditional media

CHAPTER 5

A Reference Architecture
for Developers

"Everything deep is also simple and can be reproduced
simply as long as its reference to the whole truth is
maintained. But what matters is not
what is witty but what is true."

—Albert Schweitzer

It's time to move from Web 2.0 models to a Web 2.0 Reference Architecture, exploring more technical aspects that developers and architects must consider when building applications. In the process, we'll map the model in Chapter 4 to a technology view that facilitates the new patterns of interaction that we cover in Chapter 7.

This Web 2.0 Reference Architecture does not reflect any constraints regarding implementation; it's merely an artifact that developers, architects, and entrepreneurs can use to help them design and build Web 2.0 applications. For software architects and developers, a layered reference architecture serves to align their technical views regarding various aspects. More importantly, it offers a good starting place for anyone wishing to develop applications based on the topic covered by the reference architecture (in this case, Web 2.0). As with the model in the previous chapter, you should view this reference architecture as a starting point for your technology road maps, not the one true normative architecture for Web 2.0 application development.

 We capitalize the term "reference architecture" when referring to the Web 2.0 Reference Architecture and lowercase the term when using it in the general sense.

About Reference Architectures

In general, a reference architecture is a generic and somewhat abstract blueprint-type view of a system that includes the system's major components, the relationships among them, and the externally visible properties of those components. A reference architecture is not usually designed for a highly specialized set of requirements. Rather, architects tend to use it as a starting point and specialize it for their own requirements.

Models are abstract, and you can't implement, or have an instance of, an abstract thing. Reference architectures are more concrete. They have aspects that abstract models do not, including *cardinality* (a measure of the number of elements in a given set), infrastructure, and possibly the concept of *spatial-temporal variance* (adding time as a concept).

Consider again the example of residential architecture. The domain of residential dwellings has both an implied model and a reference architecture for a class of things called "houses." The implied model for a house is composed of or aggregated from the following components:

- A foundation and/or other subfloor structure to connect the house to the underlying environment, whether it is earth or a body of water
- Floors to stand on
- Exterior walls to keep out the elements of nature and to provide structural support for the roof
- A roof to protect the dwelling's contents and occupants from the elements of nature and to provide privacy
- Some form of entry and exit (possibly implemented as a doorway)
- External links to some form of consumable energy (an interface to connect to the electricity grid, a windmill, or some other electricity-generating device)

This model for a house is minimalist and very abstract. It doesn't detail such things as the type or number of floors, the height of the ceilings, the type of electrical system, and other things that become relevant only when a more concrete architecture (perhaps expressed as a set of blueprints) is made based on a specific set of requirements, such as "a residential dwelling in Denver for a family of five" or "a one-bedroom apartment in Berlin for an elderly person."

Although this model is very abstract, we can add details to each item in the reference architecture. For example, we can specify that the foundation be built in the shape of a rectangle. Other aspects in the reference architecture become more concrete if we then specialize the model for human inhabitants. For example, the floor must be edged by exterior walls of sufficient height to allow humans to walk through the house without stooping, and interior walls must be constructed to separate the rooms of the house based on their purposes.

A reference architecture expressed as a set of generic blueprints based on the model discussed at the beginning of this section will be insufficient to actually build a modern residential dwelling. It doesn't contain sufficient detail to serve as a set of builder's plans. However, an architect can take the reference architecture and specify additional details to create the kind of plan that builders need. For example, the architect can specify the correct energy conduit to account for North American electricity delivery standards, design the interior floor plan based on the requirements of the house's inhabitants, and so on. In sum, a reference architecture plays an important role as a starting point upon which more specialized instances of a class of thing can be built, with particular purposes and styles addressed as needed.

The Web 2.0 Reference Architecture, therefore, can provide a working framework for users to construct specialized Web 2.0 applications or infrastructures from specific sets of requirements. We'll explore that architecture next.

The Web 2.0 Reference Architecture

The reference architecture shown in Figure 5-1 is an evolution of the abstract Web 2.0 model discussed in Chapter 4, with more detail added for developers and architects to consider during implementation. Each layer can contain many components, but at the top level of abstraction, they provide a foundation that applies to many different kinds of application.

The components of this architecture are:

Resource tier

> The bottommost tier is the resource tier, which includes capabilities or backend systems that can support services that will be consumed over the Internet: that is, the data or processing needed for creating a rich user experience. This typically includes files; databases; enterprise resource planning (ERP) and customer relationship management (CRM) systems; directories; and other common applications an enterprise, site, or individual may have within its domain.

Service tier

> The service tier connects to the resource tier and packages functionality so that it may be accessed as a service, giving the service provider control over what goes in and out. Within enterprises, the classic examples of this functionality are J2EE application servers deploying SOAP or EJB endpoints. Web developers may be more familiar with PHP, Rails, ASP, and a wide variety of other frameworks for connecting resources to the Web.

Connectivity

> Connectivity is the means of reaching a service. For any service to be consumed, it must be visible to and reachable by the service consumer. It must be possible for potential service consumers to understand what the service does in terms of both business and technical consequences. Connectivity is largely handled using

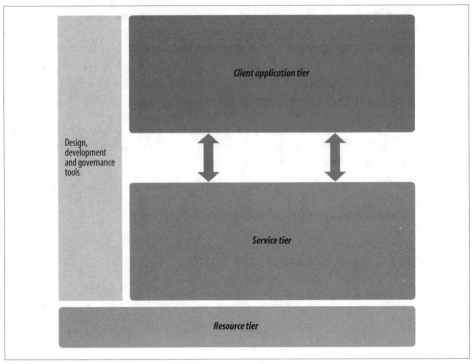

Figure 5-1. Basic Web 2.0 Reference Architecture diagram

standards and protocols such as XML over HTTP, but other formats and protocols are also possible.

Client tier

Client-tier software helps users to consume services and displays graphical views of service calls to users. Examples of client-side implementations include web browsers, Adobe Flash Player, Microsoft Silverlight, Acrobat, iTunes, and many more.

Design, development, and governance tools

This section encompasses the set of tools that enables designers and developers to build web applications. Typically, these tools offer them views into both the client and service tiers. Examples include Adobe Dreamweaver and Apple's developer tools xCode and DashCode, though there are many integrated development environments (IDEs) out there, and many developers have their own custom sets of tools.

Each of these tiers can contain a wide variety of components. Figure 5-2 shows many more possibilities in greater detail. (Tools come in so many forms that it's not easily broken down.)

This Web 2.0 Reference Architecture is very general, but it fulfills a purpose similar to that of the residential dwelling reference architecture discussed earlier. It should not

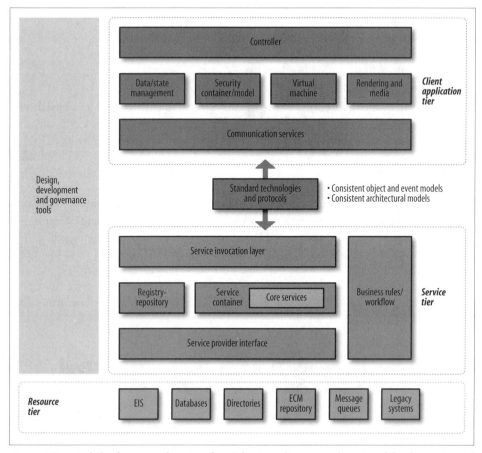

Figure 5-2. Detailed reference architecture for Web 2.0 application architects and developers (special thanks to Nabeel Al-Sharma, Dan Heick, Marcel Boucher, Laurel Reitman, Kevin Lynch, and Michele Turner for help developing this model)

be considered "the" sole authoritative Web 2.0 Reference Architecture. It is meant as *a* reference architecture that decomposes each of the concepts in Figure 5-1 into more detail. Software architects or businesspeople can use it as a starting point when designing a way to implement a certain set of design or architectural patterns over the Internet. It lets those people ask important questions that will be relevant to their purposes, such as "What type of client application do we need?" or "Where are we going to authenticate users?"

The Web 2.0 Reference Architecture is not tied to any specific technologies or standards nor is it dependent upon them. Architects and entrepreneurs can decide how to implement this reference architecture using standards and technologies specific to their needs. For example, if services need to be reachable by and visible to the largest possible segment of users, they may choose a protocol such as HTTP for its simplicity, its ability to pass through most corporate firewalls, and its widespread adoption. They could also opt for other messaging protocols to meet special requirements, such as Web Services Reliable Exchange (WS-RX) for reliable messaging, Web Services Secure Exchange (WS-SX) for enhanced security and efficiency with security, or BitTorrent for rapid distribution of multimedia content.

One last thing to note is that software implementations may choose to use all, some, or none of the individual components in each of the tiers. Figure 5-2 is based on a commonly used set of components to enable the patterns described in Chapter 7, but there are many simpler and more complex components that could be included.

The Resource Tier

This tier contains core functionality and capabilities and can be implemented in many ways depending upon the context. For example, a large enterprise might have an ERP system, an employees directory, a CRM system, and several other systems that can be leveraged and made available as services via the service tier. A smaller example might be an individual cell phone with a simple collection of vCards (electronic business cards), which are also resources and can also be made available as a service to be consumed, perhaps over a Bluetooth connection. Figure 5-3 shows a fairly complex enterprise resource tier.

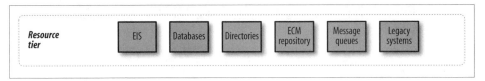

Figure 5-3. Detail view of the resource tier

The resource tier is increasingly being integrated into web applications in order to build rich user experiences. As client-side applications become richer and software rises above the level of any one piece of hardware (or device), making small computational pieces available to the client tier becomes a tangible requirement for many resource owners. This manifests as software that is no longer tied to specific operating systems or even, with large enterprise systems, operating in the cloud.

While these inner boxes are meant only as exemplars of potential resources, we'll look at each in detail to help you understand the overall architecture and some common capabilities:

EIS

> Enterprise Information System (EIS) is an abstract moniker for a component common in most IT systems. EISs typically hold various types of data for use by those who run the company. An example might be a short-term storage database or sensors feeding information into a common repository.

Databases

Databases are typically used to persist data in a centralized repository designed in compliance with a relational model. Other types include hierarchal databases and native XML databases. Each type of database is tasked with handling centralized persistence of data that may be retrieved later for a variety of purposes. Databases vary in size and complexity based on the amount and nature of the data stored, and may be supplemented by classic filesystems or other data-storage mechanisms.

Directories

Directories are lookup mechanisms that persist and maintain records containing information about users. Such records may include additional details for authentication or even business data pertaining to their purpose. Using a centralized directory is a good architectural practice to avoid errors arising from mismatches in the state of any one person's records. Examples of this are LDAP-based systems and Microsoft's Active Directory.

ECM repository

Enterprise content management (ECM) repositories are specialized types of EIS and database systems. While they typically use databases for long-term persistence, most ECM systems are free to use multiple data-persistence mechanisms, all managed by a centralized interface. ECM systems are often used for long-term storage and have several common features related to the various tasks and workflows enterprises have with respect to data management.

Message queues

Message queues are ordered lists of messages for inter-component communications within many enterprises. Messages are passed via an asynchronous communications protocol, meaning that the message's sender and receiver do not need to interact with the message queue at the same time. Typically, messages are used for interprocess communication or inter-thread communication to deal with internal workflows; however, in recent years the advent of web services has allowed enterprises to tie these into their service tiers for inter-enterprise communication. Popular implementations of this functionality include JMS, IBM's WebSphere MQ (formerly MQSeries), and, more recently, Amazon's Simple Queue Service (SQS).

Legacy systems

The last component is a catchall generally used to denote anything that has existed through one or more IT revolutions. While some view legacy systems as outdated or slated-to-be-replaced systems, the truth is that most systems become legacies as a result of working well and reliably over a long period of time. Examples of legacy systems might include mainframes and systems such as IBM's CICS.

The Service Tier

At the core of the service tier (shown in Figure 5-4) is a service container, where service invocation requests are handled and routed to the capabilities that will fulfill the requests, as well as routing the responses or other events, as required. (Java programmers will be familiar with the servlet container model, for example.)

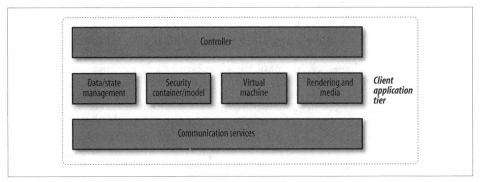

Figure 5-4. Detail view of the service tier

The service container is a component that will assume most of the runtime duties necessary to control a service invocation request and orchestrate the current state, data validation, workflow, security, authentication, and other core functions required to fulfill service requests. In this context, a service container is an instance of a class that can coordinate and orchestrate service invocation requests until the inevitable conclusion, whether successful or not.

Figure 5-4 illustrates several elements within the service tier:

Service invocation layer
> The service invocation layer is where listeners are plugged in to capture events that may trigger services to perform certain actions. It may utilize several types of adapters or event listeners to allow invocation of services; for example, communication endpoints may provide the triggers (typically SOAP or XML over HTTP), or the services may be invoked temporally via timeout events, or even via internal events such as a change in the state of some piece of data within the resource tier. While many articles and papers focus on incoming messages arriving via SOAP endpoints, other forms of invocation are often used.

Service container
> Once a service is invoked, a container instance is spawned to carry out the service invocation request until it is either successfully concluded or hits a fatal error. Service containers may be either short- or long-lived instances, have permissions to access many common and specific services (core services) within the service tier, and can communicate with external capabilities via the service provider interface.

Business rules and workflow
> All service invocation requests are subject to internal workflow constraints and business rules. A service request being fulfilled may have to navigate a certain path in order to reach its final state. Examples include forms being routed to the correct personnel for approval or parameters for a request for data being authenticated to

determine if the request meets the business's acceptance criteria. Some commercial service bus products also offer a workflow engine and designer as part of the service tier.

Registry/repository

A registry is a central component that keeps track of services, perhaps even in multiple versions. The registry may also track secondary artifacts such as XML schemas, references to service capabilities, and other key resources that are used by the service tier. A repository is a component used to persist resources or data needed during the execution of short- or long-running service invocation requests. The registry and the repository can be used both during design time, to orchestrate amongst multiple services, and at runtime, to handle dynamic computational tasks such as load balancing and resource-instance spawning and to provide a place where governance and monitoring tools can use data to give insight into the state of the entire service tier. Data stored in a repository is often referenced from the registry.

Service provider interface (SPI)

Since the service tier makes existing capabilities available to be consumed as services, an SPI is required to connect to the resource tier. The resource tier in this case is a generic descriptor for a virtual collection of capabilities. The SPI might be required to communicate with several different types of applications, including CRM systems, databases, ECM systems, plain old Java objects (POJOs), or any other resources that provide the capabilities to power a service.

Service containers are the physical manifestation of abstract services and provide the implementation of the internal service interfaces. This can require substantial coordination. If, for example, a service request proves to be outside the service policy constraints, the service container might be required to generate a fault and possibly roll back several systems to account for the failed invocation request, as well as notifying the service invoker. The service container depicted in Figure 5-4 might also use the registry/repository to help in service fulfillment.

Additionally, the core service tier ties into backend capabilities via the SPI. Implementers of Web 2.0–type applications will have to consider the following integration questions while designing their systems, some of which will affect how the SPI is configured and what protocols it must handle:

- What systems or capabilities will I want to connect with?

- What set of core services will I need to provide as part of my infrastructure? (Some examples include authentication, encryption, and email notifications.)

- What business rules will I have to enforce during the service invocation process, and how will I describe and monitor them?

- How will services be invoked? What invocation patterns will transpire within my infrastructure?

There are other complications as well. Service interaction patterns may vary from a simple stateless request/response pair to a longer-running subscribe/push. Other service patterns may involve interpretation of conditional or contextual requests. Many different patterns can be used to traverse the service tier, and the semantics associated with those patterns often reside with the consumer's particular "view." For example, if a person is requesting a service invocation to retrieve data, he may define that service pattern as a data service. From a purely architectural perspective, however, this is not the case, because every service has a data component to it (for more specifics on the relationship between a service and data, see the discussion of the SOA pattern in Chapter 7). Another person with a more specific view might try to define the service as a financial data service. This is neither right nor wrong for the consumer, as it likely helps her to understand the real-world effects of the service invocation. However, the granularity and purpose of the service pattern is in the eye of the beholder.

Service oregistries are central to most SOAs. At runtime they act as points of reference to correlate service requests to concrete actions, in much the same way the Windows operating system registry correlates events to actions. A service registry has metadata entries for all artifacts within the SOA that are used at both runtime and design time. Items inside a service registry may include service description artifacts (WSDL), service policy descriptions, XML schemas used by various services, artifacts representing different versions of services, governance and security artifacts (certificates, audit trails), and much more. During the design phase, business process designers may use the registry to link together calls to several services to create a workflow or business process.

Service registries help enterprises answer the following questions:

- How many processes and workflows does my IT system fulfill?
- Which services are used in those processes and workflows?
- What XML schemas or other metadata constraints are used for the services within my enterprise?
- Who is using the services I have within my enterprise?
- Do I have multiple services doing the same function?
- What access control policies do I have on my services?
- Where can users of my services be authenticated?
- What policies do I have that are common to multiple services?
- What backend systems do my services talk to in order to fulfill invocation requests?

This is only a starter set of questions; you may come up with many more. The SOA registry/repository is a powerhouse mechanism to help you address such questions.

It's also worth discussing the service invocation layer in Figure 5-4 in greater detail. The service invocation layer is where service invocation requests are passed to the core service container. The service invocation layer can hook into messaging endpoints (SOAP nodes, Representational State Transfer interfaces, HTTP sockets, JMS queues, and so on), but service invocations may also be based on events such as a timeouts, system failures and subsequent powerups, or other events that can be trapped. Client software development kits (SDKs), customer libraries, or other human or application actor interactions can also initiate invocation requests. In short, remember that several potential types of invocations are inherent in SOA design and to fulfill the patterns of Web 2.0 flexibility should be maintained by using the service invocation layer as a sort of "bus" to kick off service invocations. Realizing that patterns other than request/response via SOAP (what many people consider to be SOA) may be employed to invoke services will result in a much more flexible architecture.

The Client Application Tier

The client application tier of the Web 2.0 Reference Architecture, shown in Figure 5-5, contains several functional components that are managed by the controller, the core application master logic and processing component. Every client application has some form of top-level control. The concept used here is in alignment with the controller concept in the Model-View-Controller (MVC) pattern.

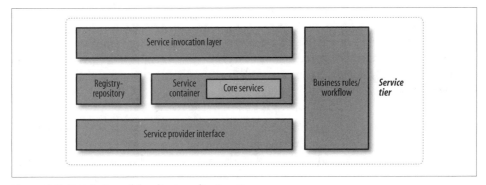

Figure 5-5. Detail view of the client application tier

Web 2.0 clients often have several runtime environments. Each runtime is contained and facilitated by a virtual machine. Thus, while the runtime environments are launched and managed by a single controller, they remain somewhat autonomous with respect to executing scripts or bytecode to control certain aspects of an application. The virtual machine itself is a specialized type of controller, but it's controlled by a master controller that's responsible for launching and monitoring virtual machines and runtime environments as they're required.

To clarify the relationships, let's break out each component in the client application tier diagram, starting at the top:

Controller
    The controller contains the master logic that runs all aspects of the client tier. If the client is a browser, for example, the core browser logic is responsible for making

a number of decisions with respect to security and enforcement, launching virtual machines (such as Flash Player or the Java Virtual Machine), rendering tasks pertaining to media, managing communication services, and managing the state of any data or variables.

Data/state management

Any data used or mutated by the client tier may need to be held in multiple states to allow rollback to a previous state or for other auditing purposes. The state of any applications running on the client tier may also need to be managed. Companies like Google and Adobe are getting very aggressive in developing advanced functionality with respect to data and state management to allow online and offline experiences to blend (i.e., using Google Gears and the Adobe Integrated Runtime, or AIR). Mozilla's Firefox browser now supports connections to SQLite databases as well.

Security container/model

A security model expresses how components are constrained to prevent malicious code from performing harmful actions on the client tier. The security container is the physical manifestation of the model that prevents the runtime enactment of those malicious scenarios. Almost every client-tier application includes some kind of security model (unrestricted access to local resources is in fact a security model), and each must have a corresponding set of mechanisms to enforce its security policies. A security sandbox in a browser, for example, prevents website authors from injecting into a web page any code that might execute in a malicious manner on the user's machine.

Virtual machines

Virtual machines (VMs) are plug-ins that can emulate a specific runtime environment for various client-side technologies. Virtual machines were the foundation for Java, including its early move to the Web as "applets," but the busiest VM these days is likely the ActionScript Virtual Machine, the core runtime behind Adobe's Flash. VMs are often built in alignment with the applications' security models to constrain runtime behavior from leaving the emulated environment.

Rendering and media

Management of the media and rendering processes is required to present a graphical interface to users (assuming they are humans). The client tier handles all aspects of rendering. For example, in a browser, HTML and CSS might first be parsed and an internal representation made in memory, which can be subsequently used to build a "view" of the web page.

Communications

With every client-tier application, communication services are required. These are often constrained in accordance with the security model and orchestrated by the controller based on a number of criteria (online/offline synchronization, small AJAX-like calls back to the server, etc.). The communications aspect of the client tier usually incorporates various stacks and protocols so that it can speak HTTP and HTTPS, supports the XMLHTTPRequest object, and more.

The client-side rendering engine handles all the "view" behavior for GUIs, as well as media integration. Rendering engines also pass information to the virtual machines and are controlled by the master controller. The data/state management mechanisms in the client tier control transformations, state synchronizations, transitions, and state change event generation during the object life cycle.

On client systems, allowing access to local resources—even read-only privileges—represents a primary security risk. A sandbox philosophy typically confines the runtime environment and keeps it separate from the local system. Access to local system resources is usually denied unless explicitly granted for browser-based applications, unlike desktop applications, which enjoy a greater deal of interaction. There's also a new breed of hybrid smart client applications that exist outside the browser, without being full-featured applications. Examples include widgets, gadgets, and Adobe's AIR applications. These applications use a hybrid security model that must be carefully thought out, as smart client and composite applications that mash up content from more than one site can experience runtime problems with mismatched security privileges between domains.

The communication services manage all communications, including between the client and server, with the host environment, and with resources in other tiers. Together with data/state management services, the communication services must be aware of the connection status and understand when to locally cache data and where to go to synchronize data states once interrupted connections are reestablished. Several of the patterns discussed in Chapter 7, such as the Synchronized Web and Mashup patterns, require a careful orchestration of these resources.

Architectural Models That Span Tiers

The SOA and MVC architectural models are key pillars of Web 2.0. The services tier and the client application tier must be built using similar design principles so that they can provide a platform for interaction. Resource tier and client application tier designers tend to abide by the core tenets and axioms of the Reference Model for SOA and apply application design principles such as MVC. The MVC paradigm encourages design of applications in such a way that data sets can be repurposed for multiple views or targets on the edge, as it separates the core data from other bytes concerned with logic or views.

Model-View-Controller (MVC)

MVC, documented in detail at *http://en.wikipedia.org/wiki/Model-view-controller*, is a paradigm for separating application logic from the data and presentation components. MVC existed long before Web 2.0, but it can be usefully applied in many Web 2.0 applications and architectures. It's a deployment pattern whereby application code is separated into three distinct areas: those concerned with the core data of the application (the Model), those concerned with the interfaces or graphical aspects of the application (the View), and those concerned with the core logic (the Controller). MVC works across multiple tiers: it allows application reskinning without affecting the control or data components on the client, and it enables Cloud Computing, where virtualization results in the controller and model concerns being distributed in opaque regions while still fulfilling their required roles.

Web 1.0 applications tended to mix together the Model, View, and Controller. Early applications were built around requests for specific pages, with every page a program of its own and data linked primarily by SQL calls to shared databases. On the client, HTML scrambled behavior with view and processing. Although HTML used different elements for these functions, the result was still a mixed-up markup language.

Declarative Programming Languages

Declarative languages tell applications what to do using a markup language. This model for programming interprets declarations into a set of functional components before runtime, and allows them to be deployed. Declarative programming languages are often much easier for beginners to use,[*] and they can be used alongside scripting languages.

The eXtensible Application Markup Language (XAML)[†] is a declarative XML-based language that defines objects and their properties in XML. XAML syntax focuses on defining the user interface for the Windows Presentation Foundation (WPF) and stays separate from the application code behind it. Although XAML presently can be used only on the Windows platform, the Windows Presentation Foundation/Everywhere (WPF/E) initiative will eventually bring XAML to other platforms and devices.

XAML syntax describes objects, properties, and their relationships to one another. Generic XAML syntax defines the relationship between objects and their children. Properties can be set as attributes or by using period notation (concatenating object names together with a ".") to specify an object as a property of its parent.

The Macromedia eXtensible Markup Language (MXML)[‡] is a complete framework for declaring Flex and AIR applications that works in the Adobe technology platform. MXML, coupled with ActionScript, is compiled into *.swf* files, the format known as "Flash." Flex and AIR are cross-platform runtimes that can tie into the capabilities tier in Figure 5-1 and let developers build rich interactive applications. MXML is a primary technology that you can use for the Mashup and Rich User Experience patterns discussed in Chapter 7.

---

[*] For more information on Flex, see *http://flex.org*.

[†] For more information on XAML, visit *http://www.xaml.net*.

[‡] For more information on MXML, see *http://livedocs.adobe.com/flex/2/langref/package-summary.html*.

There are also a number of other XML formats that define user interfaces. The Mozilla Firefox browser uses the XML User Interface Language (XUL), and the W3C-specified XForms can be built into applications through browser plug-ins. Although they are more specialized, Scalable Vector Graphics (SVG) and the Synchronized Multimedia Integration Language (SMIL) can also be read as programming languages expressed in declarative syntax.

Web application development has evolved, however. On the client, HTML still provides a basic framework, but it has become more of a container for parts that support the different aspects of MVC more cleanly. While the HTML itself still often contains much information, XML and JSON offer data-only formats that clients and servers can use to communicate their data more precisely, according to models created early in development. (This makes it easier for other users or applications to repurpose one aspect of an application, such as using the data—i.e., the Model—in a mashup.) Controllers have also advanced. Script languages such as JavaScript and ActionScript are great for client-side processing. The View components can be realized with a multitude of technologies; however, the most common are HTML/XHTML, thanks to their use of references and layout to load and position graphics in a variety of formats, including JPEG, GIF, PNG, SVG, and Flash. On the server side, new frameworks supporting MVC approaches have helped create more consistent applications that integrate more easily with a variety of clients and servers.

Ruby on Rails

Ruby has been described as many things. Dave Thomas has called it "the glue that doesn't set."[§] Steve Yegge, in comparing writing and refactoring Java code to moving earth with a Caterpillar construction machine, has called Ruby "a butterfly."[‖] The key in both of these descriptions is the notion that Ruby is lightweight and malleable: it stays out of your way, and you can adapt it to your particular problem. These traits are especially pleasant if, like myself, you've spent a lot of time as a Java developer. When famous Java gurus discuss Ruby, one word that you hear a lot is "joy"—a word I hadn't heard for a long time in the Java community before Ruby made its entrance.

I remember smiling the first time I saw "Develop with Pleasure!" in the splash screen of IDEA, when I used IDEA for Java development. This is indeed what many Java developers were looking for—but instead of finding it in a better IDE, many of them have found it in Ruby. Ruby has given many Java developers their mojo back.

Of course, the particular problem to which Ruby has most famously been adapted is web development, with Ruby on Rails. Although Ruby had existed for years before Rails, it needed a catalyst to take off.[#] Rails was that catalyst. The developer

[§] See http://pragdave.pragprog.com/pragdave/2006/06/glue_that_doesn.html.

[‖] See http://www.oreillynet.com/ruby/blog/2006/03/transformation.html.

[#] See http://www.onjava.com/pub/a/onjava/2005/11/16/ruby-the-rival.html.

productivity gains with Ruby on Rails are real, as are the reductions in the number of lines of code and amount of XML configuration required.

But beyond mere developer productivity is developer happiness, and this is where Ruby on Rails really shines.

A similar situation is occurring with the REST versus WS-* and SOAP debate. Just as Ruby is a lighter alternative to Java, REST is a lighter alternative to WS-* and SOAP. As such, it is a natural fit for Rails. With the built-in support for REST in Rails, adding a public API to your web applications is easier than ever: just use RESTful Rails controllers and routing.

Besides providing this API to third parties, you can also use it to power next-generation rich Internet applications with capabilities that go beyond anything you can do with Asynchronous JavaScript and XML. Technologies such as Adobe's Flex and AIR make it possible for the average developer to build applications that would be difficult or impossible to build with AJAX. What's more, these rich Internet applications integrate easily with Rails: they can talk to the same RESTful Rails controllers that power traditional web applications. This stays true to the DRY (Don't Repeat Yourself) principle of the Pragmatic Programmers, which has heavily influenced the design of Rails.

It's been years since IDEA first exhorted me to "Develop with Pleasure!" I have finally found a way to do so, with Ruby, Rails, and Flex.[*]

—Peter Armstrong
author of *Flexible Rails* (Manning Publications)

Service-Oriented Architecture (SOA)

The other major advance, SOA, provides a more flexible foundation than the client/server models of the past. Client/server architecture did not fully account for the variety of standards and extensible protocols that services under the control of different ownership domains could use. That wasn't a problem in the early days of the Internet, but as more protocols and ownership domains appeared, the architectural pattern of SOA became necessary to facilitate proper architectural practices among the designers of the applications connected to the Internet.

In the context of this book, SOA refers to an architectural paradigm (style) for software architecture, in much the same way that REST is an architectural style. SOA does not mean "web services," nor would every implementation of web services be automatically considered an SOA. An example of an application built using web services standards that is not an SOA would be an application that used another component over SOAP, but in which the SOAP component's life cycle was tied directly to the consumers. This concept is known as *tight binding*, and it doesn't allow repurposing of services.

---

[*] Even more ironically since Eclipse is one of IDEA's main competitors, I currently use the Eclipse-based Flex Builder with RDT as my IDE.

This definition of SOA might not be the same definition you had in mind when you picked up this book. We encourage you to decouple SOA from any standards or technologies and ask some hard questions like, "If SOA is architecture (as the name implies), how is it expressed as architecture?" and "What is unique about SOA that is not inherent in other architectural models?" Also consider SOA apart from specific implementation technologies and ask, "If X is SOA, what is not SOA?" (replacing X with your definition of SOA).

Enough of the core patterns we'll explore in Chapter 7 on SOA as an architectural pattern that SOA itself is presented as the first pattern. The Mashup pattern relies on services, the Software as a Service pattern consumes computational functionality as services, and the Rich User Experience pattern often employs SOA on the backend to retrieve contextually specific data to make the user's experience much richer.

Consistent Object and Event Models

Our Web 2.0 Reference Architecture leaves some items, such as consistent object and event models, outside of the tiers themselves. These items relate to several tiers of the reference model. For example, if a developer wishes to develop an application that listens for changes to the state of an object and catches them as events, the entire architecture must have a consistent model for objects and events, or at least a model for making them consistent eventually.[†] These models may vary slightly if the developers are using several technologies within their projects, and it is important for architects to understand and be able to account for the differences. Consider an Adobe Flex frontend (client-tier) application that is coupled with a .NET backend (server tier). If the Flex client needs to capture events, the model of how events are generated and detected and how messages are dispatched has to be consistent throughout the entire application.

Some Web 2.0 patterns, such as the Mashup and Synchronized Web patterns (described in Chapter 7), demand a consistent model for both objects and events. Those building composite applications might have to deal with events occurring on objects residing in several remote domains and different environments. SOA makes this somewhat easier by providing a clearly defined interface to the objects; however, the high-level models need to be aligned.

Over the past decade, this has become easier. The W3C recognized the need for consistent approaches to objects a long time ago and has developed several recommendations on this subject. The Document Object Model (DOM) is the base technology used to address many XML and HTML pages, and the XML Infoset provides a further layer of abstraction. Even Adobe's Portable Document Format (PDF), Microsoft's Office format, and the Organization for Advancement of Structured Information

---

[†] For more on eventual consistency, see *http://www.allthingsdistributed.com/2007/12/eventually_consistent .html*.

Systems's Open Document Format (OASIS ODF) largely correspond to the same conceptual model for a document object. Most programming and scripting languages have also evolved in a similar manner to have a roughly consistent view of events and objects.

What's new is the way in which some patterns use the events and objects across both the client and the server. Whereas in Web 1.0 many events were localized to either the client or the server, architectural paradigms have evolved whereby events on one might be caught and used by the other. Also new in Web 2.0 implementations is the ability to capture events on objects persisting on multiple systems, act on these events in another application, and then aggregate the results and syndicate them to the client. AJAX applications can support this model across systems with thousands of clients. The Google personalized home page,[‡] a prime example of this approach, syndicates data to each client based on its template. Small updates to the resulting page are made when new events are communicated to the AJAX framework behind the page view, and changes to the model result in updates to the view.

We're almost ready to launch into the patterns, but before we discuss them in detail, let's take a brief detour to explore the metamodel or template that all the patterns in Chapter 7 use.

[‡] See *http://www.google.com/ig.*

CHAPTER 6

From Models to Patterns

*"Something intended to serve, or that may serve, as a
pattern of something to be made; a material
representation or embodiment of an ideal."*

—Dic.die.net

Who should be interested in design patterns? Just about everybody who's interested in the Web 2.0 phenomenon, including:

- Business or enterprise analysts
- Those responsible for the operation of an enterprise
- Systems analysts
- Developers and web designers
- Entrepreneurs
- Architects of applications and commercial software
- You

With the approach to patterns in this book, there is room for decision makers and engineers to view the business from different perspectives. Documenting key patterns is a great way to facilitate the requirements-gathering process when embarking on any project. The architectural patterns metamodel outlined in this chapter should help guide you in the definition of the logical boundaries of a solution.

Patterns represent knowledge and provide a way to convey what's really going on in a given system. Documenting the patterns behind web portals (particularly, Web 2.0 design patterns) is therefore a logical step toward understanding what Web 2.0 really is.

Understanding the concept of patterns is useful when attempting to repurpose existing things for new uses. The pattern YouTube uses to share videos, for example, could easily be applied to music files. Recent years have witnessed a rapid decline in the cost of producing audio and video files, and tools have matured to the point where creating a great audio or video work is well within the grasp of an average computer user.

Before continuing with this chapter, consider the questions that follow. Can the patterns Google AdSense uses for ad delivery be repurposed to iPods and cell phones? Could the abstract patterns of eBay be used to set up a central portal to exchange baby and children's clothing and goods? Would it be possible to use BitTorrent's peer-to-peer (P2P) pattern for grid computing? Could Twitter's pattern of distribution of real-time text-based status updates be applied to sensors attached to athletes so that others can replay 3D wireframe models of their performances to learn more about their sports?

All these ideas involve the concept of architectural patterns. Similarly, web design patterns can be repurposed for other commercial ventures. In this book, we illustrate in detail several of the core patterns that evolved out of Tim O'Reilly's original explanations of Web 2.0, but we also weave in some additional thoughts on how these patterns might be repurposed in the future.

A Metamodel for Architectural Patterns

This section will introduce readers to a specific metamodel for documenting patterns as use cases and solution templates for software architecture. We'll use this metamodel for all the pattern definitions in this book.

The patterns metamodel we use is a variation of the Mackenzie-Nickull Architectural Patterns metamodel, which is intended for both novices and seasoned experts. It ensures a consistent form and level of documentation while appealing to the widest possible audience for each pattern.

The Mackenzie-Nickull Architectural Patterns metamodel was originally designed to facilitate quick capture of use cases from business stakeholders, with subsequent substance to be added by more technical stakeholders (architects, systems engineers, etc.). Anyone seeking to use the template can modify it for their own purposes; it's freely available intellectual property. The only major departure is that in this book we decided to abandon the Unified Modeling Language (UML) and use a less formally constrained concept map notation for graphical representations of many of the patterns.

The metamodel in this book is based on version 0.91 of the Mackenzie-Nickull Architectural Patterns metamodel. Both the Mackenzie-Nickull metamodel and the one in this book are in the public domain and may be used without restriction as long as that usage remains within the bounds of the open license. The Mackenzie-Nickull Architectural Patterns metamodel is updated periodically on no particular schedule. You can always find the latest version at *http://www.adobe.com/devnet/livecycle/articles/MacKenzie-Nickull_ArchitecturalPatterns ReferenceModel-v0.91.pdf*.

Patterns

Patterns are recurring solutions to recurring problems. Christopher Alexander first introduced patterns as an organizing principle for architecture in his 1977 book *A Pattern Language* (Oxford University Press). They became a motivating force in software architecture in 1995, when Erich Gamma, Richard Helm, Ralph Johnson, and John Vlissides (often referred to as the "Gang of Four") wrote the book *Design Patterns: Elements of Reusable Object-Oriented Software* (Addison-Wesley), leveraging Alexander's thinking and bringing it to new domain. In 1996, the book *Pattern-Oriented Software Architecture* (John Wiley & Sons), written by Frank Buschmann, Regine Meunier, Hans Rohnert, Peter Sommerlad, and Michael Stal, defined an architecture pattern as:

> ...expressing a fundamental structural organization schema for software systems. It provides a set of predefined subsystems, specifies their responsibilities, and includes rules and guidelines for organizing the relationships between them.

Work on patterns continues to evolve, and today, numerous references to many patterns appear on the Internet; however, the Gang of Four's work remains the most famous. Although they have been credited with creating the first templates for patterns, some notable templates have emerged since. If you search Google for "architectural patterns metamodels," you'll find references to several of these templates.

The model used to specify a pattern must capture the structural organization of a system, relate that to its requirements, and highlight the key relationships among entities within the system.

Architectural patterns may generally be decomposed into three main components (shown in Figure 6-1): the problem (expressed as derived requirements), the context in which the problem occurs, and the generalized solution. All of these pattern components are intrinsically interrelated.

Of course, multiple elaborations or specializations of each of the major components of a pattern (context, problem, and solution) are possible. For example, a problem may be described in both technical and business terms.

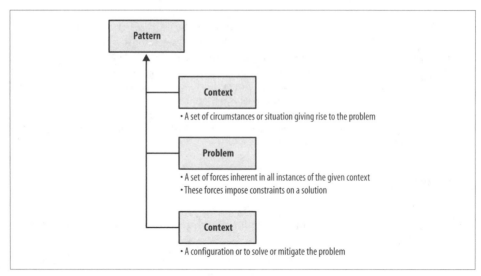

Figure 6-1. Pattern components

Context

The *context* is the set of circumstances or situation(s) in which the problem occurs. A context may be highly generalized to ensure maximum applicability of the pattern, or it may be highly specialized (e.g., the context of a specific instance).

The context should not be considered an exhaustive description of the circumstances or situations in which a problem may occur. It is highly unlikely that a pattern developer could or would bother to envision and document every conceivable context in which a specific problem might occur. Rather, it's more pragmatic to list the known situations in which a problem the pattern addresses typically occurs.

Describing the context helps document the external forces that may affect the pattern (again, this will not be an exhaustive list). Also note that patterns are likely to be useful in more than one context. Many successful entrepreneurs and inventors share the ability to understand how a specific pattern might be relevant to another context. Solutions for a given problem may also lead to solutions for other problems using the same pattern.

To take a *very* basic example, the financial services industry uses electronic forms for information collection, with paper forms as a backup. This is a simple pattern that solves the problem of maintaining current customer information. It has been reused in government, software, music, and other industries, as it's a common approach to solving a repeatable problem.

Problem

The *problem* is a documentation of issues that arise repeatedly within the context(s), augmented and expressed with a series of opposing forces. You must have a generalized description of the problem, detailed according to the requirements. A set of secondary artifacts may also be documented: the requirements, constraints, and desirable properties for a solution.

An example of a problem might be "a large corporation needs to build some kind of system to get all its customers to keep their personal account information up-to-date." This statement could encompass documentation regarding several aspects of the problem, including constraints imposed on that technology that can be used, as well as descriptions of alternative methods (e.g., walking into one of the company's offices to fill out a form, or using a computer to change records via the Web). We'll use this example to help us explore the patterns metamodel throughout this chapter: we'll call it the Customer Records Management pattern.

You can use different viewpoints to facilitate greater comprehension of a specific problem. In our descriptions of each Web 2.0 pattern, we'll outline the problem in language that businesspeople will find easy to understand and follow.

Solution

The *solution* solves the recurring business problem and/or indicates how to balance the opposing constraints and forces. The static structure of the generalized solution can be expressed in multiple architectural description languages (ADLs), including simple drawings. For the sake of readability and to appeal to a wide audience, we thought it would be useful to allow concept maps as well as some simple UML. The dynamic behavior section of the generalized solution documents how classes (objects or components) collaborate with each other and captures the dependencies and relationships among them.

Introduction to Concept Map Notation

Concept maps are a simple convention for brainstorming concepts during the development of software systems and/or architectures. A concept map is a 2D format composed of concepts (objects) and associations (relationships). Associations may be named to provide clarity (see Figure 6-2).

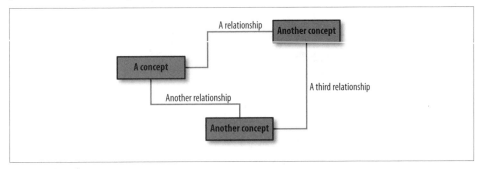

Figure 6-2. A basic concept map

Unlike other, more specific types of architectural artifacts, concept maps may mix and match components that do not typically appear together. The advantage of having fewer constraints is that concept maps are freer to depict a robust picture of what the architect wants to declare. Although many architects tend to stick to classic architectural diagrams such as the Data Model View, the Component/Technology View, and so on, occasionally a concept map may be used to supplement the other formats and provide a more cohesive view.

Each rounded rectangle in Figure 6-2 represents a concept. Concepts may be abstract; they do not have to be actual physical objects. A real-world implementation of a specific concept could be an object, element, process, or technical infrastructure component; alternatively, a concept may not have an implementation (abstract concepts cannot be implemented).

Concept maps may also mix and match things that do not normally coexist in other architectural views, such as abstract concepts and concrete components. Figure 6-3 illustrates an abstract concept, a concrete object, and an event and shows the relationships between them.

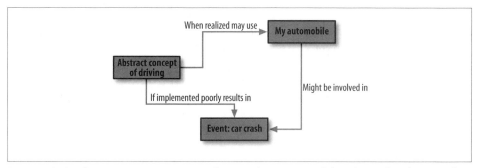

Figure 6-3. An abstract concept, a concrete object, and an event, and the relationships between them

 A good practice when developing concept maps is to use the same shape and color for similar items.

For our Customer Records Management pattern, for example, we might create artifacts to illustrate the multiple variations we described earlier, in "Problem" on page 104. These would include both electronic and paper forms to present to customers whose records required updating or validation.

The Pattern Presentation Template

Each pattern instance should be composed of the components described in the following subsections and illustrated in Figure 6-4. This patterns metamodel is used for

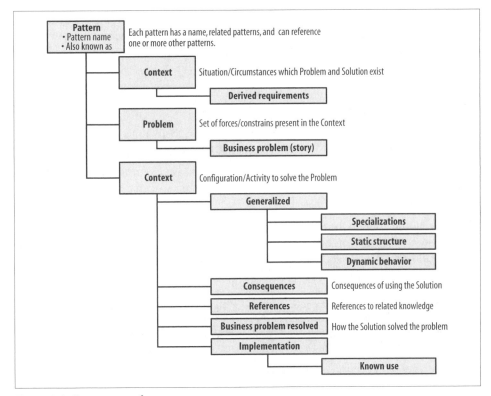

Figure 6-4. Components of a pattern

all the patterns presented in Chapter 7, and understanding it will help you digest the content in that chapter.

Pattern

Each pattern, while composed of a context, problem, and solution, also has some additional attributes that can help identify it and its characteristics to those who might benefit from using the pattern. These attributes include its name, which is unique within the patterns domain (in our example pattern, this would be "Customer Records Management pattern"), and any alternative names or terms that are commonly applied to it. These names and terms are outlined in "Also Known As" on page 113.

A pattern can have as many `alsoKnownAs` attribute instances as required. For example, Rich Internet Applications (RIAs) are also sometimes called Rich User Experiences (RUEs), and the Asynchronous Particle Update pattern is analogous to the AJAX and REST architectural styles.

For our present example, we might use some related pattern terms such as Customer Relationship Management (CRM). When listing such terms we'll often provide a reference for further information; for instance, in this case, we might reference the CRM archetype pattern diagram from Jim Arlow and Ila Neustadt's *Enterprise Patterns and MDA* (Addison-Wesley), available online at *http://safari.oreilly.com/032111230X/ ch06lev1sec2*.

Problem (Story)

A problem can be described in many ways. To appeal to a wide audience and to help convey the reasons the pattern exists, a story format may be used.

The Problem (Story) section details a specific, illustrative example of the problem to document its requirements. Told in a "story" manner, no special architectural skills are required to describe a problem.

The story should contain the text required to capture the scope of the problem. It should identify the actors who interact with the system (whether applications or humans), as well as outline the basic user experience or desired experience.

We can use the following story for our example:

> A large company needs to maintain records for all its customers. Some customers have computers and may be able to do this electronically, and others can do this only manually in our offices. But because some of the customer information is wrong, we may have no way to reach all customers to ask them to update their information.

Of course, there can be more than one story for each pattern, depending on the context.

Context

The Context section explains a situation or set of unique situations in which the pattern may apply (i.e., in which the problem occurs). The higher the degree of generality, the higher the likelihood the pattern may be reusable, and vice versa.

Derived Requirements

The Derived Requirements section provides a summary of the business problem and the context. Whereas the business problem is often specific, the derived requirements are an extrapolation of the general concepts, described in a more technical manner. Requirements derived from the problem should include a list of any constraints associated with the problem.

Building on our example, we could state the following:

1. We must identify one system or group of systems that can be used to manage and persist customer records.
2. We must have a manual process that enables customers to change their information.

3. We should have an optional process for letting customers use computers to change their information.

4. We must have a method for identifying customers who haven't recently confirmed that their information is correct and forcing them to either confirm or update it.

5. We must identify some business rules and parameters by which to expose customers to the method described in item 4. For example, if a customer has not been asked to review his records in the past year, we should flag him for such a request.

The goal of this section of the patterns template is to turn the business story into text that speaks to a software architect or developer who can infer meaningful design constraints from the derived requirements.

Generalized Solution

The Generalized Solution section explains the generic solution to the problem as it occurs within the described context. The solution can be further subdivided into two components, explored in the following sections: the overall structure of the solution as a static diagram, and its dynamic behavior.

In our example, we could state the generalized solution as follows:

> Run a match against our customer database, and then make a list of customers who haven't updated their record information in the past 12 months. When these customers log on to our website, interrupt their user experience by forcing them to update or verify their record information. Flag their accounts so that if these customers come into a physical office branch, the clerk dealing with them will ask them to either update or verify their information.

Static Structure

The Static Structure section provides a generalized description of the static components of the solution, their organization, and the relationships among them. For a formal architecture, most people will use a normative ADL such as UML. It is equally acceptable to use other forms of graphical notations to capture the concepts within the patterns, although some, such as concept maps, tend to be somewhat ambiguous.

Dynamic Behavior

The Dynamic Behavior section describes the runtime interactions, sequences, and behavior of the pattern's solution. We use UML sequence diagram syntax to depict these views. UML sequence diagrams are a part of the Object Management Group's UML Version 2.0 specification; they provide a standard notation for specifying dynamic behavior among concurrently operating objects and processes of hardware components. Within this architecture specification, we use UML sequence diagrams to illustrate the relationships between components of the pattern at runtime.

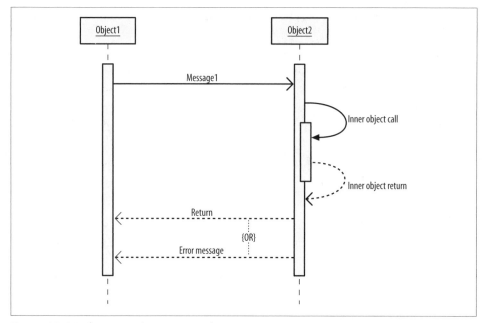

Figure 6-5. UML sequence diagram example

The UML sequence diagram in Figure 6-5 shows two objects. You should interpret the sequence diagram starting from the top-left corner.* Object1 makes a call to Object2; Object2 performs some internal process, and then sends either a return or an error message back to Object1.

For our example pattern, we would construct several of these diagrams to denote scenarios such as a user being intercepted when he logs into the website or comes into a branch office and presented with a digital or paper form either to verify or update his records. These diagrams are normally supplemented with some explanatory text.

Implementation

The Implementation section contains notes for implementing the pattern. Care should be taken to avoid constraining the implementation to any specific platform or programming language or to any specific standard or protocol. The Implementation section of each pattern is therefore somewhat more vague than you may be expecting. Idioms, for example, may be tied to such specifics.

In general, the Implementation section is considered a nonnormative suggestion, not an immutable rule or requirement. For those familiar with RFC 2119, "Key Words for Use in RFCs to Indicate Requirement Levels," the implementation is of RECOMMENDED or MAY status, meaning it is optional to anyone using the pattern. That said, the

---

* For more on UML sequence or class view diagrams, visit *http://www.uml.org*.

implementation notes do help make the pattern much more useful to a technical audience.

Continuing with our example, we could state the implementation notes as follows:

> The solution can be implemented using Adobe PDF forms that were mailed via regular post to all customers who, according to our records, had not updated their records. The same PDF form was also linked to the company website so that any customers who log into the front portal will be redirected to the electronic version of the form to update their records. Customers who do not get tracked with either of these methodologies will be flagged in the mainframe system so that when they enter a branch to conduct any transaction, the form will pop up on the clerk's screen and she can prompt them to update their records manually.

If further implementation details need to be caught, the level of implementation detail can be more specific. An example might be to note the specific version of the PDF form and what software the users would require (e.g., Adobe Reader or Apple Preview) to access the form.

Business Problem (Story) Resolved

The Business Problem (Story) Resolved section of the pattern reconciles the pattern's solution with the business problem (story). This section may contain additional details not covered in the various solution sections and the Implementation section.

For our example pattern, we would probably make statements such as "An electronic form will be presented to any user right after the user logs into our website. The user will not be allowed to access any other services until he either confirms or updates his records." Similar statements would be made about the manual methods.

Specializations

Specializations of the solution can also help provide further clarity. The Specializations section lists specific or customized instances of the generalized solution. This is where we might actually bind the solution to a specific set of technologies. Continuing with our example, we might make a statement such as this:

> When a customer logs into our website, he will be presented with an HTML page informing him that all other actions are suspended until he either updates or confirms his records. JavaScript will be employed to keep the user on the same page and provide him with two options. The first option will be a link to an HTML form that is prefilled with his current record information, which can be updated as necessary. That form will have two buttons at the bottom enabling the user to either "confirm as correct" or "submit changes" after he's modified the form. The second option on the initial HTML page will enable the user to download a PDF file to either fill in electronically or print out and fill in with a pen and send back to the company via regular mail. That form will have a LiveCycle 2D barcode printed on it so that the company can scan it to take the electronically entered information and changes from the document and put them back into XML format onsite. Alternatively, penned-in values may be scanned.

This is, of course, a very rudimentary example; it could be far more detailed.

Known Uses

The Known Uses section provides references to examples of specializations of the pattern in use. In our example, this section could give pointers to other companies that have implemented the pattern and to Adobe's LiveCycle 2D barcoded forms,[†] mentioned earlier.

Consequences

For certain audience members, it's useful to know the consequences of implementing a pattern. The Consequences section details any potential liabilities or caveats associated with using the pattern to architect your system (i.e., the potential consequences of implementing the generalized solution).

The consequences of specialized solutions may also be discussed here. For our example, we may wish to note that some customers will be angry if they are forced into this type of interaction. We could also document scenarios that may not work with the solution we've outlined, such as customers whose records are inaccurate and who therefore are not reachable either electronically or via regular mail.

References

The References section includes references to other patterns or information relevant to the problem, context, and solution.

Now that you've had a chance to peruse the structure of the metamodel, it's time to jump into the actual patterns themselves.

[†] See *http://www.adobe.com/products/livecycle/barcodedforms/*.

CHAPTER 7

Specific Patterns of Web 2.0

*"Art is the imposing of a pattern on experience, and our
aesthetic enjoyment is recognition of the pattern."*

—Alfred North Whitehead

It's been a long climb, but it's finally time to explore some Web 2.0 patterns. This chapter could not feasibly contain an exhaustive list of all patterns associated with Web 2.0; new patterns are likely evolving as you read this sentence. Nonetheless, the patterns presented here should continue to provide a foundation for applications well into the future, even as the bigger picture continues to change.

Unlike the rest of this book, the pattern descriptions in this chapter are meant as reference material. We do not expect that you will read the chapter from start to finish, but rather that you'll refer to sections on certain patterns as the need arises. You should feel welcome to read, re-read, and circle back over the individual pattern discussions.

Finally, a note about ordering. This chapter presents the more foundational patterns first, so that the main patterns on which other patterns depend will appear before their dependencies. For example, the Mashup pattern relies upon the Service-Oriented Architecture (SOA) pattern, so we discuss the SOA pattern first.

The Service-Oriented Architecture Pattern

Also Known As

Other terms you may see in conjunction with the Service-Oriented Architecture pattern include:

Services Oriented Architecture
> The extra *s*, often used by nontechnical users, doesn't change the meaning.

Services
> Developers who work outside of the enterprise development world often just think of SOA as "services," building them into individual applications without worrying

about the connecting architecture between applications. The lessons of SOA, especially those of opacity, still apply even in simpler contexts.

Event-Driven Architecture (EDA)

All SOAs are, by design, *event-driven*; however, a series of new architectures are emerging that actually take note of the events, and even add the concept of *event causality* (the relationship between two or more events). The pattern of Event-Driven Architecture, defined by the analyst firm Gartner,[*] is the most prominent of these.

Event-Driven Architecture

When your friend calls you to invite you to her wedding and you accept and update your calendar, this is an example of a traditional one-iteration interactive SOA. When she posts an announcement of her wedding in the newspaper and you read the announcement and cross her off your list of single female friends, this is a simple example of event processing.

Event-Driven Architecture is a style of software architecture that is built around the model of event processing; that is, a model in which the movement of information is facilitated by the detection, notification, and processing of events. Events of relevance include notable changes of state and discovery of facts. In IT systems, the manifestation of an event is marked by the creation and publication of an *event object* (also called an *event message*, an *event descriptor*, or, unfortunately, sometimes simply an *event*).

Both SOA and EDA are about modularity, encapsulation, business-driven software partitioning, agility of application composition, and sharing of software resources. Sometimes EDA is referred to as "event-driven SOA" to highlight these commonalities of purpose. However, the two architectures are vastly different.

Unlike traditional requests for services in an interactive SOA, which involve requests to perform some work in the future, in an EDA events enter the system as records of things that have already occurred. This fundamental premise is what separates the two architectures. SOA (or "interactive SOA" or "object-oriented SOA," which are different naming attempts to denote the request/reply nature of the basic SOA) is about making requests on behalf of requestors (clients) to the services that are thus subordinate to the clients. In EDA, however, the posting of an event by the source and the detection and processing of the event by the sink (or "event handler") are fully decoupled, independent activities performed by peer software modules. (Of course, the client, the service, the source, and the sink are just roles; the same software module can play multiple such roles in relation with multiple other software modules.)

EDA removes from the originator of an event the burden of knowing what to do, and whom to call to do it, when action is required. It also removes the burden from the middleware of preserving the availability of and connectivity between parties so that the response can be delivered and the context of the encompassing unit of work can be

---

[*] See *http://www.gartner.com*.

preserved. By pairing two event postings, EDA can easily simulate interactive SOA. It is, on the whole, a more powerful architecture.

Complex event processing is a special case of EDA that deserves a mention. Simple event processing involves detecting an event and processing its consequences. Complex event processing involves correlating multiple events, generating derived events, and then processing their consequences. The correlation of events can be across multiple categories of events, as in event-driven business intelligence or business activity monitoring; it can also be across a temporal (spread out in time) sequence of events of the same type (an event stream). Multiple vendor products are offered today to handle temporal stream processing or business activity monitoring. These should be seen as advanced forms of event sources, as their ultimate objective is to detect patterns and generate derived events (i.e., events composed of multiple other events) of business consequences to be processed through the EDA network of sources and event handlers.

Interactive SOA in its core architecture follows the traditional remote procedure call (RPC) model. Its implementations typically rely on request/response-style middleware (such as Java RMI or .NET Remoting) and enjoy the benefits (and the overhead) of a single atomic logical unit of work for all client/service exchanges on behalf of the original client. Most event-driven systems today use the message queuing and, especially, publish/subscribe programming models. They rely on messaging middleware and enjoy the scalability and manageability of the queued distributed systems. Both Java EE and the .NET Framework support the messaging and publish/subscribe models, though both remain grossly underused by mainstream applications.

Thousands of production IT systems are built using EDA principles, but these systems are concentrated in a few industry verticals: securities trading, telecommunications, transportation, systems management, the growing RFID field in retail and manufacturing, and some others. Business in these areas is decidedly event-driven, and the disconnect between the business requirements and the technology architecture when RPC-style SOA middleware is used to process what in the real world is intensely event-driven is an issue. The additional mainstream system engineering remains mostly in the camp of interactive SOA, which is better understood, is much better supported by vendor products, and, unlike the EDA approach, seems safe and proven to mainstream projects' leaders. This state of affairs is likely to last until technology vendors begin to offer development and deployment tools that make design of event-exchange systems as easy as or easier than design of request/response-exchange systems.

My longstanding advice to software architects is this: when you can choose between event-driven and request/response-driven forms of interaction, event-driven should always be the preferred choice. Event-driven systems will prove more scalable, more amendable, and more resilient in the long run. They will serve your organization longer, cost less over time, and offer greater opportunities for new use.

—Yefim Natis
analyst at Gartner

Business Problem (Story)

The SOA story is most easily told within the context of a single organization, though once the problems have been broken down into more manageable pieces, those pieces can be more widely distributed and shared with ease, in particular over the Web.

Consider an enterprise that has a set of systems or applications that its employees use to accomplish various tasks. Each system is large and encapsulates a lot of functionality. Some of the functionality is common to more than one system, such as authenticating users before granting them access privileges to the system. Figure 7-1 shows a set of systems, each containing its own module for logging in and authenticating users, a persistent record of the users' names and addresses, functionality for changing their names and addresses, and some human resources (HR) information. Each vertical grouping represents an application that fulfills a process. The only thing that differs between them is their central focus: payroll, insurance, or employee relations (ER).

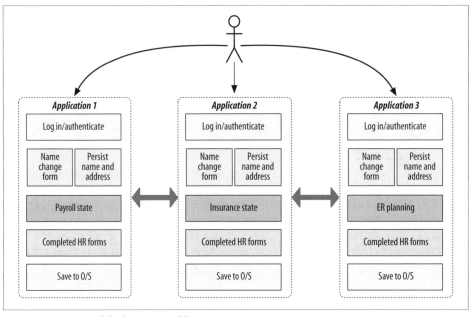

Figure 7-1. A view of the business problem

The systems also sometimes communicate with each other. They are arranged in a *stovepipe*: communication between specific systems takes place according to rules specified for those systems. The natures of the relationships for connected systems vary greatly, but they are often bound to the specific application environment used to create the systems. In some cases, the integrations are *tightly coupled*, which denotes that the systems have certain dependencies on each other's environments.

Maintenance of these systems has become a very expensive task for the enterprise, repetitive and fragile. Each time an employee changes her password, she has to log into every system and reset that password. Replacing a system or upgrading it to a newer version requires an extensive series of studies to understand what impact this upgrade might have on other connected systems.

The enterprise is tired of the repetition and fragility, and is starting to realize another cost: it implements a variety of functions that other organizations provide at lower cost. By creating IT "hooks" into which external companies can tie their systems, the enterprise can take advantage of those companies' services.

Corporate acquisitions and mergers raise similar issues. When two companies come together, it makes little sense for the combined enterprise to maintain two customer relationship management (CRM) systems, two authentication directories, two payroll systems, two enterprise resource planning (ERP) systems, and so on.

Context

This pattern occurs in any context in which IT systems or functionality must be made usable for a large group of potential consumers (those with needs), both inside and outside a specific domain of ownership.

This pattern also occurs anywhere enterprises need their IT to be agile in support of their business strategies, such as outsourcing, acquisitions and mergers, and repurposing functionality to save IT budgets.

Derived Requirements

Each system that the enterprise owns and maintains must have a clearly defined interface so that it can be repurposed and used by multiple other applications, including external systems. Each interface should be linked to a specific policy whose terms a consumer must agree to comply with in order to use the service, thereby entering into a contract of sorts.

Because the exposed services may exist in different domains of ownership, several key artifacts must be present to facilitate interoperation with the enterprise's guidelines. These include being able to declare policies on services, being able to describe what services do in both technical and business terms, security, governance, and several other related functions.

To facilitate coupling to the services, a common set of protocols and standards must be used alongside a standard model for the services. Ideally, use of common protocols and standards will create a service bus within the organization, enabling most applications to talk to each other without being hardwired together. Agility also arises from being able to orchestrate multiple services to facilitate an automated workflow or business process.

It's also important that all consumers use the same data formats as the service providers. This requirement logically encompasses the artifacts that describe various aspects of a service (e.g., the use of WSDL as the format for describing a web service).

To alleviate problems with managing the functionality behind the services, the service interfaces should be as opaque as possible, preventing service consumers from tying into the application delivering the services any more deeply than required. This makes it easier to manage the functionality and capabilities behind the services, including replacing systems or changing external providers, without endangering the functionality of the systems using the services. Ideally, service consumers should know only about the service interface, and nothing about how the functionality is being fulfilled.

Generalized Solution

SOA is an architectural paradigm used to organize capabilities and functionality under different domains of ownership and to allow interactions between the consumers of capabilities and the capabilities themselves via a service. It can also be defined as an abstract action boundary that facilitates interactions between those with needs and those with capabilities. Organizations adopting this strategy can make all of their core functionality that is shared by two or more consumers available as opaque services. *Opacity* isolates the service consumer from the internal details of how a capability is fulfilled and helps keep the components of a system from becoming too tightly bound to each other. (Most public services will want to be opaque in any case, for security reasons.)

Static Structure

The Organization for Advancement of Structured Information Systems (OASIS) Reference Model for Service-Oriented Architecture depicts SOA as an abstract pattern —not tied to any specific technologies, standards, or protocols—built from the components shown in Figure 7-2.

The *service* is the core action boundary that enables consumption or use of the capabilities lying behind it by consumers or users in need of the functionality it provides. Those who deploy services manage opacity and transparency, meaning that the services fulfill invocation requests without necessarily allowing the consumer to know the details of how the request was carried out behind the service interface.

Because services fall under various domains of ownership, each service has a set of policies in place that govern its use. Failure to comply with the terms of those policies may result in service invocation requests being denied, whereas agreement and compliance with them implies that a contract has been built between the consumer and the service provider, possibly involving one or more proxies in the middle. Examples involving proxies include services that are consumed and then offered to another

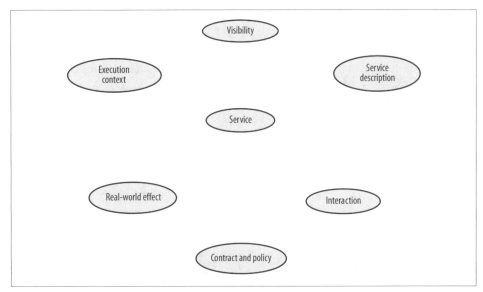

Figure 7-2. The core reference model for SOA

consumer. We describe such a scenario in our discussion of the peer-to-peer (P2P) models in Chapter 3 (see Figure 3-15 in that chapter).

For a service to be consumed, it must be reachable by and visible to the consumer. This is typically accomplished via some common network fabric or bus, such as the Internet, although it can be implemented in other manners, such as via Bluetooth, radio broadcast/multicast/unicast/anycast, and many other means. The most common implementations of SOA use web services over HTTP, Asynchronous JavaScript and XML (AJAX), and several variations of Representational State Transfer (REST)-style (sometimes referred to as "RESTful SOA") services using different technologies, including plain old HTTP.

A service provider must describe a service, including all its relevant details (properties, location, policies, data models, behavior models, and so on), in such a manner that potential consumers can inspect and understand it. Web services are commonly described using a W3C recommendation called the *Web Services Description Language*, an XML language for declaring relevant aspects of a service's operations. Simple HTTP services might, in contrast, be described via a URL and/or simply through documentation.

The real-world effect of consuming a service is a tangible change of state based on interactions with that service. For example, the real-world effect of invoking an Amazon.com web service to purchase a book might be that you create a real-world contract to complete the purchase by paying for a book that will arrive at the delivery destination. Real-world effects are, of course, dependent upon the type of service with which a consumer interacts. In some cases, a real-world effect may happen even when the service invocation is not completed successfully. For example, you might not complete the book ordering process, but due to some internal error the service might deduct the book from its internal inventory, or your credit card might be billed even though the book was never scheduled for delivery. (Or perhaps in a nicer situation, you might receive a notification that the process wasn't completed.)

The service interaction model is much more complex than we've shown so far and is worth decomposing further. We can subdivide it into two smaller components: the information model and the behavior model (see Figure 7-3).

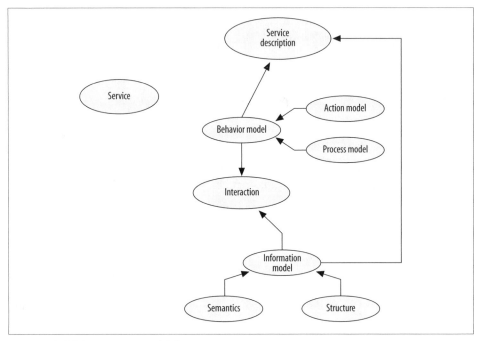

Figure 7-3. SOA interaction model decomposition

The information model governs all the data passed into and out of a service. Typically, the data is constrained using some form of declaration. An example might be an XML schema that constrains data going into a service to only two signed integers, serialized as XML.

The behavior model governs all the patterns of interaction or service invocation, on both sides of the service interface boundary. The model might be a simple idempotent request/response pair or a longer-running subscribe/push pattern where the service keeps sending responses back to the consumer until the consumer sends another message to unsubscribe.

The service's *execution context* is the overall set of circumstances in which the service invocation life cycle plays out. A service's execution may be affected by business rules, legislative rules, the role of the service consumer, and the state of the service provider. We used Starbucks as an example in Chapter 4 to illustrate this concept (see "Services" on page 67).

Dynamic Behavior

The dynamic pattern of interaction with a service describes the behavior of all actors working with the service at runtime. Potential consumers must first be aware of the service's existence and purpose, including its real-world effects, before they can consume the service. In the electronic world, it's best to use a specific, standard set of protocols and technologies across all service and consumer interfaces, creating an ad hoc service bus. There are many interaction models with services, but those described here are the most common.

Request/Response

Request/Response is a pattern in which the service consumer uses configured client software to issue an invocation request to a service provided by the service provider. The request results in an optional response (see Figure 7-4). Request/Response is by far the most common interaction pattern on the public Web.

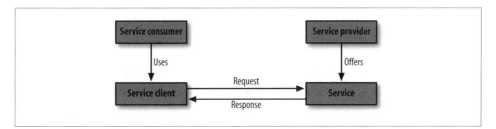

Figure 7-4. SOA Request/Response pattern

Request/Response via service registry

An optional service registry can help the service consumer automatically configure certain aspects of its service client. The service provider pushes changes regarding the service's details to the registry to which the consumer has subscribed, which sends the consumer notifications about the changes. The service consumer can then reconfigure the service client to talk to the service. Figure 7-5 represents this process conceptually.

Subscribe/Push

A third pattern for interaction is called Subscribe/Push. In this pattern, one or more clients register subscriptions with a service to receive messages based on some criteria. Regardless of the criteria, the externally visible pattern remains the same. The

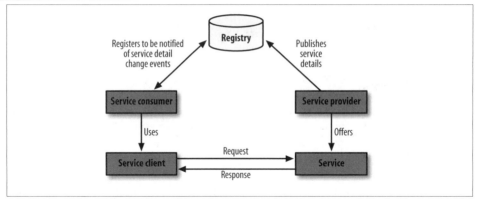

Figure 7-5. SOA Request/Response pattern with a service registry in the equation

Subscribe/Push pattern can be as simple as clients subscribing to a mailing list, but it supports a wide range of much more complicated functionality.

 Readers who are familiar with Message-Oriented Middleware (MOM) may wish to contrast this pattern with those systems. MOM usually is configured to push asynchronous messages rather than always adhering to the Request/Response pattern. These types of patterns are becoming more common within SOA infrastructure, and you can read about them in David A. Chappell's *Enterprise Service Bus* (*http://oreilly.com/catalog/ 9780596006754/*) (O'Reilly).[†]

Subscriptions may remain in effect over long periods before being canceled or revoked. A subscription may, in some cases, also register additional service endpoints to receive notifications. For example, an emergency management system may notify all fire stations in the event of a major earthquake using a common language such as the OASIS Common Alerting Protocol (CAP).[‡] An example of the Subscribe/Push pattern appears in Figure 7-6.

Probe and Match

The Probe and Match pattern is used for discovery of services. In this variation, shown in Figure 7-7, a single client may multicast or broadcast a message to several endpoints on a single network fabric, prompting them to respond based on certain criteria. For example, this pattern may be used to determine whether large numbers of servers on a server farm are capable of handling more traffic based on the fact that they are all scaled at less than 50% capacity. This variation of the SOA message exchange pattern

---

[†] See *http://safari.oreilly.com/0596006756*.

[‡] CAP is a standard from the OASIS Emergency TC (*http://www.oasis-open.org/committees/tc_home.php?wg _abbrev=emergency*).

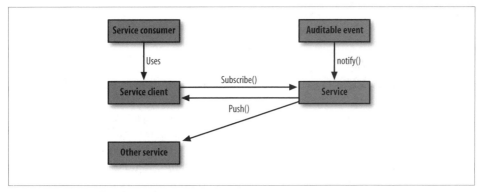

Figure 7-6. SOA Subscribe/Push pattern

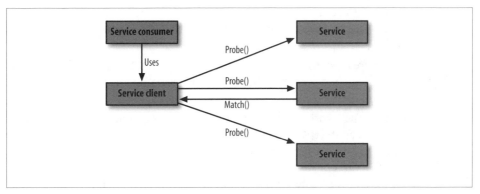

Figure 7-7. SOA Probe and Match pattern

may also be used to locate specific services. There are definitely caveats with using such a pattern, as it may become bandwidth-intensive if used often. Using a registry or another centralized metadata facility may be a better option, because the registry interaction does not require sending `probe()` messages to all the endpoints to find one; by convention, registries allow a query to locate the desired endpoint using a filter query or other search algorithm.

In the Probe and Match scenario in Figure 7-7, the service client probes three services, yet only the middle one returns a successful match message. A hybrid approach could use the best of both the registry and probe and match models for locating service endpoints. For example, registry software could implement a probe interface to allow service location without requiring wire transactions going to all endpoints, and the searching mechanism could probe multiple registries at the same time.

There are several other variations of SOA message exchange patterns; however, an exhaustive list would be beyond the scope of this book.

Implementation

When implementing SOA, architects have to deal with several key issues:

Protocols and standards

> Implementers need to make sure that a common set of protocols and standards is employed to ensure that users can communicate with all services without requiring custom client software for each service. Such noninteroperability would constitute an anti-pattern of SOA. For example, if all of a provider's services use Simple Object Access Protocol (SOAP) over HTTP to communicate, it's much easier to wire together multiple services for a common purpose. If each service uses a different protocol and the service responses came back in differing data formats (e.g., one in XML, another in EDI, another in CSV, and another in plain ASCII), the work required to make the service bus operate might be disproportionately greater than the work involved in building a self-contained application from the ground up. On the public Web, the cost of variations tends to fall on consumers. Applying common practices and protocols makes sense and will help adoption rates.

Security

> Some services are open to anyone, but most have a limited number of acceptable users and roles, and service providers try to limit use to that list.

Denial-of-service (DoS) and other attacks

> Implementers must work to minimize the impact of potential DoS attacks on mission-critical services. Keeping the impact of a failed connection as small as possible is a good foundation. In more intricate systems, one safeguard may be to require every service consumer to use a registry to get the endpoint coordinates for the service and to configure its service client appropriately before talking to the service. In the event of a DoS attack, this will allow the service provider to dynamically redirect legitimate traffic to a new service endpoint that is unknown to the attacker in order to avoid interruptions in service provision. It will deny DoS attackers the ability to even send a message to the new endpoint, and a ring or proxies on the perimeter will drop them. Of course, a smart attacker might then target the registry, so a hybrid approach would be more secure.

Governance

> Service providers monitor service invocation requests during their life cycles to make sure they can scale the number of active service endpoints to meet demand in peak times. This is particularly important if the services perform some mission-critical function (like routing a 911 telephone call during a major emergency such as Hurricane Katrina). Additionally, service providers need to monitor the real-world effects of what their services are allowing consumers to do. For example, if you typically build a product at a rate of 1,000 units per month and you receive a purchase request for 30,000 units via one of your services, you'll need to carefully consider the impact of the request because you will not be able to deliver the product in a timely manner.

Business Problem (Story) Resolved

The architects can apply the SOA pattern and refactor their IT system to be service-oriented, as illustrated in Figure 7-8. The core service platform contains several components, each with specialized tasks to fulfill. The core service container governs service invocation requests during their life cycles. This container keeps track of the state of each service invocation request and monitors any conditions that may affect service fulfillment. If a service request must use some capabilities in another system, such as the database (depicted at the bottom of Figure 7-8), the service container may route the service request to the relevant component and track timeouts or other errors that might result in unsuccessful service invocation. The invocation layer is where all service requests are started. It can contain multiple types of mechanisms for kicking off service requests. The human actor may simply use a form to log into a system or systems. Note that, unlike in Figure 7-1, now a single authentication service is shared across all applications within the enterprise's platform. This is known as *single sign-on* (SSO). Likewise, there is only one data persistence component. This saves the IT staff money as well as time because now it has to look after only one system, rather than several.

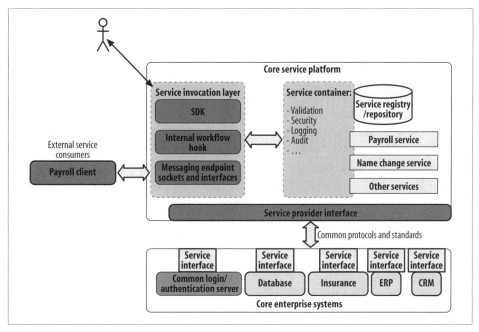

Figure 7-8. The enterprise's systems, previously shown in Figure 7-1, refactored as an SOA

The runtime service registry/repository can also aid in directing requests to the appropriate core enterprise systems to handle the functional aspects of service fulfillment. Any number of enterprise applications can be added to the core service platform via the service provider interface, which uses a common set of protocols and standards to enable interoperability with the service platform. This, in effect, forms a special type of bus often called an *enterprise service bus* (ESB).

In our example, the enterprise has also outsourced one function, payroll, by allowing a third party to hook into its system via a messaging endpoint. Similar hooks could be added should the company decide to outsource other functions or act as a resource for other enterprises in the future.

The SOA infrastructure is very nimble, and new services can be added with relative ease. If an application has to be replaced, as long as the new application supports the existing service interface, there will be no interruptions to the rest of the system.

Specializations

There are too many specializations of the SOA architecture to list in this book. Some add service aggregation (also known as *service composition*) to combine services or build composite applications. Others use workflow engines to orchestrate multiple services into a business workflow. Business process automation is another consideration that is built on SOA, but it is not part of SOA itself.

Known Uses

There are several known uses of the SOA pattern. For instance, Microsoft's .NET architecture exemplifies many of the concepts we've discussed. IBM, Oracle, JBoss,[§] Sun Microsystems, Red Hat, TIBCO, and BEA also have similar ESB SOA functionality built into their application servers.[‖] JBossESB is based on a loosely coupled message pattern approach in which contracts between endpoints are defined within the messages and not at the service interface boundary. It uses SOA principles within the ESB.

J2EE application servers offered by various vendors can be used alongside secondary web applications (such as Adobe's LiveCycle Enterprise Suite) as a core SOA platform to provide business-related services and aggregate them into processes. Although many software vendors offer SOA infrastructures or components, it is also important to note that a thriving open source community is rapidly building many components for SOA, and many standards bodies are making protocols, standards, and technologies available to the masses.

The technology family most often used for implementing SOA is referred to as "web services." However, simply using web services standards does not necessarily mean that a service-oriented architecture has been built.

[§] See *http://labs.jboss.com/jbossesb*.

[‖] ESB is a specialized set of patterns within an SOA infrastructure or context. For more on ESB, see Enterprise Service Bus (*http://oreilly.com/catalog/9780596006754/*) (O'Reilly).

Options for the payloads are too numerous to list; most are based on XML. The more commonly used payload formats are binary formats and specialized XML constraint languages from groups such as OASIS, including the Universal Business Language (UBL) and Common Alerting Protocol (CAP).

On the public Web, the SOA pattern is also used to create public services. While public services typically act to connect users outside of a process boundary, the same best practices apply. Consistency, ease of use, and reliability are just as important (if not more so) for public services as they are inside of an enterprise.

Consequences

SOA architectures allow the elimination of many dependencies between systems, because the service acts as an action boundary to cleanly separate the consumer from the provider. Duplication of systems can be reduced or possibly eliminated if services can be repurposed among multiple consumers. IT management should become easier if SOA is used to architect systems that can be cleanly separated so that functionality can be easily isolated for testing when things go wrong.

Many other Web 2.0 patterns in this book depend on SOA. The Mashup and Software as a Service (SaaS) patterns, for example, rely on a layer of services that can be mixed and matched to create new and powerful applications and experiences for users.

Unauthorized access to key systems is a real risk that service providers take when exposing their services via the Internet. Overuse of a single service might also become a factor that results in a service no longer being functional for its intended users.

Architects have to consider which interfaces or systems (capabilities) are potential candidates for becoming services. If a capability is used by only one other system, it may not be a suitable candidate. On the other hand, if it is used by more than one process (for example, login/authentication), it might be ideal for implementing as a service that can be repurposed for several processes or clients.

The Software as a Service (SaaS) Pattern

Also Known As

Terms often associated with the Software as a Service pattern include:

Utility Computing and Cloud Computing
Cloud Computing is not the same as SaaS; rather, it is a specialized pattern of virtualization. Utility and Cloud Computing refer to treating computing resources as virtualized, metered services, similar from a consumer's perspective to how we consume other utilities (such as water, gas, electricity, and pay-per-view cable).

On-demand applications

On-demand applications provide access to computing resources on an ad hoc basis when the functionality is required. Using the *http://createpdf.adobe.com* service to create a single PDF document online rather than having to download and install a version of Acrobat is a good example.

Software Above the Level of a Single Device

This pattern relates to software that spans Internet-connected devices and builds on the growing pervasiveness of the online experience. It touches on various aspects of the SaaS pattern; in particular, the concepts of distributed computing of tasks via network connections.

Model-View-Controller (MVC)

Some people consider SaaS a specialization of the MVC pattern that distributes the Model, View, and Controller (or parts thereof) over multiple resources located on the Internet. It is strongly related to SaaS, and most SaaS providers follow the MVC pattern when implementing SaaS.

Business Problem (Story)

Consider a software vendor that wishes to develop spam removal software to keep spam from reaching its clients' inboxes. This can be achieved by writing algorithms that analyze incoming local email messages, detect possible spam messages, and flag them in such a way that the mailbox owners can filter them out automatically without having to manually sort through all the messages.

The business problem arises from the fact that spam is constantly changing, which makes it difficult to detect and flag. Spam is typically sent from a variety of spoofed email addresses, and the specific text patterns are changed frequently. For example, if you wanted to detect any spam that had the word "Viagra" in it, you could simply use Perl's regular expression matching syntax:

```
if ($emailString =~ m/viagra/;)
{
 $SpamScore =+ 1;
}
```

However, all the spammer would have to do is alter the case of some of the letters to thwart this detection, as in the following:

```
"ViAGRA"
```

You could counter this in Perl by adding an i flag to ignore case, as follows:

```
if ($emailString =~ m/viagra/i;)
{
 $SpamScore =+ 1;
}
```

However, the spammer could then substitute an exclamation point, the number 1, or the letter *l* for the letter *I*, capitalizing on the face that the human mind will perceive

"Viagra" if it sees "V!AGRA," "V1AGRA," or "VlAGRA." To a human these terms might semantically be the same, but changing the one byte from an *I* to another character will render useless the efforts of a computer trying to filter spam based on a string of characters. Each possible mutation would require the software vendor to write and distribute new patches to detect the latest variations to each client, possibly on a daily or even hourly basis. In this case, the Perl syntax could be changed to:

```
if ($emailString =~ m/v*gra/i;) {
{
 $SpamScore =+ 1;
}
```

The ballet between those who create and send spam and those who try to detect and delete it is a constantly morphing work in progress, with new steps being introduced every day. Each individual the company serves could attempt to create these rules by himself for his own mailbox, but this would be both ineffective and inefficient. Users would each sample only a small subset of all spam, would not be able to easily create heuristic filters to detect spam, and would likely spend an inordinately large amount of time on this activity.

Context

The SaaS pattern is useful any time a customer base has needs that could be addressed more efficiently or reliably by creating a service all of them can share across organizational boundaries.

This pattern occurs whenever a person or organization is building an application whose model, control, or view aspects must be refreshed based on dynamic circumstances or instances in which specialized functionality of the application must be delivered. The pattern could apply anywhere a static application does not easily lend itself to frequent specialization of the model, view, or control aspects required to make it function properly.

The pattern is useful in situations in which users need more computer resources than they can easily support on their local systems and in those situations where users need particular computing resources only occasionally.

Derived Requirements

Computing resources should be architected to be reachable (as discussed in the section on SOA) over whatever network or fabric the architect designs the application to work with. For example, most web-enabled SaaS applications use a common transport protocol, and most ham radio operators use a common frequency to broadcast information or pass it along in a chain.

Functional components of the core computing resources must be usable via a well-defined interface. Such an interface should not be bound to a single client or single model for delivery (such as installation of an application) and should support multiple options for building the user interface (e.g., web-based or client application interface).

Generalized Solution

SaaS is a model of software delivery in which the manufacturer is responsible for the daily technical operation of the software provided to the clients (including maintenance and support), while the clients enjoy the full benefits of the software from remote locations. SaaS is a model of "functionality delivery" rather than "software distribution." Most of the functionality can be delivered over the Internet or made available in such a way that the end user can interact with the application to get that functionality without having to install the software on her machine. This approach can deliver functionality to any market segment, from home consumers to corporations, and hybrid solutions can deliver small pieces of client-side software that make certain tasks easier.

Static Structure

The basic deployment pattern for SaaS involves deploying different aspects of the model, view, and control components of an application to multiple physical locations. The deployment approach may vary greatly depending on the software and its complexity and dependence on other aspects. Figure 7-9 shows how the basic deployment pattern for SaaS differs from traditional software distribution.

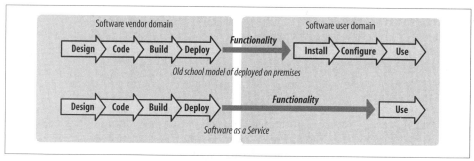

Figure 7-9. Deployment patterns contrasted (SaaS versus conventional approach)

The service should also be able to learn from its users when appropriate. This concept of "software that gets better as more people use it," a hallmark of Web 2.0, has many advantages. For example, in the business story shown in Figure 7-10, if enough email flows through a pattern detector, spam recognition becomes much more accurate based on the collective interactions of thousands of users. As more and more users flag the same messages as spam, the server will begin to recognize those messages as spam, and the global filter will then prevent them from being delivered to other end users. Many readers probably use this type of functionality already without really knowing it.

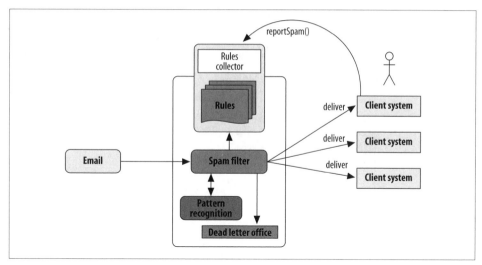

Figure 7-10. Spam filter software as a service

Google's Gmail is a prime example of this pattern in action. Google Search is another dynamic example of Software as a Service that gets better the more that people use it. Google actually tracks the links users click on to determine how many people seek the same resource for the same search term. This system is much more sophisticated than a simple adaptive algorithm, yet the principle benefit of large-scale use is that the system learns and adapts based on users' behaviors.

This functionality is a side benefit of SaaS rather than a core aspect of the pattern.

Dynamic Behavior

The dynamic behavior of the SaaS pattern can vary greatly depending on which protocols, standards, and architectural approaches are chosen. Figure 7-11 shows a common depiction of the pattern.

First, a user identifies his requirements for consuming computing resources. This pattern can be implemented at many levels of complexity, from a secure web service to a simple user interface such as an HTML web page in a browser. The user will interact with the service (the service in this case is a proxy), which will then invoke the core functionality. The responses are appropriately directed back to the user, as required.

Note that this pattern becomes very interesting when multiple users employ the resources and implementers have capabilities that do not exist for their non-SaaS counterparts. First, the functionality provider can detect and act on patterns in runtime interactions. An example of this might be the detection of some error state that is occurring for multiple users of the system (e.g., the email clients are crashing because of a nefarious script contained within some emails). Rather than waiting for enough users to contact the software provider with enough information to enable it to fix the error,

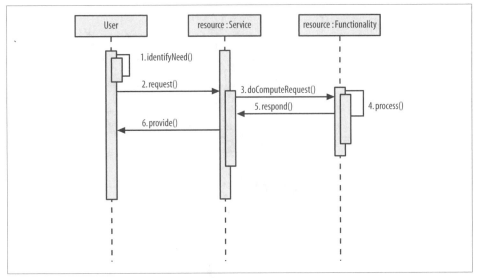

Figure 7-11. A dynamic view of one way to visualize SaaS

the provider can detect the condition itself at an early stage and has access to sufficient information to enable it to trace the source of the error. Ultimately, all users of the software will have a much better user experience if problems are mitigated sooner rather than later and before they feel compelled to complain about them.

Second, a provider may want to consider scaling the system in the backend to handle large numbers of requests. Sudden traffic spikes can adversely impact the user experience, making the system seem unresponsive. Service providers may want to investigate other services, notably those of Cloud Computing providers, if they need to support widely varying usage levels. Most Cloud Computing providers offer automatic scaling to support the amount of processing power and storage needed by an application.

Implementation

As shown in Figure 7-12,[#] designers of software provided as a service rather than as a static, installed entity must consider several new nuances of the industry, as these changes in how users interact with software vendors are affecting the way we should design and architect SaaS.

When implementing SaaS, you may need to ensure that no one can take advantage of your license model. For example, if you license only one user, what keeps that user from simply sharing her username and password and reselling your service? There are various types of license models for SaaS. Some are single-enterprise licenses, with the

---

[#] This figure was provided courtesy of Fred Chong. See *http://blogs.msdn.com/fred_chong/*.

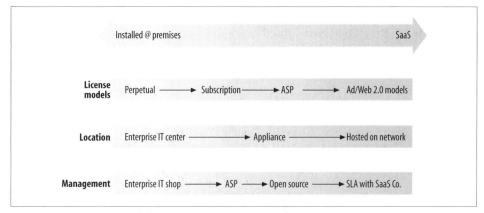

Figure 7-12. Distinctions of the SaaS pattern

cost based on the size of the enterprise. Spam software and Microsoft Exchange Server are reported to use this model. By contrast, Adobe Systems uses a "per use" model for *http://createpdf.acrobat.com*, where users can either create PDFs one at a time or protect them with a persistent policy. Other software business models (e.g., for Google Search and other widgets) are built around advertising revenue models.

A software vendor implementing SaaS also can react swiftly to bugs in the system. The vendor can monitor all users concurrently to detect software glitches that may require immediate attention and may be able to fix them before most users even notice.

Business Problem (Story) Resolved

The spam detection software is housed in a federated server environment, and users' incoming email can be automatically pre-passed through the filters to detect spam. Any spam that sneaks through can be recognized and trapped by secondary mechanisms (including human users) and reported back to the spam detection infrastructure, enabling the system to adapt to the latest spammer tactics. There is no discernable delay or lag in incoming email, and most spam email gets eliminated.

Sampling a very large cross section of all mail makes it easier to detect patterns indicating spam emails. This results in the entire system performing better, to the benefit of all users.

Specializations

SaaS may be specialized by using advanced computer algorithms to perform reasoning tasks such as inference. These ultra-advanced systems may one day be able to use cognitive skills to recognize and act on certain patterns of events. For example, these hybrid systems could use a combination of the Bayesian Theorem (conditional probability) and lexical heuristic filtering (finding evidence to support a hypothesis) to dynamically change their functionality. Such specializations will also benefit from adoption of the Collaborative Tagging (a.k.a. folksonomy) pattern, discussed later in this chapter, as it will help foster computational intelligence applications that can reason and infer hypotheses.

Known Uses

Postini, Inc. (which Google acquired in 2007[*]) figured out quite a while ago that centralization and offering its security, compliance, and productivity solutions as a service would result in better spam detection for end users. Recently, many other email companies have begun to use similar SaaS models. Apple's iTunes music application is perhaps one of the most prominent examples of a hybrid approach to the Software as a Service pattern. The iTunes application has some predetermined functionality and user interfaces (the "V" and "C" components of "Model-View-Controller"); however, much of the information presented to the user is based on information (the "M" in "MVC") the application receives from the iTunes servers during runtime. This hybrid approach can link user profiles to service calls to offer users better experiences.

Adobe Systems recently launched a service that allows people to manually create small numbers of PDF documents online and optionally link to them other functionality for things such as enabling rights management. Google continues to expand its SaaS offerings. Initially, its search service used algorithms to vary search result rankings based on user interaction patterns. Recently, Google has added multiple other SaaS offerings, including creation and manipulation of online documents, spreadsheets, and more. Note that most of Gmail has always been provided as a service rather than as an application.

Consequences

The negative consequences of using the SaaS pattern are minimal, but they need to be addressed from the outset. Offering software as a service may create additional complexity in supporting computing resources for large numbers of users. The ability to dynamically scale an offering based on surges in the number of users requesting the functionality is also an issue.

In addition, authentication—especially when used to force compliance with software licensing—can be difficult to implement and to police.

The most noteworthy consequence of implementing this pattern is that the software may have a dependency on an Internet connection. In many cases, if the connection does not work, neither will the software. When such a mechanism is possible and makes sense, the best way to avoid such issues is to employ client-side caching. The appropriateness of this strategy varies by application. Caching Google Search is

---

[*] See *http://www.postini.com/goog/google.php*.

difficult, and would be mostly useless in an environment where readers couldn't go to the linked articles anyway. On the other hand, technologies like the Adobe Integrated Runtime (AIR) and Google Gears are steps in the right direction.

Denial-of-service attacks can also be a threat. A malicious user may be able to overpower the bandwidth or computational capabilities of software implemented as a service and effectively deny or greatly slow down other users' experiences.

End users often prefer to keep their software in a controlled and secure environment. Because SaaS applications are not hosted or controlled by the user, the user might be subjected to occasional outages when service upgrades or other events take place on the provider side.

Also, personal security risks are inherent in passing information back and forth on the open Internet. Users should carefully assess what risks are acceptable for their purposes.

The Participation-Collaboration Pattern

Also Known As

The Participation-Collaboration pattern is related to two other patterns:

Harnessing Collective Intelligence
> This pattern, from the O'Reilly Radar report *Web 2.0 Principles and Best Practices (http://radar.oreilly.com/research/web2-report.html)*, discusses aspects of the Participation-Collaboration pattern where inputs from many users over time are combined into composite works.

Innovation in Assembly
> This pattern, also from the O'Reilly Radar report *Web 2.0 Principles and Best Practices*, is focused on the ability to build platforms where remixing of data and services creates new opportunities and markets. The Participation-Collaboration pattern and the data aggregation patterns in this book cover some aspects of this and of the Harnessing Collective Intelligence pattern.

The Constant Beta

Another pattern sometimes talked about in relation to Web 2.0 is the Constant Beta pattern. Many companies are benefiting by releasing products (including software or other digital assets) earlier in the design and development cycle, allowing users to directly interact with these assets and help provide direction toward finishing the work.

Companies we studied that were considered "Web 2.0 companies" tended to act in a very agile manner. Some of them were flexible by design, in stark contrast to many of the larger companies existing in their space in years gone by. Ruby on Rails[†] gets a great deal of attention as a flexible technology; however, the Getting Real design and development process perfected by 37signals[‡] (a variant of the Agile software development methodology) can be considered the agile manifesto. The Getting Real process is about paring things down to the bone, practicing YAGNI (You Aren't Going to Need It) wherever possible, involving users in the design process as early as possible, and then pushing back hard on new feature requests to stay focused.

The Constant Beta concept is about really being agile, releasing often, and making small gains in functionality (as opposed to waiting up to two years between software releases and doing wholesale upgrades to users' applications). Software vendors benefit from rapidly changing requirements, even if these requirements are not considered when planning the initial software, as they help to reveal the holistic direction the industry is taking.

One of the most ironic Constant Beta stories we encountered was with Blogger.com, which was released to the public for use months before the owner (Google) finally removed the "beta" label. As soon as the last changes were added, it immediately received reports of multiple technical issues, prompting substantial growth in the online list of issues at *http://knownissues.blogspot.com*.

What lessons can we learn from the Blogger.com example? The "beta" label lowers users' expectations and often facilitates a friendly dialog with them as they discuss new features with you.

The number of Web 2.0 companies that are incredibly small and agile also is a testament to the fact that software vendors now have much better developer products that vastly improve garage businesses' abilities to produce world-class websites in record time. Agile development, coupled with powerful infrastructures such as Ruby on Rails, AJAX, Adobe's Flex and AIR, Python, PHP, and Cascading Style Sheets (CSS) technologies, has resulted in far higher productivity for the average developer.

[†] See *http://www.rubyonrails.org*.

[‡] See *http://en.wikipedia.org/wiki/37signals*.

Business Problem (Story)

Until recently, the easiest way to compose and distribute textual content was to have a small group of authors write some material, print it on paper, bind that paper, and sell it or give it away. Printing is a much cheaper process for large runs than copying by hand: its setup costs are considerable, but the additional costs of printing an extra copy are relatively small. The publishing business structured itself around those costs, trying to find ways of ensuring that projects that made it to the printing press could reach the largest market possible. Traditionally, publishing processes have emphasized uniformity, quality, and stability at the expense of openness, preferring controlled conversations between authors, leading predictably through a complex process that culminated at the printing press and resulted in sales.

Once something is published, if the material becomes obsolete or errors are found, there is no quick or inexpensive way to change it. The high costs of new print runs also mean that once material is published, it isn't generally possible to append contributions to the material until enough demand accumulates for a new revision to supersede the earlier edition. If a publisher prints a large number of copies of a book and then some new facts that challenge its content are uncovered, this presents a huge problem for the publisher. Pulping books (or destroying software or any other material produced this way) is an expensive waste of resources.

Consider a small company that wants to create a manual covering the use of one of its products. The traditional approach is to gather a small set of experts to write it, hopefully minimizing the potential for costly errors. Manuals face a market of readers with different skill levels, though, and the company's writers may not always get everything right. For example, they may assume that everyone reading the manual has a deep technical understanding about how alternating current works in relation to direct current, and fail to give the average reader enough information to make informed decisions. Customers often know what they need better than the company does, but the flow of information has traditionally gone from the publisher to the customer, rather than the other way around.

Context

The ease of distributing information on the Web makes it possible to discard most of the constraints of earlier publishing processes, opening them up to include contributions from many more participants. The Participation-Collaboration pattern can appear wherever a group of people has a common interest in sharing and appending to information about a specific subject. This pattern recognizes that an open process may provide better results than having only a few people present their knowledge. This pattern lets a wider group of people collaborate on and contribute to a work, so that it reflects a wider set of experiences and opinions. This many-to-many participation model has worked very well for the development and maintenance of open source software for years. It has also been applied to website and portal development, as well as publishing.

Derived Requirements

To operate, this pattern requires a system or platform where collaborative input can be collected and shared in a way that enables people to interact with it. Participating users generally need to be able to write, not just read, the material. These systems must also have some form of overrule mechanism to guard against common threats such as spam and vandalism, as well as mechanisms allowing users to validate the points of view contributed by other participants.

A community must self-organize to police the collective works and ensure that common interests are protected. This is a nontechnical issue, but it has far-reaching technical implications. For example, Wikipedia.org has been widely criticized by many people for its lack of a common set of standards implemented across all articles. People often contribute to articles on Wikipedia only to later find that the editors have removed their contributions. It can be extremely frustrating for people who consider themselves experts on a given subject to have an editor who is not familiar with the subject unilaterally decide that the information they've contributed is not worthwhile. Sometimes errant information also gets published on Wikipedia, and when knowledgeable people try to correct it, the editors keep the accurate information from being published.

Version control over content is also a common requirement for those implementing this pattern. Keeping track of multiple versions of shared edits helps participants to see and discuss the process, and adds accountability.

Generalized Solution

The generalized solution for the Participation-Collaboration pattern is to implement a collaborative platform through which humans or application actors can contribute knowledge, code, facts, and other material relevant to a certain topic. A seed discussion or starter text can be made available, possibly in more than one format or language, and participants can then modify or append to that core content.

Static Structure

In the static structure depicted in Figure 7-13, a contributor can come in and review published content, possibly aggregated from a content management repository. The contributor can add to or even change some of the published material. The magnitude of the changes can vary greatly, from as minor as adding a small "tag" (see the discussion of the Collaborative Tagging pattern, later in this chapter) or fixing a typo to as major as erasing or rewriting a complete section of content. The actions are fully auditable, and in most such solutions, the users' identities can be verified. This helps to prevent contributors from deleting material and replacing it with content that is abusive or

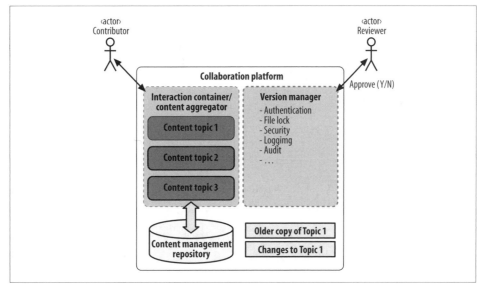

Figure 7-13. The Participation-Collaboration pattern

misleading in nature (e.g., a Wikipedia user erasing a page that discusses online poker and replacing it with an advertisement for his online poker website).

Each time content is changed, it generates an auditable event. In systems such as Wikipedia, volunteer *reviewers* are notified of these events and may subsequently inspect the content and, if they see fit, change it back to its original form. Most such solutions provide mechanisms to lock content so that more than one collaborator cannot edit it concurrently.

Figure 7-13 uses the term "Topic 1," but you can replace this with almost any other type of artifact, whether it be text, code, audio, video, or something else entirely. The number of Contributor actors can range from one to infinity.

Dynamic Behavior

The simplified UML sequence diagram shown in Figure 7-14 indicates the order of activity during the Participation-Collaboration process. There are many nuances to each step of the sequence. For example, when a logged-in user first requests the content, by retrieving a copy of the content she may place a "lock" upon it that prevents other participants from concurrently accessing it with write privileges. In the case of wikis, this lock is acquired as soon as a participant clicks the Edit button and begins to edit a section of content.

The reviewer may not necessarily accept or reject the user's changes wholesale; in fact, he may take on a role similar to that of the collaborator and further change the content.

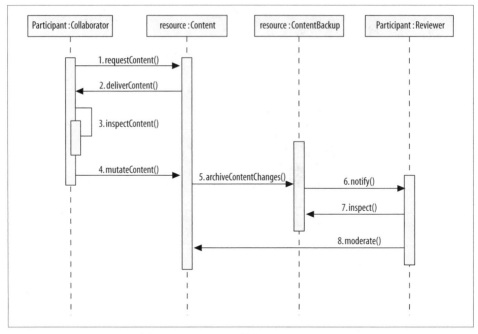

Figure 7-14. The sequence of the Participation-Collaboration pattern

During this process, most implementations normally keep a copy of the original content in case the changed copy becomes corrupted or otherwise unusable.

Implementation

The Participation-Collaboration pattern can operate on any type of content. The pattern is certainly not limited to text, although wiki and publishing examples might give that impression. Several websites, for example, allow video content to be remastered, or allow other changes whereby a user can reproduce the original content, add new video and audio, and create an entirely new piece of work. Several collaborative music sites use the same pattern to allow amateur musicians to mix their tracks with those of professionals, creating unique audio content.[§]

As an implementer of this pattern, you will probably want to have some form of editorial control over content within your domain, but you should realize that some interactions may result in content being moved outside your domain. Having clearly stated and scoped licenses for all contributions is a prime concern that many legal experts have expressed. Legal jurisdiction is another primary consideration. Some countries have not signed or agreed to, or do not enforce the terms of, various international legal instruments (such as treaties from the World Intellectual Property Organization, or

[§] *http://mix2r.com, http://www.splicemusic.com*, and *http://www.mixmatchmusic.com* are three examples.

WIPO||) to mutually respect intellectual property rights. This could create legal problems around ownership and derivative works.

Implementers will likely want some way to identify their contributors and participants. Those who demonstrate consistent wise judgment (as judged by the collective community) in content participation may be good candidates for reviewers. Those who repeatedly abuse such systems should be barred from further participation until they can demonstrate a better understanding of the activity. Of course, much of this is subjective, and implementers should also place a great level of trust on the user community as a whole. Communities can generally police themselves when their common interest is challenged.

One criticism of Wikipedia is that a select few editors end up in control of the collective knowledge that was originally contributed by many diverse contributors. Some Wikipedia pages have disappeared completely, much to the dismay of subjects of those pages, and some content has been ruled unworthy or improper. Trusting one or two people to control the content related to a specific topic may lead to contributor frustration. Proponents of this argument claim that mechanisms like Wikipedia represent a clear danger to society: if considered authoritative and beyond reproach, they could effectively be used to rewrite portions of history, at least for people who don't look beyond these sources.

Archiving older copies of content is also a consideration for implementers. The ability to examine audit trails and older versions of content can be critical for custodians of mutable digital content. Some watch for a pattern of change and reversion to the original, followed by the same change and reversion over and over again. Think about the Wikipedia problems we just discussed. Multiple users logging in and repeatedly attempting to add the same reference to a specific page could indicate that content really needs to be added. Alternatively, if the editor repeatedly rejects the content, it might be because the same user is logging in under different names, attempting to make the same change. An archived content set might also be of interest to those who study public perceptions as they change regarding certain topics. For example, the American cyclist Lance Armstrong became a hero and won millions of fans by coming back from a deadly form of cancer to win the world's toughest cycling race a record seven times. The public's attitude regarding this feat and their admiration for Lance went back and forth on several occasions, and a historical perspective might be a crucial part of any analysis of his career. Edits, though, likely reflect perspectives current at the time they were made.

This pattern has also assisted the rise of *microformats*, or small snippets of syntax that can be used to mark up existing web pages to declare that certain pieces of content are formally structured using the syntax and semantics defined by those microformats. An example might be a *vCard* (a formal syntax for describing a business card), or a

---

|| See *http://www.wipo.int/treaties/en/*.

declaration to help attribute an author to a specific piece of content. We describe the microformats phenomenon in more detail later in this chapter, in the section on the Structured Information pattern.

When working with non-text content, implementers will have to employ extra metadata to ensure that the content can be mixed and matched. Such metadata might include the beats per minute (BPM) on audio files, the codec on video content, and the timestamps on aggregate audio-visual content.

Business Problem (Story) Resolved

The online manual for a product becomes far more useful if customers and users can contribute material (e.g., filling in details that the manual's original authors may have left out because they made faulty assumptions about the readers' level of technical expertise). Instead of publishing a static manual for its customers, the company could allow existing users to participate in creating a more comprehensive and useful information set, to help new users who have purchased the product as well as people considering purchasing it. Free and open information carries with it much more weight when it comes from users who are outside the company, and reading positive feedback from existing customers often encourages others to buy the company's products. Another benefit is that users can include useful workarounds to potential problems or even describe alternative uses of the product that its designers may not have foreseen (say, how to use an ordinary steak knife to perform an emergency tracheotomy on someone who is choking).#

To achieve this, the company might set up a special online manual using a wiki that allows contributions by many people. In this scenario, all users must register and log in each time they visit. There are also forums where users can help others with questions pertaining to products and services. Note that such an infrastructure might be implemented by the user community itself rather than by the company that manufactures or distributes the devices, although, generally speaking, the company would be wise to participate. Users may gain status points each time they help other users and append materials that are accepted into the wiki. The company can track these status points and use them to provide special promotions to top users for future sales campaigns or even beta tests of new products (several technology companies use this bonus scheme now and offer users who make large numbers of helpful bulletin board posts early access to alpha versions of their software).

The company itself can employ participants who try to let the community run as autonomously as possible, but who also make sure that all questions are answered in a timely manner and that no errant or abusive information is posted to the company's website. A consumer can download a printable manual or section thereof at any time,

---

Inspired by Katey on United Airlines Flight 446 to Charlotte, North Carolina.

thus eliminating the wasteful process of the company printing static and rapidly outdated materials for every product.

A dynamic publishing platform could also allow content owners to incorporate content provided by their user communities or based on customers' wishes (notifications of product news, new reviews, new tech bulletins, and updates to user manuals) that could ultimately make for a better user experience for everyone.

ENTREPRENEUR ALERT

Entrepreneurs may have already sensed that providing a common platform that companies wishing to publish their manuals online could use as a base might be a good idea. If you built a platform that had all the features necessary to enable companies to manage and publish manuals online, plus added functionality to let members of the public contribute to the manuals, it could prove a very useful software package. A smart entrepreneur could carry this idea further by modifying an existing open-document publishing platform and marrying it with a common set of tasks and labels for various types of information (the folksonomy approach). The information could be further specialized for publishing to the Web or paper, or it could be just a direct conduit to the company itself to provide useful feedback.

An employee might monitor what pages were requested most often, resulting in an understanding of where the company's manual was lacking information. A common rating system employed by multiple companies would ultimately be far more useful than scattered approaches to ranking information (e.g., one company asking users to rate its product on a scale of 1–5, with 1 being not good and 5 being good, and another company asking people to rank its product on a scale of 1–10, with 1 being the best in the marketplace and 10 being the worst).

Employing a common set of metrics for all such Participation-Collaboration implementations for public feedback of company-written materials might help consumers worldwide to locate more useful information. Additionally, coupling this pattern with other Web 2.0 patterns, such as the Rich User Experience pattern discussed later in this chapter (for example, by providing a place for 3D Flash videos of products in use), might also help companies better communicate certain uses of their products to their customers.

Specializations

There are many specializations of the Participation-Collaboration pattern, including *blogs* (web logs), *blikis* (blogs with wiki support), *blooks* (books that are collaboratively written), *moblogs* (mobile blogs), and *vblogs* (video blogs), among others. Each uses the same basic pattern, where participation and collaboration in a shared work is a core theme.

The same pattern is also used for open source software development, where many programmers contribute code to evolving projects.

Known Uses

Wikis—including many specialized wikis such as Wikipedia and RIApedia,[*] a site devoted to Rich Internet Applications—are probably the best-known use cases of this pattern. SourceForge, Apache, and other open source software processes use the same pattern for code rather than text.

In addition, the specialized content management system Drupal,[†] built in PHP, supports many aspects of Participation-Collaboration right out of the box. (And its manual is written in precisely the way that we outlined earlier.)

Meanwhile, some cool new websites are applying this pattern in a different manner. As noted earlier, at least three companies—Mix2r.com, Gluejam, and MixMatchMusic—have collaborative sites where music is open sourced and new tracks can be mixed with existing ones to create new audio projects. Artists and musicians can contribute loops and original audio tracks to works that others can download.

In the video world, similar companies are pursuing this pattern. MixerCast.com, MovieSet.com, Brightcove.com, and others have used the same approach with video, letting people remix video clips and even provide audio clips to create new works. MovieSet.com also allows users to view the behind-the-scenes aspects of content creation, and in the future it may allow the audience to provide input regarding the plot.

Consequences

As mentioned earlier, this pattern has many benefits. It does, however, require the domain owner to take care not to give the appearance of dominating the community, yet at the same time to try to collectively guide the community toward a common goal.

The Asynchronous Particle Update Pattern

Also Known As

The Asynchronous Particle Update pattern is related to two well-known architectural styles:

Asynchronous JavaScript and XML (AJAX)
> AJAX, which has made web pages much more interactive, is a well-known implementation of this pattern and has been credited with being a major force behind the Web 2.0 movement.

---

[*] See *http://www.riapedia.com*.

[†] See *http://www.drupal.org*.

Representational State Transfer (REST)

REST is a strongly related architectural style, one that often supports the update mechanism. Roy Fielding, one of the principal authors of the Hypertext Transfer Protocol (HTTP) specification, introduced the term *REST* in his 2000 doctoral dissertation on the Web, and it has since come into widespread use in the networking community. Like the Asynchronous Particle Update pattern, REST is a pattern or architectural style and principle of networks that outlines how resources are defined and addressed. The term is often used in a looser sense to describe any simple interface that transmits domain-specific data over HTTP without an additional messaging layer such as SOAP or session tracking via HTTP cookies. In true pattern style, it is possible to design any interchange in accordance with REST without using HTTP or the Internet. It is likewise possible to design simple XML and HTTP interfaces that do not conform to REST principles.

Business Problem (Story)

During the first iteration of the Internet, most clients retrieved content using HTTP GET requests, which returned complete HTML web pages. In true REST style, the web pages were built with information that represented *snapshots* of the state of information at a certain point in time. For some exchanges this did not represent a problem, as the content was updated rather infrequently. But in many instances some of the information changed within moments of the web page being delivered, and some web page users required more dynamic content delivery. These users had to resort to clicking the browser's Reload button, causing the entire page to be resent from the server to the client. In many such cases, the ratio of bytes that needed to be updated compared to the number of bytes in the page that remained static made this a very inefficient operation to force on users. Requests for popular web pages that were normally updated several times per minute could completely overload the providers' servers. Examples included web pages that provided the latest information regarding sporting events such as the Tour de France cycling race, news reports, stock market quotes, and news headlines, among others.

Beyond performance concerns, the page-by-page approach also drastically limited interface possibilities, making it more difficult to replace desktop applications with web applications.

Context

The Asynchronous Particle Update pattern is likely to be useful in any situation in which exchanging a small number of bytes rather than an entire document will save both server and client (and owner) resources.

The pattern is also applicable where the Synchronized Web pattern (discussed later in this chapter) is implemented and multiple users must have regular data updates sent to or pulled into them.

Anywhere there is a stream or supply of rapidly changing data that subscribers want to receive, this pattern will help. There are specialized expressions of it, such as real-time protocols (RTPs) for online collaboration and communication.

Derived Requirements

This pattern requires building or working with a small methodology that is capable of loading a small portion of the document object model (DOM) by making a small, asynchronous request, waiting for a return to the request, and then using the return to update a portion of the page without having to load the entire page. The browser itself must have some form of processing power and access to some way of updating a portion of the page content.

The requests for transfer of data from one point to another should be loosely coupled to the trigger mechanism to allow maximum flexibility in implementation. Being able to trigger updates on events such as user interactions, server events, state changes, or timeout events will provide maximum flexibility for this pattern to be applied over a gamut of contexts.

For this to work, the architecture must have a consistent model for objects (including document objects), events, event listeners, and event dispatchers across multiple tiers of any solution pattern. This means that architects must analyze the event and object models (including the dispatch mechanism) across all technologies, standards, and protocols used within their infrastructures.

Building an application that adheres to the Model-View-Controller pattern is also likely to be an advantage for developers and architects who can manipulate both the server and the client frameworks and code.

Generalized Solution

The generalized solution to this pattern consists of four parts. The first part is a small method built-in to browsers that allows a small structured message to be sent to a remote address and, optionally, waits for a reply. The second part of the solution is a server component that waits for the browser's request and fulfills it by replying based on the incoming parameters. The third part is a small runtime environment within the browser that can manipulate the returned value and make post-retrieval changes to the data. The fourth component is a plug-in (or the browser engine itself) that uses the result of the operation to update the view presented to the user.

The solution should support message exchange patterns other than straight Request/Response (see the discussion of the SOA pattern for more on message exchange patterns). For example, several clients should be able to subscribe to event or state changes, perhaps with one change federating out to several clients.

Static Structure and Dynamic Behavior

Several views of the static structure of this pattern are interspersed with sequence information; therefore, we have combined the static and dynamic depictions of this pattern in this section.

The scenario in Figure 7-15 depicts an asynchronous request/response message exchange based on a user event trigger. In this case, the user clicks her mouse over a button labeled "Update stock quote" and a small `request()` message is dispatched to the server side. The server retrieves the stock quote from the stock quote data provider and returns it to the client side via the response. The service client uses the information to update the browser view.

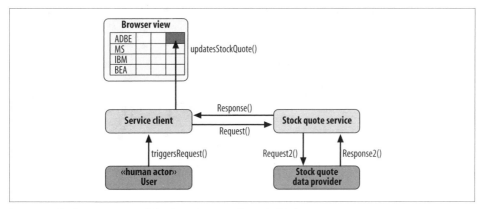

Figure 7-15. Variation one of the Asynchronous Particle Update pattern

In Figure 7-16, the same sequence of events is kicked off by a `timeElapsed()` event, which is set to automatically update the stock quote at certain intervals. In this case, the `timeout(90)` event is triggered from the client to update the node of the DOM every 90 seconds.

A third variation exists in which the timeout is placed on the stock quote service. Note that in this variation, which is shown in Figure 7-17, communication between the client and the stock quote server goes from server to client, something not presently supported by AJAX. It is assumed that the client has somehow registered that it wants to receive events from the stock quote service every 90 seconds. The advantage of this pattern variation is that the client does not have to send a `request()` message to each stock quote service it might be using (remember, this pattern shows only a 1:1 ratio; in reality, the number may be 1:*n*, or one to many). In this case, the `timeElapsed` event triggers a server-side request. The server-side request then triggers the messages to be pushed to each client that has registered to receive messages of that type or for that event.

Yet another variation of this pattern, shown in Figure 7-18, is based on an actual state change (in this case, the change of the value in the stock quote). When the state of a

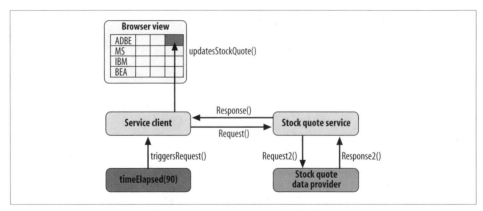

Figure 7-16. Variation two of the Asynchronous Particle Update pattern, based on an elapsed time event on the client

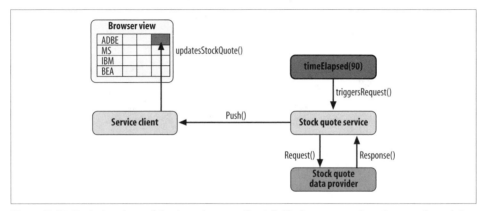

Figure 7-17. Variation three of the Asynchronous Particle Update pattern, based on an elapsed time event on the server

stock price changes, it triggers an event message to be fired to the stock quote service, which in turn pushes a message to all clients registered to receive messages based on that event.

Implementation

When implementing this pattern you must carefully consider many nuances, including the number of requests, the size of the particle, and how to present changes to users. In general, the overall goal will be to provide the best possible quality of service while using the least possible amount of network bandwidth and generating minimal processing overhead.

The sheer number of clients using a service or wanting to be notified of event changes should be grounds for deciding which of the four variations to employ. Each pattern

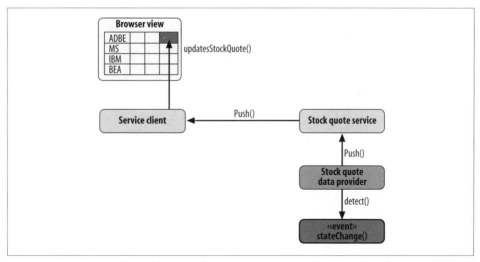

Figure 7-18. Variation four of the Asynchronous Particle Update pattern, based on a state change event on the server side

has a slightly different profile in terms of how much bandwidth, system memory, and client-side processing it uses/requires, and finding an optimal balance will require analysis. An architect could further develop a hybrid approach that could dynamically change the pattern based on the number of active clients and other details, such as which common stocks they're interested in.

Business Problem (Story) Resolved

Wholesale page refreshes can be replaced with updates to minute fragments of data. Within the page, small snippets of code make asynchronous coordinate particle updates with various services and ensure that the user has access to those updates. Regardless of the actual interaction model, the pattern of updating particles rather than the entire resource can be implemented in a manner that saves bandwidth and minimizes the user's responsibility for updating the view. Users also benefit because the interfaces are more flexible, letting them make changes to information without interrupting a page refresh.

Specializations

The four different interaction models illustrated earlier each specialize (i.e., extend the basic concepts of) the main pattern. Further specializations via interaction patterns are possible as well, but it is beyond the scope of this book to account for all possible variances.

Known Uses

The AJAX manner of implementing this pattern is widely known and used in the software industry today. Although the specifics regarding how it can be implemented are largely left to each developer, the technologies used are very particular.

Adobe's Flex and AIR, for example, implement the pattern via different remote messaging methodologies, standards, and protocols. The Action Message Format (AMF) transmission protocol may be used within a Flex application. In addition, Adobe Live-Cycle data services can be used to push data to multiple subscribers (for more information, see the section on the Synchronized Web pattern later in this chapter).

REST is also a style of software architecture that is frequently used to support implementations of this pattern (REST does not mean XML over HTTP). Although not specifically dependent upon HTTP and XML, it is a frequently quoted implementation of this pattern.

Consequences

It is highly possible to implement this pattern in a way that uses more bandwidth than a simple page refresh would. Software architects and developers should assess the number and nature of the AJAX widgets on their web pages and consider the cost of the various particle updates in relation to a page refresh to ensure that there is an actual gain in efficiency. If a single web page is too heavily dependent on a large number of AJAX components, users will find its performance unacceptable.

Also, as soon as a service becomes available for its intended purpose, some users may discover it and start using it for other purposes. Architects and developers would be wise to consider the policy and security models for their services as well as thinking about what sorts of mechanisms they might use to ensure only authorized use of the services.

References

For more on the Asynchronous Particle Update pattern, visit the following websites:

- AJAX—*http://www.webopedia.com/TERM/A/Ajax.html*
- Adobe Flex—*http://www.adobe.com/devnet/flex/*
- AMF—*http://osflash.org/documentation/amf/*
- W3C DOM—*http://www.w3.org/DOM/*
- MVC—*http://en.wikipedia.org/wiki/Model-view-controller*
- JavaScript—*http://en.wikipedia.org/wiki/JavaScript*
- W3C XML—*http://www.w3.org/XML/*
- REST—*http://www.webopedia.com/TERM/R/REST.html*

The Mashup Pattern

Also Known As

Other terms you may encounter in discussions of the Mashup pattern include:

Whole-Part pattern
> The Whole-Part pattern, a pattern of composition and aggregation, is well established in software architecture. In many instances, there are specific nuances. For example, sometimes a whole does not know or cannot see that it is composed of parts, while in other cases it may hide this fact from those that interact with it. An example of the latter might be a software system that uses all open source software internally, yet hides this fact and all the interfaces that the software provides so that other software entities cannot use the functionality.

Aggregate relationship (as described in UML 2.0)
> Aggregation is a specialized type of Whole-Part pattern in which individual parts can exist independently without the whole, yet can also be aggregated into the whole. If the whole ceases to exist, each of the parts can still exist.

Composite Relationship pattern (as described in UML 2.0)
> In a composite relationship, a whole is composed of individual parts. In the Composite Relationship pattern (often summarized as a "has a" relationship), the whole cannot exist without the parts, nor can the parts exist without the whole. The life cycle of the parts is tied directly to the life cycle of the whole.

Composite applications
> The concept of creating applications from multiple particles of computing resources is similar to the concept of aggregating data from many resources. This is a further specialization of the Whole-Part pattern, although possibly an anti-pattern of SOA.[‡]

Business Problem (Story)

An insurance company wants to supply maps to its branch offices, overlaid with demographic data to present agents with the information they require to write specialized policies. It has access to detailed data about median income, automobile accident statistics, and snowfall accumulation, as well as statistics regarding the threat of natural disasters such as earthquakes, tornados, forest fires, and hurricanes, and many more data sets. Some of these data sets are available via the insurance company's infrastructure, while external parties provide others. Individual agents will need slightly different content for their work depending on what types of policies they are writing and where they are located. The corporate insurance office wishes to allow agents to download

---

[‡] See *http://technoracle.blogspot.com/2007/09/soa-anti-patterns-service-composition.html*.

and display data from various sources at their convenience with little or no overhead so that the agents can write insurance policies that both protect the homeowner and act in the best interests of the insurer by cutting risks to known events.

The insurance company wishes to use online statistical data as well as delivering the maps and other information via the Internet. The statistical data comes from many sources that can be accessed over the Web. The data sources are in multiple formats, and each source may or may not be available at any given moment. This makes hard-coding the data into an application undesirable, and a "best effort" quality of service is the highest possible outcome of any interaction.

To complicate matters further, each agency has its own technology, and the insurer cannot count on any standard technical infrastructure or specific platform across its agents' offices. Insurance agents may have different browsers, different operating systems, and even different levels of bandwidth, thus making content delivery challenging.

The data required cannot be hardcoded into the agents' applications because it is constantly changing. Pushing newer information is not desirable given the fact that not all agents require the full set (an agent in Mexico city, for example, does not require heavy snowfall warning data, whereas agents in Alaska do not require heat wave or hurricane warning data). Nor can pushes of data be reliably scheduled because the data sources update infrequently and on completely different schedules.

Context

This problem occurs anywhere a common, user-controlled view to disparate remote data is required and the data is delivered via services over a network connection or other communication formats and protocols. The Mashup pattern may be applicable well beyond the business model outlined in the preceding section.

Derived Requirements

The Mashup pattern depends on the SOA pattern; services that can be consumed must exist. Additional recommendations also apply:

- Data encoding should generally be in a format that does not depend on any specific operating system, browser, or other hardware or platform (other than a common class of business software, such as browsers). Languages such as XML are commonly used to encode data for mashups, as these languages are easy to interpret and manipulate.
- On the client side, there should usually be some way for the user to manipulate the mashup content. However, this is not always necessary.
- Where major computational resources are required to manipulate data, a third tier may be introduced to help reduce client-side processing.

Generalized Solution

An application is built to load a map and template onto a user's system upon request. The application then detects remote data sources that are online and presents the user with a control button object to allow the user to render the data sets over the top of the map application. The data is retrieved using web-based protocols and standards to connect to a set of services that supply the data.

The data sets may alternatively be cached locally on the client to allow more efficient launching and operation of the client-side application.

Static Structure

A mashup uses one or more services and mashes together aspects of those services. An optional view may be generated for human users. Figure 7-19 depicts the most basic pattern for mashups.

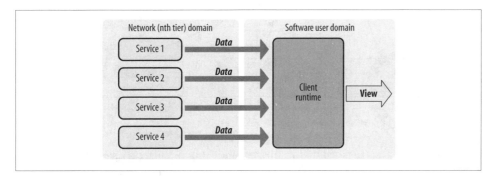

Figure 7-19. The basic Mashup pattern

A specialization of the Mashup pattern involves letting users configure the mashup's view component. This is done in many implementations and has been built-in to content management systems such as Drupal and many PHP sites. There are also examples in which users can mash up content from their own sources, such as photos from their Flickr sets or their own blog content. Note that the UML convention, shown in Figure 7-20, is written in a manner that recognizes this variant.

For those who do not read the OMG's UML notation, Figure 7-20 shows that a mashup is an aggregation of services, other mashups, or both. A mashup may provide a view (commonly a graphical user interface, or GUI), although this is not mandatory; mashups may simply aggregate data for another application to ingest.

Several patterns exist for how and where content is mashed up. One variation is that all services are mashed up on the client side. This approach, depicted in Figure 7-21, is commonly used for Internet-based mashups.

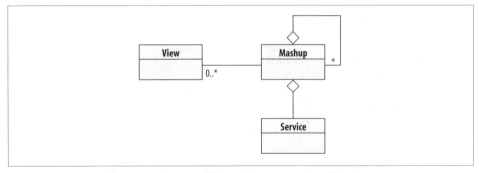

Figure 7-20. A UML class view diagram of the Mashup pattern (simplified)

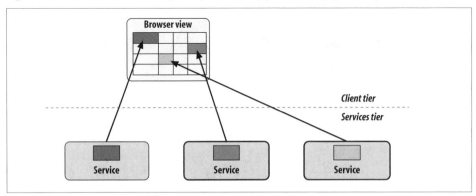

Figure 7-21. A simple two-tier mashup pattern

Sometimes content is mashed up in a proxy middle tier or even on a server before being delivered to the client. In this case, the fact that the application is a mashup might not be readily visible to its users. Figure 7-22 depicts this variation.

Implementation

When implementing the Mashup pattern, developers must carefully consider the many standards and protocols that may be used to build the final application. Developers and architects also have to understand the availability of and policies regarding content they wish to mash up. Policies are important considerations if certain user classes might not ordinarily be free to access particular resources, or might have to submit credentials for authorization to prove their identities before being granted access to a system's resources.

Another top concern of mashup developers is the post-acquisition manipulation of data. This is much easier if the data is provided in a manner that is consistent with the Model-View-Controller pattern (i.e., is pure and not encumbered by a markup language pertaining to information presentation or control). One consideration that has received much attention in recent years has to do with the granularity of a service's

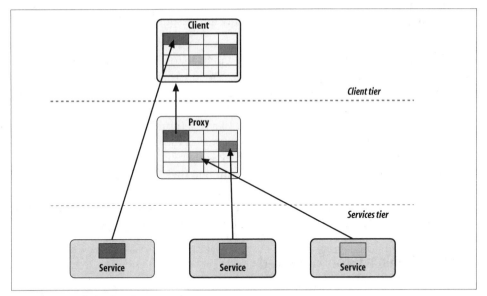

Figure 7-22. A hybrid multitier mashup

content. A coarse-grained data chunk from any service might require a lot of processing before most clients can use it, generating excessive overhead. An example might be a newspaper's website where you can request content, but you can only get the full newspaper for any given day returned as a large XML file with binary attachments. This system would not be ideal for service consumers who need only a small portion of the content, such as stock market reports. A better option would be to implement a tiered service model in which content may be accessed at a much more granular (fine-grained) level. Alternatively, if a single runtime environment (such as Adobe's Flash) is used on the client, the data can be made available in a format such as AMF that is already serialized into an efficient binary format to reduce rendering time on the client. Architects will have to weigh both options before making decisions.

Developers of services that want to provide mashable data should strongly consider using common data formats such as XML, as well as the client-side overhead of processing various standards and protocols. For example, if an implementer chooses to provide a single photograph for mashing into various client-side applications, he should consider using the PNG, JPEG, or GIF format because most browsers support these standards.

Browsers don't, however, provide much support for SOAP with extensions such as the OASIS WS-SX and WS-RX standards. The processing overhead needed to comply with the SOAP model might eliminate the possibility of services using this model being consumed on mobile platforms or other devices with constrained resources. In these cases, the Representational State Transfer architectural style, implemented by using XML over HTTP, may be a natural fit for many mashups. *RESTafarians* (the name given to those who enthusiastically evangelize the benefits of REST) promote the view that dividing application state and functionality into resources and giving them unique identifiers makes content easier to mash up.

On the client side, architects and developers will have to choose their target technologies very carefully. In many implementations, a consistent rendering experience or manner in which data can be shown to end users will be desirable. Achieving this in multiple versions of disparate browsers is somewhat difficult; a lot of testing and design iterations are required to get it right, especially if a large number of browsers is targeted. Some may choose to implement the pattern outside of the browser in a custom, stand-alone application to avoid any variable-display issues. In particular, many AJAX developers have been struggling with trying to maintain their applications and keep them working well in multiple versions of various popular browsers, such as Internet Explorer, Opera, Google Chrome, Firefox, and Safari. To add to the complexity, all of these browsers may have to be tested on multiple platforms or operating systems.

Business Problem (Story) Resolved

By offering several services via web-based interfaces, the insurance company lets branch offices and other resellers consume data and mash it together to build custom views of the data required to write insurance policies. Each branch office can pick and choose the right mix of data for its purposes. While the company could provide maps as one of its services, it could also use public services (such as Google or Yahoo! Maps) as a foundation.

Making this data accessible for mashups could also benefit the insurance company beyond this particular application—for example, by helping the company's customers choose where they might wish to live based on criteria from data services providing information on median temperatures, crime rates, financial census data, and so on.

Specializations

Mashups themselves are inherently customizable, and an infinite number of specializations are possible. Some allow users full control over the user interface, so they can see only those aspects that interest them. Allan Padgett's Tour Tracker (discussed next) is a primary example of this. Google and Yahoo! have also done wonderful things to allow developers to write code to use their maps for a variety of possible applications.

Known Uses

When we think about mashups, Allan Padgett's Tour Tracker application (written to allow users to view information about the Tour of California bicycle race in real time) often comes to mind. Figure 7-23 shows a screenshot of Allan's application from the 2007 race.

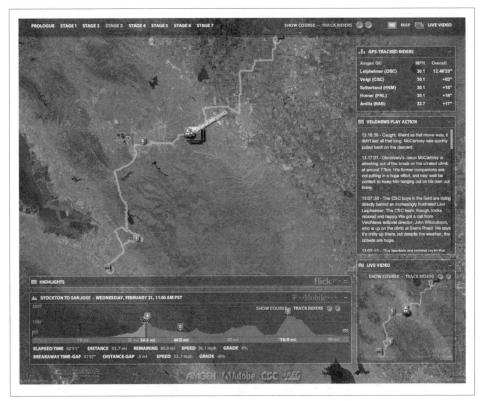

Figure 7-23. An excellent mashup example: Allan Padgett's Tour Tracker, circa 2007

The mashup in Figure 7-23 uses the Yahoo! Maps Flash API to build an overhead aerial view of a section of the bicycle race. The map is overlaid with sprites depicting where specific riders are in real time, and the entire map moves as the tracked riders progress through the race. The bottom-right box shows a live video feed of the bicycle race (basically the same as TV coverage), and the other layers contain data about the course profile and about the cyclists, such as their average speed, distance remaining, and overall standings. Go to *http://tracker.amgentourofcalifornia.com* for a demo of this mashup.

For a vast list of mashups, as well as much more information on how to create and apply them, see *http://www.programmableweb.com/mashups/*.

Consequences

Mashups depend on the services that feed them. Anyone implementing a mashup must take this into consideration, especially if those services are not under his control.

Content used in mashups may carry with it certain copyright privileges or restrictions. Material licensed through Creative Commons§ under a license allowing free distribution is a perfect fit for mashups. In the Tour Tracker application shown in Figure 7-23, thumbnail photos are tiled onto the course based on geocoded photographs that spectators have contributed to Flickr.com. The Tour Tracker uses the Flickr API to retrieve the license data; however, the licenses may not be immediately apparent to end users.

The Rich User Experience Pattern

Also Known As

Often discussed in conjunction with the Rich User Experience (RUE) is the Rich Internet Application (RIA). The term itself suggests a type of application that is connected to the Internet and facilitates a RUE. Some people (most notably, industry analyst Bola Rotibi)‖ expand the RIA acronym as Rich *Interactive* Application, which is a far more descriptive term in our opinion.

Business Problem (Story)

Websites evolved as static pages (documents) served to those who requested them. The document sets were largely modeled on real-world artifacts such as sales brochures, help manuals, and order forms. However, the real-world documents themselves were only part of the full interaction (process) between the company and the customer/user; typically, a human working for the company provided additional input, contributing to the richness of the interaction concerning the document or artifact.

For example, if you walked into a travel agency in Northern Canada in January and started looking at brochures for Mexico and Hawaii, an observant employee might infer that you were sick of the Canadian winter and want to get some sun. She could then enhance your experience by asking questions to clarify this inference and offering you contextually valuable information (such as details on a sale on a one-week all-inclusive trip to the Mayan Riviera).

Many interactions with customers, suppliers, and partners are good candidates for migrating to electronic interactions and patterns of engagement. The problem is that human-to-human interaction is most often an ad hoc interaction, with boundaries wide enough to allow the entities involved to fork or change the conversation at will. Although the entire range of conversation (engagement) can be scoped to include only

---

§ See *http://creativecommons.org*.

‖ See *http://ukwebagencies.wordpress.com/2007/04/14/2007-the-year-of-the-ria/*.

those topics that are relevant to the actual business task at hand, the two entities can still discuss multiple topics and engage in a variety of activities.

For an electronic interaction to measure up to human-to-human interaction, the application has to be able to let a human actor dynamically engage with it in multiple manners, at her discretion. The application's task is to present the available interaction choices to the human and to react to the human's stimuli in a manner that mimics the interactions between two humans, while simultaneously hooking those interactions into various business systems. Amazon.com, where other users' interactions are studied and used as enriching data to present likely choices to those who are in the process of buying books, is an excellent example (this manifests as "Customers who bought this item also bought...").

Visual and design aspects of this engagement are very important, as some tasks are more complicated than simple data interchange. Simple exchanges of data can be accomplished via electronic forms in HTML or PDF. For example, an interactive website that shows a customer how to build a custom Harley-Davidson motorcycle, style it with custom accessories and colors, and view the end result cannot be created effectively using forms. Visual components for Web 2.0 are being developed so cleverly now that some of the interactions possible between applications and humans would be hard to mimic in the real world with two human actors. The Amazon.com functionality mentioned earlier is one example of this—a human being would have to conduct very quick research to gather the data about other customers' purchases, formulate a hypothesis about which other item the current customer would be most likely to buy, and then retrieve and present a visual rendition of that item. An application can do this much more quickly by running a quick database query to arrive at an answer.

The Harley-Davidson Customizer

The Harley-Davidson example mentioned in the text is actually a real-world Web 2.0 application in which users can log in, custom-configure a Harley, and even park it in a virtual garage. This is a forward-thinking application that accomplishes several things. First, it gives the user a way to see how his bike actually looks based on various configuration options. Second, it gives the company insight into popular options, which it can use to create a better user experience in the future. The company could also use the data gathered as a quantifier for its research and development efforts, by looking at the marketplace reactions to various options.

You can try the application for yourself at *http://www.harley-davidson.com/pr/gm/cus tomizer/launchCustomizer.asp*.

Context

The Rich User Experience pattern can be applied anywhere a user might need to interact with an application in a way that optimizes the experience in terms of visual presentation of data and information relevance. This pattern is likely to occur where multiple remote resources are used to interact with and present the state of the applications as seen by the user.

Derived Requirements

Modeling and understanding the real-world process that accompanies the exchange of documents as part of a human-to-human interaction can help make rich user experiences genuinely rich. For example, if a human passes a sales brochure to a customer and at the same time collects information from the customer to guide her to a specific set of options in the brochure, the electronic interaction should support that extra interchange. To perfect this sort of interaction, alpha architects might want to make the information exchange invisible and seamless from the user's perspective, perhaps by detecting the user's IP address, using it to map the user's locale, and then using that information to contextually specialize the user experience. A *contextually specialized experience* is one in which the user interacts with an application that has functionality, data components, and visual components uniquely configured for that user.

 Many companies do this by directing customers to a national website from their main web page. The corresponding national page is then contextually specified for the user. This is a common "entry-level" application of the RUE pattern.

In architecting a rich user experience, developers and others have to consider that different users may require different presentations to derive the most benefit from the interaction. This is a strong reason to look at developing the application using the Model-View-Controller pattern, which will enable different application views to share the control and model components.

An application supporting rich visual experiences should be capable of rendering content in a variety of media-rich formats, each tied to a common shared view of the state of the core model (see the next section, on the Synchronized Web pattern, for an example of this concept).

An application delivering a rich user experience should also be capable of tying into a variety of backend system services to provide the richest data exchange possible.

Some other considerations for development of RUEs include the following:

- RUEs should use an efficient, high-performance runtime for executing code and media content and for managing communications. Efficiency is a key attribute of a "good" user experience. If an application is viewed as taking too long to produce results or to change view states, it will not be very enticing to the user. Developers should note that sometimes the illusion of good performance and good user feedback (such as busy cursors) can mitigate perceptions of bad performance.

- RUEs should be capable of mashing up and integrating content, communications, and application interfaces into a common runtime environment.

- RUE technologies should enable rapid application development through a component library that is available during the development phase as well as at runtime. Although this trait is not specific to RUEs, it potentially frees developers' time to make more prototypes, resulting in more options to choose from.

- RUEs should enable the use of web and data services provided by application servers and other services.

- RUE technologies should support runtime scenarios for both Internet-connected and disconnected clients, including features for synchronization.

- RUEs should be easy to deploy on multiple platforms and devices.

Generalized Solution

To deliver rich user experiences, developers should try to model the processes used in the real world (human-to-human interactions) and create workflows to facilitate similar, successful interactions within websites or applications. These processes may have various start and end states as well as decision and elevation points. A process might initiate with the user requesting the website, in which case the developer has to be able to understand as much about that user as possible before the user advances to the next step. Alternatively, a rich user experience may involve a complex backend system that pushes relevant and timely information to the user based on some event in which the user is interested. Some of the first questions the process modeler and developer should ask in this case are:

- Where is the user located?
- Has this user been to the site before (cookie check)?
- Is the user a regular customer (or other partner) of mine?
- What are the user's technical capabilities (browser, bandwidth)?
- Do I already have information stored about this user so I don't have to pester him to re-enter data on every form he fills in?
- What is this user likely to do as a next step? Developers can monitor interactions and apply Bayesian Theory to predict likely interactions based on the user's initial knowledge.

An example

Competent architects and developers must also account for possible forks or deviations from the process's main path. For a very simplistic example, let's consider registering as a new user or logging in as an existing user.

In our example, there are several paths and states to consider. The design constraint is that our user will require only two tokens to log in: a username and a password. For the username, using a working email address with validation is a good practice because it can accomplish several things at once. Before we get into that, though, here is a list of possible sequences or states:

Normal

User remembers the username and the password and logs in with no issue.

Lost password

User remembers the username but not the password and needs to have the password reset.

Lost username

User remembers the password but forgets the username. Using email addresses as usernames can mitigate this problem, but a lost or forgotten username event can still happen if the user has multiple email addresses.

Everything gone

User forgets both the username and the password. While the user can get around this by signing up for a new account, that approach may lead to the presence of orphaned accounts that should be cleaned up.

Lost password, email changed

User lost the password and control of or access to the email address where the password might ordinarily be sent after a reset.

Unregistered user

User has neither a username nor a password and needs to log in.

Phishing

User is directed to a fake site and asked to enter his username and password. You can help guard against phishing-style attacks by allowing users to design custom skins for the login page, so they can instantly tell the real site from fakes. This customizing also lets the user choose a custom color scheme that appeals to him.

Double registering

User is already registered and tries to register again.

For a simple first stage of the process, designing mechanisms to mitigate most of the potential problems should be relatively easy. However, in more complex applications, your options may be less obvious. For example, if you are designing an Internet application where a user's history of previous interactions is available as a series of tabbed panes, figuring out how to present them in a logical manner that is intuitive to all users might be difficult.

Static Structure and Dynamic Behavior

Figure 7-24 shows the Web 2.0 Reference Architecture from Chapter 5. Architects and developers can use this reference architecture as a guide when considering the various aspects of creating a rich user experience.

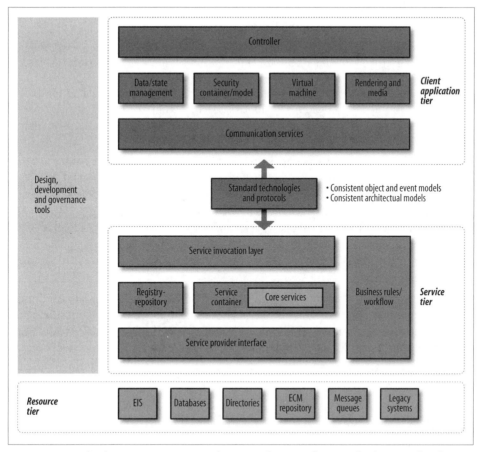

Figure 7-24. Technology component view reference architecture for RUE developers and architects

Architects and developers should first map out the interactions and experiences they wish their users to have. This may involve creating a series of storyboards using various GUI elements. During this activity, some artifacts should be developed to provide a map of the various paths moving forward.

Model-Driven Architecture

Model-driven architecture is a style of architecture in which requirements and solution behavior are strongly documented. Model-driven architecture comes in several flavors, including the Object Management Group's Model-Driven Architecture (MDA), IBM's Rose Unified Process (RUP), and the United Nations Centre for Trade Facilitation and Electronic Business's UN/CEFACT Modeling Methodology (UMM). They all share similar concepts, although the specifics and artifacts are sometimes different. Most use UML as the modeling syntax for capturing and preserving knowledge.

Most model-driven approaches to software architecture are also compatible with frameworks such as the Zachman Framework for Enterprise Architecture and benefit from the use of a catalog of architectural patterns such as those expressed in this book.

Any organization developing a rich user experience should consider some form of model-driven approach to the application architecture. These methodologies will allow architects to understand whether they have captured all the potential variants of the user experience, as well as the full lexicon of the system.

The challenge is that a system must be built to handle all the potential conditions, without forcing the user to strain her memory or have to try too many times to log in. The data model of the user profile is a good place to start to think about how to architect the application. The following items should be associated with each user account:

- A unique identifier (username)
- An email address at which the user can receive any information (such as a reset password token) that is sent back
- A password
- Other details (such as the state of the interface the user sees when she logs in)

Upon reading the preceding list, a pragmatic architect might quickly realize that the first and second items can be combined by using the email address as the unique identifier, given that email addresses are guaranteed to be unique (except in situations where multiple people share an email account, but for the purposes of this example we will leave that condition out of the scope). This illustrates many of the benefits of a model-driven approach to software architecture: architects can ask questions such as "How many email addresses does a user have?" (zero to infinity) and "How many people might use the same email address?" (one to many), rather than assuming that everyone has exactly one email address.

A problem with using the email address is that some users have multiple email addresses. To simplify the user experience, it might be helpful to specify the type of email address. For example, depending on the type of application, you might want to prompt users to enter their "primary personal email" or "primary work email" addresses.

You could build the interface for the application to look something like that shown in Figure 7-25.

Figure 7-25. A simple login user interface

Without such guidance, users with several email addresses may be uncertain about which one to use. Understanding this user point of view does not itself constitute a rich user experience, but it is a small aspect of creating one.

What Web 2.0 Users Will Demand of User Interface Designers

The next generation of Internet users will not likely be as forgiving of ill-conceived, poorly designed interactions as the current and previous generations. New users have come to expect more.

Websites make several common mistakes or violations when collecting user information. Here are the top 10 that we noted:

1. Having a long, unwieldy form through which a user must navigate, filling out every form field. If interacting with the form seems like too much work, users may feel overwhelmed and turn and run.

2. Resetting the form (erasing all the information the user just entered) if the user has made a mistake in the submitted form. Very few logic conditions would suggest that it is good to reset all fields of a form rather than just the few that contained mistakes.

3. Validating the form fields based on a national model (e.g., invalidating a non-U.S. postal/zip code if the mask does not match exactly five numbers). This is often done when form designers do not expect people from other countries to use their forms.

4. Not incorporating form elements that prevent users from entering incorrect information. An example of this is the date field: instead of using a text box (which lets users enter a string or set of integers in any order they choose), you could use a specialized date chooser, such as the one shown in Figure 7-26.

Using a component such as this eliminates the need to interpret a user-entered date. Of course, this assumes that all users use the Gregorian calendar (see mistake #3).

5. Collecting information unnecessarily. For example, if the user is registering, why ask him the date of his registration? You can read that from other sources. Likewise, it shouldn't be necessary to ask an already registered and logged-in user for personal information entered during the registration process (although asking one or two questions to validate the user might be OK).

6. Having the wrong "tabbing" order on forms. Although this is a finicky principle, people do tend to fill out chunks of information in a logical order. For example, if you ask someone her "first name," when she enters that and presses the Tab key having the focus go to the "last name" box would be a logical progression. Asking the user to instead enter an unexpected piece of information, such as her mother's maiden name, may cause confusion or even errors.

7. Not presenting users with the information they need as they are entering values into the form. An example of this might be asking a customer how much money she wishes to transfer from her bank account without showing her how much is available. Another example is asking the customer a very specific question without providing a link to information he might need to know before he answers.

8. Asking the user to enter duplicate information. For example, if you are asking a user for his billing, ship to, and home addresses, all of which might be the same, do not make him enter this information three times. Instead, put a "same as" function into the interaction.

9. Illogical presentation or poor graphical layout. For example, in the form in Figure 7-27, the choice fields are not grouped together logically, making the presentation difficult for the user to digest.

   In the figure, it is not clear what choices are legitimate for or linked to "Paper." What effect does the "Tabloid" form field have in this dialog? It seems to be randomly placed at the top of the "Printer Effects" listings and have little or no relationship to the other form fields. Figure 7-28 shows the same form with a more logical presentation.

   Note that there are now four main groupings of functions, separated from the three master control buttons near the bottom. The bold font makes the function headings more evident, while the choices for each heading are placed in a clear graphical layout beneath the headings, making it easy to understand which choices correspond to each heading. This clarity is a fundamental aspect of building a rich user experience.

10. Writing a script to validate multiple fields using the onBlur() event handler. This is one of our favorite top-10 mistakes, and is pure evil. If you're using the onBlur() event, you should validate only one field. You can write code to make sure the user's answers are legitimate based on certain rules. For example, if the user chooses "male" as his sex and then later answers "yes" to being pregnant, you might want to generate an error message that tells the user why that choice is not valid. Such a message could be worded as follows: "We noted that you checked

'male' earlier. As such, being 'currently pregnant' is not a valid choice. Please fix the mistake." An even better option might be to not present the option of being pregnant if the user checks "male." What is truly evil about form validation using the `onBlur()` event is requiring a user to check several values that must add up to a fixed value (say, 100). Logically, if the user enters any individual number in a form field when the others haven't been filled in, an error will be generated. If the user has to fill out five separate values and gets the same error each time ("The values must add up to 100"), she will likely be very annoyed.

Figure 7-26. A specialized date chooser

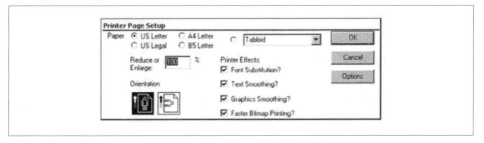

Figure 7-27. A graphically ugly way to lay out a form

We're not done with our example yet; we still haven't accounted for several use cases. First, let's consider that a user has not yet registered. Making the registration page very simple and giving it the same look as the login page has several advantages. First, users will not be scared away by having to answer numerous questions before they can register.

Second, a subconscious association between the account creation and login pages might help some users to remember their usernames and passwords later. You could easily modify the user interface in Figure 7-25 to allow users to also use it to create an account, as shown in Figure 7-29 (note the addition of the text "Need to Register?").

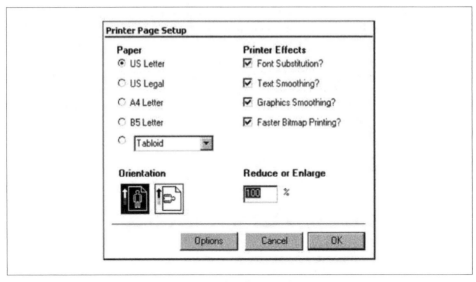

Figure 7-28. The same form designed in a graphically appealing manner

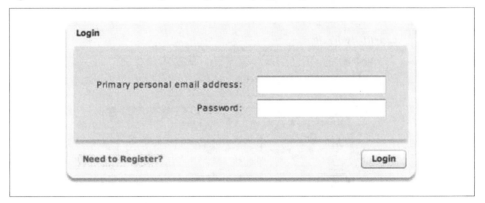

Figure 7-29. Registration added to GUI

When the user clicks the "Need to Register?" link, the GUI changes to include a password confirmation box, as shown in Figure 7-30.

This screen now allows a user to create an account. However, it could be optimized. Look at the "Return to Login" link. Why would you want to force your user, who has just registered for the first time, to log in? After all, he has just entered the requisite information. Having to repeat the process will not add any element of trust. If you are not going to verify the account creation through email, you should remove the link and simply allow the user to proceed to the site he wishes to access.

Most websites will add some form of validation. This may be done for a variety of reasons, but the best is to ensure that your user has not made a mistake when entering

Figure 7-30. A second view of the registration screen

the email address. There are good and bad ways to do validation. Figure 7-31 shows a bad way—having to enter an email address twice is *annoying* to most users, and it's also a bad architectural choice. Your user could be having a bad day and enter her email address incorrectly both times; even if both email values match, they could still be wrong. Our advice is to never use the interface depicted in Figure 7-31.

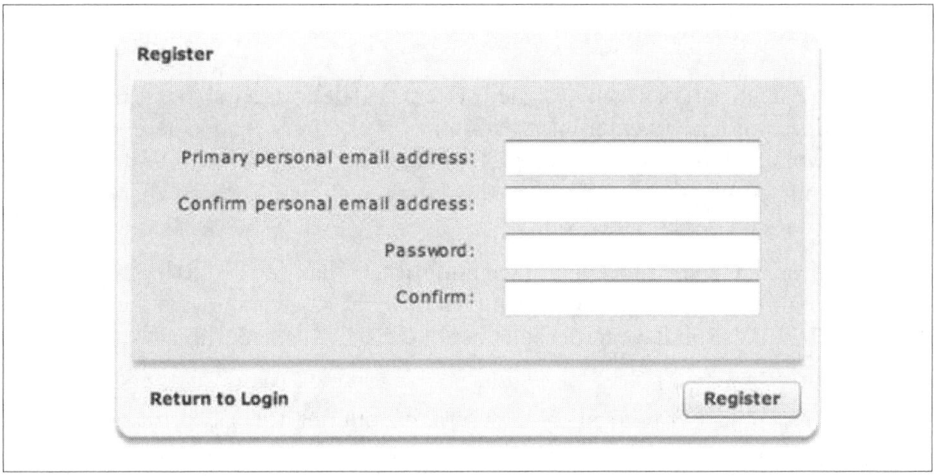

Figure 7-31. A good way to annoy your user while possibly not validating that his email address is correct

The best way to validate that an email address is correct is to collect it once, and then send an email to that address with a link that the user has to click to complete the registration process. The sequence is simple, as shown in Figure 7-32, and if the user makes a mistake, it will be caught right away.

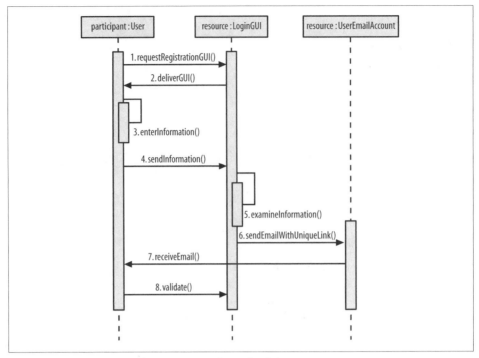

Figure 7-32. The sequence of registration with email validation

This is also a small part of a well-designed system that delivers a Rich User Experience. The user does not have to enter information any more times than is necessary, and a lot of the work is done in the backend. (This example isn't unique to Web 2.0 applications, but hopefully the process of getting here has shown some of what's involved in creating a Rich User Experience.)

Now, suppose that some time has passed and the user has decided to log in. Use case 1 (normal login) is simple and can be completed via the screens shown in Figures 7-29, 7-30, and 7-31. We still have to consider use cases 2, 3, 4, and 5, though:

Use case 2: Lost password

In this case, the user remembers her username but not her password and needs to have the password replaced. Because we have the user's email address (and we know it is valid), all we have to do is add a small link that says "Forgot your password?" to the login screen. The user can simply enter her username (email address) and click the link, and the system will send her a new password. A general security pattern here is to automatically reset the password to a random one and email it to the user rather than emailing her the old password. The reasoning is that she may also use the same password for other accounts, and exposing it via email could allow a clever hacker to use that information to gain access to other accounts (such as PayPal). A good architectural pattern to employ here is to also force the user to change her password upon logging in again for the first time after the lost password incident. Because most email travels in plain text over the Internet, letting the user keep the generated password is a bad idea.

Use case 3: Lost username

In this case, the user remembers his password but forgets his username. Although it's rare for this to happen if email addresses are used as usernames, such an event can still occur if the user has several email addresses. By prompting the user for a specific type of email address at registration time, you can mitigate the likelihood of such incidents. In the user interface we designed, we used the phrase "Primary personal email address," which should provide a sufficiently strong hint for most users. In this use case, it is a bad idea to allow users to enter their passwords and look up their email addresses because passwords are not guaranteed to be unique. Using OpenID[#] is a good solution here.

Use case 4: Everything gone

In this case, the user forgets both her username and her password. This is a special case that is most likely to arise with services in which users log in only infrequently (e.g., a domain name registration service, where users may log in only once and then not visit the service again for several years). In this case, often the best you can do is to ask the user to create a new account. If she enters an email address that matches an existing account username, you may be able to catch the mistake.

Use case 5: Lost password, email changed

In this case, the user has lost his password and has lost control of or access to the email address where the password might ordinarily be sent after a reset. An alternative to re-registration in this case may be to ask the user to provide a secondary email account, email the temporary password to that account, and then give the user a fixed amount of time to log in and change the primary email address.

As you can see, Rich User Experiences don't follow one specific pattern. In the rest of this section, we discuss designer and architect considerations.

Implementation

One of the primary activities of any architect or developer should be to model the entire system, including subartifacts for things such as use cases, technology component views, sequence diagrams, and data models used within the application. If more than five people are working on a project, consider adopting a consistent modeling syntax and methodology for designing the interface and interactions, not just for the code.

Using a modeling methodology when implementing a RUE application will likely help everyone involved to understand where issues may arise. Adopting UMM, MDA, or RUP, as discussed earlier in the sidebar "Model-Driven Architecture" on page 164, will likely benefit your end users.

[#] See *http://openid.net*.

Capturing the knowledge of the application independent of technology is another consideration worth pondering. Technologies come and go; however, most business patterns remain fairly stable. Adopting a consistent modeling syntax and library of artifacts, including business patterns, processes, and other artifacts, likely will help you build rich applications.

Business Problem (Story) Resolved

In "Generalized Solution" on page 161 , we caught a small glimpse of how a technical solution can be used to enhance the overall user experience by encouraging careful consideration of the entire lexicon and scope of the interaction: every possible combination of initial situations was considered, and a solution was developed to account for each one of them. This approach was applied to only a small aspect of the overall experience (login), yet the methodology is applicable to the wider scope of application development.

Specializations

The Rich User Experience pattern has so many potential specializations that it would be hard to provide an exhaustive list. Here are some variations with strong architectural departures from the websites of yesteryear:

Getting away from the browser
> Several new technologies are arising from various companies that let Rich User Experiences be delivered beyond the browser. This is not an attempt to kill the browser, but rather to cross a chasm between compiled desktop applications and web-based applications. Two of the leading technologies in this arena are the Adobe Integrated Runtime and Sun Microsystems's JavaFX. Microsoft's Silverlight is presently constrained within a browser, though that may change.

Virtualization
> Virtualization is about presenting the user with an interface that appears to be his native system without actually having him directly connect to that system. An example would be to turn an operating system into a web-based application so that a user can log in to any public terminal in the world and get the appearance of having logged into his own system.

Skinnable applications
> This evolution allows users to custom-skin their applications. In the past, only software developers were able to do this; however, more recently some applications have been delivered that allow users to add their own skins or "chrome" to have a custom view of the application. As well as being visually enticing to the user, this specialization also helps to prevent certain types of fraud, such as phishing—the phishers will not know what skin the user applied, so it will be easy for the user to detect phishing attempts.

Known Uses

This pattern has thousands of known uses. Here are some of the more notable ones:

- iTunes—*http://www.apple.com/itunes/*
- Kuler—*http://kuler.adobe.com*
- The Harley-Davidson Bike Customizer—*http://www.harley-davidson.com/pr/gm/customizer/launchCustomizer.asp*
- The Canadian Government Electronic Passport renewal form, which pre-fills many fields based on existing knowledge of the person who is applying rather than forcing the user to enter all the data manually —*http://www.ppt.gc.ca/cdn/form.aspx?lang=eng&region=Canada*

Consequences

The biggest consequence of using this pattern to architect your system is a positive realization of a good user experience. Those who implement cutting-edge applications raise the standard, setting a higher bar for other developers to follow. It may also have a positive impact on your business. For example, online sales traditionally have a very high abandon rate. However, a recent piece of research into the return on investment (ROI) of RUE done by Allurent on Borders.com[*] showed the following results after migration:

- 62% higher conversion from website visitors to paying customers
- 41% more products viewed
- 11% more likely to recommend

Technical considerations range from increased system complexity to limiting users to only those who have a specific set of capabilities required to interact with the applications. Increased complexity can be addressed by using the Software as a Service, Mashup, and Service-Oriented Architecture patterns (discussed earlier in this chapter) to help keep systems from becoming too interdependent. Limiting users to those who have certain required capabilities is an issue that must be addressed much more carefully. When building a Rich User Experience, you do not want to lose a sizeable portion of your users due to limited technical capabilities. Each developer and architect must assess this consequence individually based on the specific requirements.

---

[*] See *http://technoracle.blogspot.com/2008/10/defining-ria-borders-case-study.html*.

The Synchronized Web Pattern

Also Known As

Names and terms you may see in conjunction with the Synchronized Web pattern include:

Office 2.0
> The term is given collectively to a group of new synchronized applications that provide the same sort of functionality as people collaborating on one instance of a document. The documents (or other digital files), as well as the applications that create and show them, are often online, and all users have a consistent view of their state. The term is so popular that an Office 2.0 conference has been formed and continues to grow and prosper as of this writing.[†]

The Online Desktop pattern
> Many companies (Google, Yahoo!, Facebook, Firefox, Salesforce.com, and others) are changing the software we use by shifting applications from the desktop operating system to a model of being on a server and accessed via the Web (the Online Desktop pattern). It also merges in the pattern of SaaS.

Rich Internet Applications and Rich User Experiences
> Rich Internet Applications and Rich User Experiences, both of which are defined and discussed elsewhere this book, are relevant to but are not themselves manifestations of the Synchronized Web pattern. Many applications that embrace the Synchronized Web pattern also embrace the RUE pattern (discussed in the preceding section). Arguably, synchronization is in itself a facet of a good user experience.

The Observer pattern
> The Observer pattern is a well-known computer science design pattern whereby one or more objects (called *observers* or *listeners*) is registered (or registers themselves) to observe an event that may be raised by the observed object (the *subject*). These are commonly employed in a distributed event handling infrastructure or system. See *http://en.wikipedia.org/wiki/Observer_pattern* for more information.

REST
> The Representational State Transfer model (REST),[‡] originally put forward by Roy Fielding for his doctoral thesis,[§] treats application state and functionality as resources to be manipulated with a constrained set of commands, boiled down to GET and PUT. REST describes a method for building large-scale hyperlinked

---

[†] An impressive list of companies sponsoring the conference is available at *http://office20.com*.

[‡] See *http://en.wikipedia.org/wiki/Representational_State_Transfer*

[§] See *http://en.wikipedia.org/wiki/Roy_Fielding*.

---

systems, and it's an ideal architectural style to use for getting and putting information required to synchronize the state of disparate resources.

Business Problem (Story)

Many web-based services are designed to be consumed in pure online mode, and have no value to their consumers when the consumers are decoupled from the Internet. Although some would argue that we're on the verge of pervasive, reliable broadband access powered by Wi-Fi, 3G networks, WiMAX, and wired connections, 100% online connectivity is not yet pervasive. One of the authors of this book, who recently experienced his broadband being switched off and had to work using a dial-up connection, can attest to the fact that ubiquitous high-speed Internet connectivity is not yet a reality. The business problem involves how to synchronize the states of multiple applications connected to the Internet when you sometimes can't reach the required services online.

Some people use "small things, loosely joined," a mantra originally created by David Weinberger, to describe the aspects of Web 2.0 dealing with application and service usage patterns. Those who live and work on the Web use many different online services, each with its own usefulness. Such systems often contain a great deal of redundancy, which is not necessarily a bad thing. An individual user might have redundancy in his Flickr, Facebook, WordPress, and other accounts. As our society increasingly comes to rely on these web services, however, it becomes useful to establish some synchronization between them. This is where an API for service-to-service synchronization might prove useful. Such multiservice synchronization will underpin much of the next generation of web applications, intermingled with desktop experiences in the context of Experiences (see the preceding discussion of the Rich User Experience

hronized Web pattern generally occurs wherever an application has both a ktop) component and a network-bound server or service component, and required to fulfill the functionality of the whole application. In some ways, ariant of the Software as a Service pattern; however, this pattern relates specifically to state management in terms of synchronization.

The pattern can also occur anywhere information is persisted in two or more locations in a mutable form. If the information changes state in only one physical form, the other form(s) must be synchronized when possible.

 The term *synchronization* is not used here in the same way it is in traditional database terminology. The term is used a bit more loosely for Web 2.0 purposes, and it touches on the related database concept called *replication*.

Anyone who has ever signed up for a new online service and asked, "Why can't I just move data from my existing service to here?" is, in essence, asking the question, "Why don't these applications support the synchronized Web?"

Derived Requirements

At a minimum, you need replication and synchronization services, a local web application server, and a data persistence tier with state-change reporting functionality. Such a data store must be more than a "bucket of bits," and you need some form of data-state manager to use this pattern. Such audit trails are necessary to enable a rollback to the last known synchronized state should something go wrong during the process.

Other possible requirements include modules to ensure the performance of the core components of the system.

You must have a high-level set of instructions or other methodology, and declare the rules for how unsynchronized components should become synchronized. For example, you can check the timestamps to determine the most recent information.

Although an embedded relational database such as JavaDB or SQLite is the obvious replication service provider for this pattern, it makes no sense for synchronized web developers to limit themselves to relational databases. Web 2.0 is currently experiencing a data management revolution, with a far greater tolerance of heterogeneous data layers.‖ *Database* doesn't necessarily mean *relational*.

Generalized Solution

A lightweight embeddable data persistence mechanism provides for service-to-service synchronization, as well as letting data be stored and indexed in and retrieved from either remote or local locations. A database is not the only required data-handling mechanism, however. AJAX-like functionality to enable updates of specific data fields rather than entire web pages is another foundational aspect of the Synchronized Web pattern. AJAX can be made even more efficient using the binary JavaScript Object Notation (JSON) format supported by all modern web browsers, although other approaches are acceptable for most architects and developers. Any technology that makes data transfer between services more efficient is useful in a synchronized web application, and local AJAX is now finding its way into more and more applications. Google Gears, for example, provides WorkerPool, a module designed to allow JavaScript processes to run in the background without having to wait for script updates on the web app UI.

The clients may be offline during some phases of the Synchronized Web pattern. In such times, they can be prepared for use in service-to-service synchronization once a

---

‖ See *http://redmonk.com/sogrady/2006/04/28/heterogeneous-data-layers-check-whats-next/*.

connection is re-established. During this preparation, special data-handling routines may be used for any translations that are required.

In some cases there is no offline phase, and the synchronization happens in real time between connected clients. The pattern is still the same, as the communication interaction is one of asynchronous messages as updates become necessary.

With this pattern, it is important to minimize the complexity of the API. Synchronized web solutions should use standard web methods (such as HTTP GET and PUT) wherever possible, generalizing the web development and deployment experience for client-side use. Several basic message exchange patterns exist; however, the more common ones are get, put, subscribe, and push. Supplemental methods exist for event notifications for changes in state in most applications embracing this pattern.

Although not always in machine language form, a set of rules regarding how unsynchronized resources can reattain a synchronized state is imperative to the overall success of this pattern. Rules should carefully outline how to avoid issues when there are conflicts and misalignments.

Static Structure

With the Synchronized Web pattern, multiple clients may be synchronized to a single object's state or multiple states. Although this pattern may appear to be enterprise-oriented, it is equally applicable to individual servers or even peer-to-peer interactions. The underlying concept is the same.

Figure 7-33 depicts one manner in which a pattern of synchronization can occur. In this variation, the state misalignment originates in data on the client at the top left. This is pushed to a centralized service and federated down to multiple tiers in the enterprise's architecture. Other clients that have subscribed to the change in state can be pushed notifications when the state changes fall outside permissible tolerances.

During the phase depicted in Figure 7-34, the change in state is pushed up to every subscribed client that needs to know.

This pattern can facilitate many different types of software, ranging from online video games to financial services. The electronic stock markets of this decade use this pattern on a daily basis to ensure that stock prices are accurate.

Implementation

The industry is currently at a very early point in the synchronized web evolution, and standards have not yet shaken out, which makes decisions somewhat more difficult for architects, developers, and businesspeople. A thousand flowers are currently blooming, and standards are emerging; however, some flowers grow faster than others.

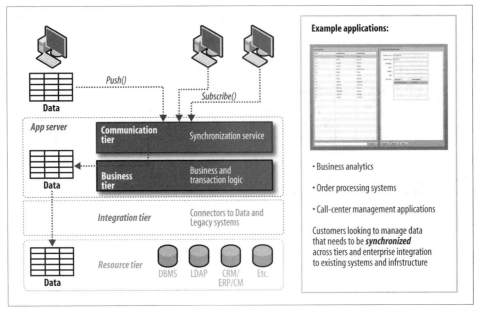

Figure 7-33. Synchronized web clients registering to an object's state (courtesy of James Ward)

The proposed HTML5, for example, includes web sockets that allow for a much wider range of communication possibilities between browsers and servers, simplifying the process of keeping information synchronized.

In actual deployment, service-to-service synchronization has become a popular feature of Facebook and even of the new Pulse service from Web 1.0 player Plaxo. (To be fair, Plaxo was always about synchronization, so in some respects it's well positioned for what comes next; it has synchronization in its DNA.)

Synchronization also certainly matters in the online world. One example of a compelling synchronized web application is Dopplr.# With this travel management application it is simple to import Twitter information (an example of the Mashup pattern), which is useful because information from both sites can be combined to provide a more meaningful set of information to those who read it.

Perhaps the most pressing concern in building what comes next is enabling offline use of online services. Both Adobe and Sun Microsystems have recently made new runtime environments available to enable synchronized web-style offline access for client-side apps (or vice versa), in the shape of AIR and JavaFX, respectively. Several smaller companies now offer online word processing, spreadsheet, or other data-grid applications that can be used in both online and offline modes and can themselves detect and account for changes in connectivity, effectively *synchronizing* the desktop with a service.

See *http://www.dopplr.com/main/login*.

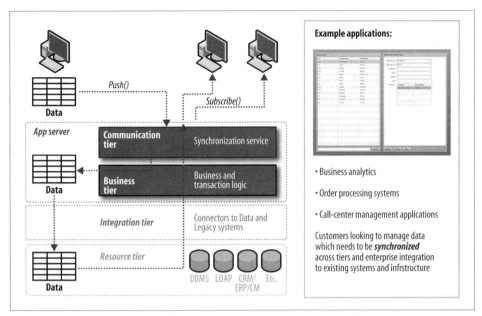

Figure 7-34. Multiple interaction services being synchronized via one application

AJAX has long been used to build synchronization functionality into Rich Internet Applications. Zimbra was one of the first vendors to demonstrate an AJAX web application synchronized for offline access using standard database technology.[*] It used the Derby (otherwise known as JavaDB) database. The announcement of Google Gears in May 2007 was the tipping point, when the synchronized web "arrived" and developers were given some great tools to work with. Google Reader was one of the first applications to benefit. Google even used the offline use cases (the set of requirements for being able to use software when not connected to the Internet, increasingly common in most document-reading software) as the basis for a humorous blog announcement for Google Reader offline titled "Feeds on a plane!"[†] The following quote is from a related article in the Google Developer Blog titled "Going offline with Google Gears":

> One of the most frequently requested features for Google web applications is the ability to use them offline. Unfortunately, today's web browsers lack some fundamental building blocks necessary to make offline web applications a reality.[‡]

Another player is Joyent, with its Ruby on Rails-based Slingshot platform. Slingshot is designed to let developers build web applications using Rails that offer a somewhat desktop-like experience: when a user is offline, she can use the app, accessing a local

---

[*] Although BackWeb, an enterprise software vendor that offers offline access for web-based enterprise apps such as JEE-based portals, definitely deserves a mention here.

[†] See *http://googleblog.blogspot.com/2007/06/feeds-on-plane.html*.

[‡] See *http://gearsblog.blogspot.com/2007/05/posted-by-aaron-boodman-and-erik.html*.

copy of the data, and the next time she goes online any changes will be synchronized with the server.

The Dojo AJAX framework, an open source DHTML toolkit written in JavaScript, is also working toward synchronized web functionality in the shape of the Dojo Offline toolkit, which includes API calls for synchronization and network detection, and even a widget to indicate successful synchronization (see Figure 7-35).

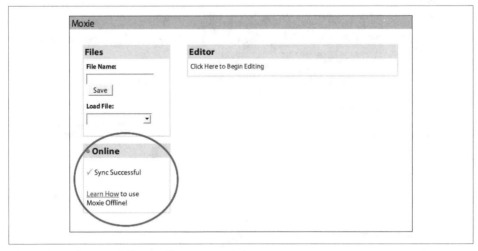

Figure 7-35. The Dojo Offline toolkit

One particularly useful Dojo function is `slurp()`, which works out the resources, Java-Script, Cascading Style Sheets, image tags, and so on that the developer needs to consider in offline-enabling the app.[§]

On the client side of a synchronized web application, you will see a more bounded experience than in the web-dependent version. Introducing and managing constraints will be one of the keys to making the synchronized web work.

From an architectural perspective, a common model for objects, events, and event management is required. If clients are to subscribe to an object's state, they need a consistent model for what represents an object. Likewise, a framework for listening to and handling events and other exceptions is a requirement. Many individual programming languages embrace a common model today, and architects need to be very clear when building applications that may touch components in disparate environments and domains of ownership.

For Ruby on Rails shops, Slingshot is an obvious choice for offline access to synchronized web applications. Developers targeting the Adobe AIR or JavaFX runtimes,

---

[§] This application's functionality is described in greater detail at *http://docs.google.com/View?docid=dhkhksk4_8gdp9gr#widget*.

meanwhile, have effectively already chosen a programming model that supports the synchronized web.

One important implementation detail to consider is the rise of the small database SQLite, which Adobe, Google, and Joyent Slingshot are adopting for storage and synchronization services. Adobe and Google are now explicitly partnering in this arena, and Mozilla Firefox 3.0 offers SQLite services out of the box.

When implementing this pattern, you should first build your synchronization services, and then work to optimize performance. The patterns of usage may not be obvious or even fully known until later, as they will be shaped by how users decide to interact with the applications.

The more standards you support in building an application or service, the more easily "synchronizable" it will be.

"Freedom to leave," a concept championed by Simon Phipps at Sun Microsystems,[ll] is automatically built-in to any true synchronized web application. In his blog, Phipps lamented the fact that a lot of user-owned data (such as bookmarks in a browser and email address lists) was not easy to port from one application or platform to another. This placed undue pressure on people to stay with the applications they used rather than allowing them to migrate to newer applications or platforms. It's not enough to merely be able to transfer or import this data to the service; the user must be able to transfer it away again. This pattern for software is referred to as "lock-in," and it is the enemy of the synchronized web, to be avoided at all costs. Open data and open standards underpin the synchronized web.

Business Problem (Story) Resolved

Establishing services that allow the free transfer of information between applications creates a much more functional environment for users to share and store data and for businesses to emerge around it. The synchronized web will allow online software offerings such as Google as well as other Software as a Service companies (such as Salesforce.com) to compete on more than equal terms with self-contained software applications. Whereas once Microsoft had a seemingly unassailable advantage when it came to rich clients with offline storage for continuous productivity, with local processing for number-crunching and so on, Google and other synchronized web players are demonstrating that rich applications need not be 100% client-side, and that there are benefits for having some types of documents online. Adobe Systems's September 2007 acquisition of Buzzword, an online word processing utility, shows the validity of such business models in the industry.

---

ll See *http://blogs.sun.com/webmink/entry/freedom_to_leave*.

Specializations

Offline access to online web applications is one specialization of this pattern. For example, the Adobe Integrated Runtime made it easy for most developers to migrate over Flash, HTML, AJAX, and PDF-based web applications, effectively allowing any online web application to locally cache data so it can work both online and offline. Early examples included a Salesforce.com application[#] built by Nitobi that allowed sales personnel to enter data while in offline mode; the application on the salesperson's computer would then automatically synchronize with the main Salesforce.com database when the client application reconnected. Although they are not synchronized with each other while one is offline, the fact that they do resynchronize is evolutionary for web-aware software applications.

Video gamers who play online also embrace a specialization of this pattern. Microsoft's *Halo 2* (one of the first applications that gave users the ability to compete online in real time against opponents anywhere in the world) really is one of the major technical marvels of modern times. *Halo 2* is no longer unique in this capability; numerous other games, such as *World of Warcraft*, have embraced this pattern.

Distributed development repositories also replicate this pattern and specialize it for the field of software development. Most commonly, it is used to enable people in disparate locations to check in and out code using the same Subversion repository. The code repository keeps the state of the overall project synchronized and everyone's views aligned.

Known Uses

This pattern is very common, and this section lists only a few additional examples. Google Reader and Google Gears both use this pattern, as do YouTube and other Flash-based video upload sites.

Teknision's Finetune, a music discovery service with an AIR-based rich client to enable client-to-profile synchronization, also embraces this pattern.

Walled Gardens might be deemed an anti-pattern of sorts, as data and objects within the Walled Garden are often not visible to applications outside that environment.

Consequences

Synchronization and replication across loosely coupled web services have considerable benefits. For example, users can:

- Take web applications offline
- Take client applications online

[#] See *http://blogs.nitobi.com/andre/index.php/2007/07/20/offline-salesforcecom-with-air-and-ajax/*.

- More easily move from one service to another by making changes in one place and having the data automatically be synchronized in another place

Although not providing a single view of the combined state of a process or application per se, the synchronized web brings the user closer to it. We're emphatically not talking here about what enterprise software companies would call "master data management." The synchronized web doesn't involve a massive data cleansing and normalizing exercise, to create a single canonical view of "the truth." One way to think of the distinction is in the context of the differences between formal taxonomy and the Web's community-defined equivalents: tagsonomy and folksonomy. Formal ontologies such as the Suggested Upper Merged Ontology (SUMO)* are rife with a pure and untainted first order of logic in which each concept is defined as a distinct and undeniable truth. This logic deals with some of the problems that architects face, such as the requirement for consistent models for objects and events mentioned earlier. The beauty lies within the incontrovertible idealism and universally true axioms and tenets. Folksonomies, on the other hand, are rife with inconsistencies and a system of sometimes illogical instances, yet they flourish and have been adopted (arguably) faster than most formalized ontology work.

The synchronized web is supposed to make users' lives easier, not harder. So, when users act in one place, this pattern allows applications to update in another. When you update a Dopplr trip, for example, it also updates your WordPress blog. Or you can update your profile in Twitter, and the changes get syndicated to Facebook. No one entity needs to own and manage all the data to create huge benefits for users.

Matt Biddulph, the CTO of Dopplr, explains how this kind of synchronization should change the way that developers create web applications:

> The fundamental web concept of Small Pieces, Loosely Joined is finally reaching maturity. It's no longer necessary for every new webapp to re-implement every feature under the sun. Instead, they can concentrate on their core product, and share data with other sites using web APIs as the connectors.

The flipside of the "small things, loosely joined" mantra is that it can be a challenge to manage all the intermingling and data redundancy. To emphasize this point, consider how many profiles the average Internet user might have, including ones on MySpace, Facebook, Twitter, Flickr, Gmail, Yahoo!, the Microsoft Developer Network, various conference websites, and more. All contain the same basic semantic building blocks, yet they will inevitably become somewhat unsynchronized if some details change. The Synchronized Web pattern can be employed in software design to manage these states for you.

References

For more on the Synchronized Web pattern, please see the following sources:

---

* See *http://en.wikipedia.org/wiki/Classes_(SUMO)*.

- Google Gears blog and architecture—*http://code.google.com/apis/gears/architecture.html*
- Zimbra Desktop—*http://www.zimbra.com/products/desktop.html*
- "Synchronized Web Surfing: A Web-Based Application for Interaction Between Online Users," by Tao Sun, Yang Li, and Bill Tucker—*http://www.cs.uwc.ac.za/~btucker/academic/research/publications/SunLiTucker-AIDIS2004.pdf*
- Ruby on Rails—*http://www.rubyonrails.org*

The Collaborative Tagging Pattern

Also Known As

Terms and patterns associated with the Collaborative Tagging pattern include:

Folksonomy
> Folksonomy is a popular term used to capture part of this pattern (as documented in the O'Reilly Radar report *Web 2.0 Principles and Best Practices (http://radar.oreilly.com/research/web2-report.html)*. There are multiple definitions of folksonomy; however, the one given in the O'Reilly Radar publication is closest to this pattern.

The Semantic Web Grounding pattern
> We discuss the related pattern of Semantic Web Grounding later in this chapter. Such a pattern may use a collaborative tagging system as the basis for tagging resources; however, it may be implemented without this pattern.

The Declarative Living and Tag Gardening pattern
> The Declarative Living and Tag Gardening pattern, which we discuss in the next section, is also highly relevant to this pattern.

Business Problem (Story)

Often, we need to use a search system to find resources on the Internet. The resources must match our needs, and to find relevant information, we need to enter search terms. The search system compares those terms with a metadata index that shows which resources might be relevant to our search.

The primary problem with such a system is that the metadata index is often built based on resources being tagged by a small group of people who determine the relevancy of those resources for specific terms. The smaller the group that does this is, the greater the chance is that the group will apply inaccurate tags to some resources or omit certain relationships between the search terms and the resources' semantic relevancy. Furthermore, as written in an O'Reilly Radar brief:

Hierarchies by definition are top-down and typically defined in a centralized fashion, which is an impractical model poorly suited to the collaborative, decentralized, highly networked world of Web 2.0.

Rich media, such as audio and video, benefit from this explicit metadata because other forms of extracting meaning and searching [are] still a challenge.

The Collaborative Tagging pattern represents a ground-up style of semantic tagging that, by its very nature, will represent a larger cross section of society's consensus regarding how to describe resources.

 The following definitions apply only to this pattern:

- To *tag* means to apply labels to an object or resource. When we say "tagging an object," we really mean adding a label to an object to declare what that object represents.

- *Resource* is used as a catchall term to denote any digital asset that can have an identifier (this is the W3C definition from the Web Services Architecture Working Group). Examples of resources include online content, audio files, digital photos, bookmarks, news items, websites, products, blog posts, comments, and other items available online.

- An *entity* is any human, application, bot, process, or other thing (including agents acting on behalf of one of these entities) that is capable of interacting with a resource.

In ontology circles, a triangle with the terms *referent*, *term*, and *concept* at its three points is often used to capture relationships between them. We use the word *tag* in a way that is synonymous with *term*, and *referent* is likewise similar to *resource*. The third term in the ontology triangle, the *concept*, is the abstract domain in which the lexicon or central meaning exists. This is noted as the *conceptual domain* in Figure 7-36. The *entity* is the agent or actor that makes the declaration linking all three of these concepts together. In this respect, the context in which that entity makes the declaration is an immense factor in the overall semantics, and in folksonomy implementations it can result in vastly differing tags.

Consider a person tagging a photograph of broccoli. One person might label it "cruciform," "vegetable," or "nutritious," while another might tag it "gross," "bitter," or worse.

Context

Collaborative tagging adds a community-based natural language semantic layer to other searching and indexing mechanisms, and therefore it is useful anywhere and in any context in which people want to search for and communicate about information. Tagging enables better *findability* without requiring top-down metadata annotation;

with tagging systems, users generate their own metadata. Tagging allows for resources to be described and used in communities in a way that mimics real life. If you observe a child learning to speak, you will see tagging (and later, tag gardening) in conjunction with the community—parents, other kids—in action.

Derived Requirements

Resources must be associated with a metadata infrastructure that lets anyone interacting with the resources add tags to them to make declarations about their relevancy. The system must be bi-navigational so that searchers can find all the tags attached to a specific resource and find other resources tagged with the same terms.

The tags themselves must be part of some normative or natural language to represent meaning.

Generalized Solution

To solve the business problem discussed earlier, a mechanism that lets users declare tags for specific resources should be in place, and its use should be encouraged. This pattern builds on the fact that some software mechanisms (such as folksonomies) become increasingly useful as more people use them. Additionally, collaborative tagging system users should be able to see the tags others have used to declare attributes or properties of a specific resource, to promote reuse of terminology and to increase the semantic understanding of the tags or of the resource.

To explain the pattern, Scott Golder and Bernardo A. Huberman authored "The Structure of Collaborative Tagging Systems."[†] In this great resource, they wrote:

> Collaborative tagging describes the process by which many users add metadata in the form of keywords to shared content. Recently, collaborative tagging has grown in popularity on the web, on sites that allow users to tag bookmarks, photographs and other content. In this book we analyze the structure of collaborative tagging systems as well as their dynamical aspects. Specifically, we discovered regularities in user activity, tag frequencies, kinds of tags used, bursts of popularity in bookmarking and a remarkable stability in the relative proportions of tags within a given URL. We also present a dynamical model of collaborative tagging that predicts these stable patterns and relates them to imitation and shared knowledge.

Users tag resources with keywords to classify them in alignment with their perspectives, yet in terms of their own choosing. The tags themselves are indexed, and a search on the index can yield a list of resources that may be relevant for a specific tag. Alternatively, the relationship can be traversed in the other direction to determine what tags have been applied to a specific resource.

[†] "The Structure of Collaborative Tagging Systems," by Scott Golder and Bernardo A. Huberman, *Journal of Information Science*, Vol. 32, 198–208 (2006); *http://arxiv.org/abs/cs.DL/0508082*.

Static Structure

The Collaborative Tagging pattern's static structure is simplistic in design. Resources (e.g., digital photos) are examined by entities (usually people interacting with those resources) that then tag those resources according to their own interpretations of what they represent. What one person might tag as "dog" another might tag as "friend," and yet another might tag it as "pooch" or perhaps "Pomeranian." All these tags might have value for someone wanting to find that picture. Flickr is the exemplar service of this pattern. Communities have emerged that play games using Flickr tags, such as finding "orphan" tags that have been used just once. Collaborative tagging doesn't require artificial intelligence or normalization. It keeps things simple by convention.

The tag, although freely chosen by the entity, is grounded in some form of conceptualization of a domain and represents that entity's view of the resource based on the conceptual domain. This concept is referred to in Ontology circles as "pragmatics." The resource is linked to the tag. This relationship is illustrated in Figure 7-36.

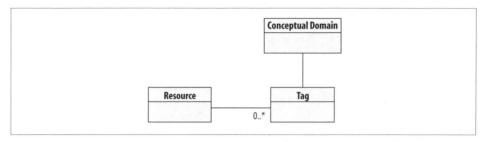

Figure 7-36. Resource-tag relationship

Dynamic Behavior

The primary sequence of activity in the Collaborative Tagging pattern is as follows. A user (an instance of an entity) makes a call to get a resource. The user then inspects the resource. After the user has inspected the resource, she can make a semantic declaration about the resource by adding a tag that references it (see Figure 7-37). Note that this diagram illustrates only the application of the tag, not the subsequent use of the tag for discovering related resources.

Implementation

Some tags have multiple meanings. In such cases, using an ontology or other higher order of logic to disambiguate meaning will help users find the correct resources. Implementers should also do what they can to encourage users to add tags to content, as the entire search and retrieval process benefits from more minds contributing tags. A synonym mechanism might be useful where tags or terms are interchangeable within

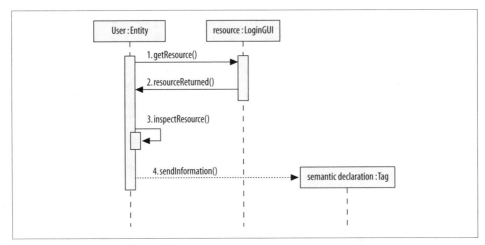

Figure 7-37. Sequence of events for tagging a resource

a certain context. For example, those seeking "rental cars" might also be interested in finding resources tagged with "automobile for hire" or "vehicle leasing."

You might also need some form of post-tagging analysis to avoid having entities thwart the Collaborative Tagging pattern by making illegal or unjustified declarations for their own benefit. For example, many website developers use or have used the HTML specification's `meta` tag's `content` attribute[‡] to make inaccurate declarations about their sites' content in an attempt to attract visitors; some were even taken to court and fined.

Business Problem (Story) Resolved

Increasing the user population usually makes a service more effective, and collaborative tagging is no exception. Semantics requires agreement and convention: the wider the agreement on a folksonomy term, the more useful the term becomes. As user populations grow, it becomes increasingly likely that someone else will also use a particular tag.

Many people don't know how Google's spell checker works.[§] The service doesn't actually know anything at all about the words it checks. It does, however, know that a lot of people use them in a particular way: the right way. That's the basis for programming collective intelligence in many contexts, and the same "learning by observation" approach can be applied to tags. Most, if not all, of the type-defining Web 2.0 web services use this pattern. Search indexes built using this system will likely appeal to a larger cross section of society. This is because, unlike taxonomies that were developed by very few people with a specific view of the world based on their own social

---

[‡] See *http://www.w3.org/TR/REC-html40/struct/global.html#h-7.4.4.2.*

[§] See *http://www.google.com/support/bin/answer.py?answer=1723&topic=10192.*

upbringing, folksonomies are defined as they are created, by the majority of society. Logically, they stand a very good chance of being accurate to a large segment of users.

Terms also morph over time. For example, saying something or someone is "sick" in some contexts is slang meaning "really good" or "cool," rather than an indication of suffering from an illness.

Specializations

There are ways to specialize this pattern. One way is to couple it with an *upper-level ontology* to classify tag terms that have multiple meanings. An upper-level ontology is a common, shared conceptualization of a domain. Two common examples are the Laboratory for Applied Ontology's Descriptive Ontology for Linguistic and Cognitive Engineering (DOLCE)[||] and Adam Pease's Suggested Upper Merged Ontology (SUMO).[#] By mapping SUMO to terms in Wordnet, ambiguities can be avoided in cases where words have multiple meanings. Imagine searching for the term "Washington." You would likely get results for George Washington (a president), Denzel Washington (an actor), Washington, DC (a city), the Washington Monument (a large monument), Washington State University (a school), and more. If folksonomies can be mapped in a manner that disambiguates pluralities of meanings, it might be a valuable mechanism to advance Semantic Web interests.

Other ways to specialize this pattern could be to include human actors to monitor and build a massive thesaurus. This project could be of interest to entrepreneurs who want to do something in the field of semantics.

Known Uses

Flickr, Google Earth, Technorati, and Slashdot are all notable uses of this pattern.

In particular, Flickr has implemented the capability to have many humans provide tags for digital photographs. Flickr has often been heralded as a pioneer in Web 2.0 in terms of folksonomy development. Technorati is likewise a pioneer in terms of letting individuals use tags for blog articles, and Slashdot's beta tagging system lets any member place specific tags on any post. Technorati has even published a microformat for tags in blog entries and indexes blogs using those tags (and category data). Even when an explicit tagging mechanism isn't available, users often create them, as in the *#tag* syntax common on Twitter.

[||] See *http://www.loa-cnr.it/DOLCE.html*.

[#] See *http://www.ontologyportal.org*.

Consequences

Collaborative tagging has created controversy. For example, some ontologists have argued that folksonomy approaches are worthless due to their inherent flaws and the lack of a formalized ontology to provide context for the declarations (i.e., the lack of a higher level of formal logic to help classify all things in the folksonomy). Tag clouds, for instance, can help people find resources relevant to what they're seeking.[*] Although this itself may seem to prove that tag clouds work, the logic for making such an assumption is flawed. Most people who find items that seem "relevant" to their search terms via tag clouds have no way of knowing whether those items were in fact the *most* relevant, because in most cases they don't see all the choices. A further problem is that some actual tag cloud categories cannot be audited from an external perspective (an example of this might be "most popular").

In spite of these flaws, it appears that several uses of collaborative tagging actually are semantically useful to those seeking articles or resources, even though not everyone may agree on the validity of the tags used. One example we encountered involved an article on Slashdot, a famous discussion board that bills itself as providing "news for nerds." The article, which discussed cell phones and some hybrid technology approach, was tagged with the word *stupid*.[†] Although this tag represents a personal point of view and is in itself rather nondescriptive of the article's content, it turned out that several people (including some of the authors of this book) who searched Slashdot for *stupid* felt that the tag accurately described most of the posts to which it was attributed. Despite the lack of a formal ontology and first order of logic, it appears that there are patterns of use in folksonomy approaches that have fairly consistent results among large groups of users.

References

Several other patterns are related to the Collaborative Tagging pattern. The following two sections (describing the Declarative Living and Tag Gardening pattern and the Semantic Web Grounding pattern) are particularly relevant. There are also several sections in Chapter 3 that deal with folksonomies and collaboration that may be of interest.

The Declarative Living and Tag Gardening Pattern

Also Known As

Terms associated with the Declarative Living and Tag Gardening pattern include:

---

[*] See Figure 7-42 for an example of a tag cloud.

[†] See *http://hardware.slashdot.org/article.pl?sid=06/06/03/1311231*.

Ambient findability

The pattern of Declarative Living and Tag Gardening is similar to the concepts discussed in Peter Morville's book *Ambient Findability (http://oreilly.com/catalog/9780596007652/)* (O'Reilly). In this book, Morville describes several of the problems related to semantic declarations.

Social networks

While many people think of social networks as the rage of Web 2.0, social networks are in fact as old as society itself. What is truly new are the ways we have found to "declare" our social networks, or fractions thereof, on several Web 2.0 platforms. Most notable of these have been MySpace, Facebook, Twitter, Plaxo, LinkedIn, and YouTube.

Business Problem (Story)

In conversations around the world, people are constantly expressing their preferences and opinions. In other words, we live *declaratively*. We declare who our friends are and who our acquaintances or business colleagues are. We talk about the videos, music, books, art, food, and so on that we've encountered, the people that inspire us, and the people we'd rather avoid. It's no different on the Web, except that on the Web we can make these declarations explicitly through common formats and technologies (such as *tags*, as discussed in the preceding section on the Collaborative Tagging pattern), or we can leave a trail of digital breadcrumbs and let other people draw their own conclusions. In both cases, others can capture these declarations and make use of them. That is, the breadcrumbs can be aggregated and given to actors (either human or machine) who can make *inferences* from these declarations.

Before the Internet, a lot of our declarations were never put to any use; many of them dissipated (quite literally) as hot air. But when people began to have conversations online, a new possibility arose. Because people's preferences could be explicitly imprinted on the Internet's memory as auditable bits, they could be aggregated and mined. Rather than trying to harvest the entire Internet, which would be like trying to catch a waterfall in a thimble, specific dedicated services have been created to optimize both the declaration and the aggregation of these preferences as "tags," which can then provide rich semantic information (in a process known as *tag gardening*).

The next stage in the evolution of declarative living is the continued creation and adoption of standards—for example, microformats—giving the user more control and freedom to make declarations and the tag garden a richer, more formalized vocabulary and structure with which to work.

Context

This pattern occurs in any context where declarations are made or where mechanisms are used to harvest those declarations for some computer functionality. The declarative living aspects of the pattern embrace the concept of metadata (data about data), and the tag gardening aspects embrace *inference*, a component of artificial intelligence. *Pragmatics* (the implications of information in the context in which it is encountered) are also inherent in any such design.

Additionally, we see declarative living at work in any system in which the user can make a public statement, either explicitly or by leaving an unintentional audit trail of his actions. Declarative living and its corollary, tag gardening, have varying degrees of structure. A person blogging that she's currently in London (or making such an announcement via Twitter or Dopplr) would be an example of declarative living and would enable tag gardening. That person might also use Google Maps to pinpoint her location, or even broadcast her exact current geographical coordinates using Twitter.

Derived Requirements

To facilitate this pattern, you need a mechanism that lets users make conscious declarations and, optionally, associate those declarations with resources. User interfaces supporting the Declarative Living and Tag Gardening pattern must be very intuitive and easy to use, and should facilitate data entry in the user's natural language(s). The Blogger, Twitter, Dopplr, and Delicious interfaces, which allow users to enter declarations in plain text, are good examples.

When implementing the Declarative Living and Tag Gardening pattern, starting as simply as possible with the declarations aspect is preferable (you cannot garden/harvest tags until they exist). The tag gardening aspects can be built later, against either a centralized aggregation of declarations or a decentralized yet indexed collection. In the latter scenario, understanding the intricacies of mapping relational database systems to such an index is paramount to the success of the system. Employing a strategy of partial indexing early on rather than trying to build a full-blown, real-time system from scratch might help you avoid an exponential increase in bandwidth consumption.

Specific to tag gardening itself, you must also consider early on how to split and aggregate data to and from multiple machines. It's not as difficult to have eight web servers talk to one database as it would be to have one web server talk to eight different databases. This is a problem for architects to handle.

Perception of good performance is also not optional. For Web 2.0 constituents, performance is an important feature. Debugging devices, test harnesses, and other monitoring systems (such as Nagios) are likely to be important tools for developers to use.

Developers and architects should prepare for scale but should not try to do everything up-front. Using proxies between services and the actors consuming them is likely to be beneficial, as proxies can cache and deliver the bytes more efficiently (think of Akamai, discussed in Chapter 3). Declarations can be harvested by talking to proxies who aggregate them and offer services at some logical level of granularity.

Generalized Solution

Any successful declarative living service must, by definition, be extremely easy to use, as well as self-contained in terms of providing value to the end user; otherwise, it will not be adopted. Delicious.com exemplifies this pattern. Josh Schachter, the founder of the service, constantly refuses feature requests that might make people less likely to actually use the service for declarative living and web annotation. Formal Semantic Web technologies such as the Ontology Web Language (OWL) and Resource Description Framework (RDF) force too much work onto the user. People are unlikely to spend time annotating content or relating their terms to nodes in a formal ontology. Even if some did this, the chances of this work being consistently performed are very minimal. Most new Internet users seem to prefer to get their declarations online quickly and tag resources in their own way. For those building a service, a key design principle should be to remove as many barriers to participation as possible. The service should require as few clicks and field fill-ins as necessary. (It may, of course, make sense for applications to keep track of these declarations using RDF internally, allowing them to apply RDF tools to user-provided information.)

Unlike Ma.gnolia.com (see Figure 7-38), a Delicious competitor with a five-star rating system similar to that of iTunes or Windows Media Player, Delicious provides a more binary choice: is this web resource interesting or not? Delicious doesn't allow for degrees of interest (at least, not at the single-user level). The key point here is that if more granularity is available for declarative living, more care must be taken when making decisions to keep choices consistent.

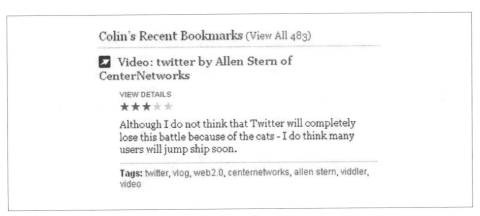

Figure 7-38. The ability to add degrees of interest indicated by stars, in Ma.gnolia.com

Last.FM, which CBS acquired earlier this year for $280 million, is a social service that brings music lovers together. The masterstroke for Last.FM, from a business model perspective, was acquiring Audioscrobbler, a plug-in that listens to a user's music player and uploads a logfile of that user's choices. Thus, rather than you sitting there entering a bunch of data about what music you like, Audioscrobbler runs in the background and does it for you, creating a constant stream of musical breadcrumbs. Last.FM users can also use the plug-in to add additional metadata tags to the track listings, but just as with Delicious, the fact that you've downloaded a track is pretty good evidence that you actually like it. If you allow someone to harvest the fact you listened to the same song between one and five times per day, she may reasonably infer that you thought it was a good song.

Taking the automated agent-based tagging approach to its natural conclusion, it's now time to consider the notion of tag gardening as applied to objects, rather than people, that "live" declaratively. Radio Frequency Identification (RFID) tagging and monitoring is an enterprise-oriented implementation of this pattern. When every instance of a class of things starts to make harvestable declarations, an exponential explosion of tag gardening may occur. When we can label many of these devices with our own tags as well, human and machine tags will be intermingled and harvesting will be required.

The ability to aggregate all the tags is not an enterprise-scale requirement or a web-scale requirement; it goes far beyond both scopes. Arguably, developers and architects haven't even begun to tackle the really thorny scaling problems in our industry (the ability to implement patterns such as this one across the whole Internet, or a large subset of it). Sun Microsystems CTO Greg Papadopoulos has recently begun to talk about what he describes as a Red Shift, arguing that it will take a hardcore computer science foundation to build scalable next-generation services (which is, of course, Sun's core competence). One of the defining characteristics of Web 2.0 developers and architects has been a dismissal of many traditional enterprise architecture patterns. But to move forward, they're likely going to need to scale up, and scale out, server-side managed session state in some cases, along with coming up with new approaches to data integrity and referentiality. Web 2.0 patterns don't change the fundamental challenges of computer science.

Smart objects aren't the only things that will need to be marshaled in declarative living. All kinds of digital assets, including documents, images, videos, audio files, users, real-world objects, and other entities, will likely benefit from this pattern. All of these resources have lives and functions, can be marked up, and can contain embedded declarations along the lines of "X is worth Y" and "A has a business relationship with B." The notion of declarative resources can lead us into some mental gymnastics. For instance, Peter Morville talks about the notion of an antelope as a document. Using the work of Paul Otlet and Suzanne Briet as background, he explains that in certain conditions, even an antelope could be considered a document—that is, if a photo is taken of the animal and is used in an academic setting, the animal has become, in effect, a document because it has been "marked up." Continuing in this vein, Morville asks:

> What if we leave the antelope in the wild, but embed an RFID tag or attach a GPS transponder or assign it a URL? What if our antelope is indexed by Google?[‡]

[‡] *Ambient Findability*, by Peter Morville (O'Reilly), page 149.

These are really interesting questions, and once we internalize the notion that anything we tag becomes a document (or other resource) to be added to a global body of knowledge, we can begin to understand the deep implications of declarative living and tag gardening.

Recently, we have seen an explosion of Apple iPhone applications that use location services to make declarations about *where* you did something. An example of this is the application iMapMyRide.com, which uses the GPS data from your phone to track or tag your movements and can overlay this data on a map. More novel uses are certain to emerge, and the pattern of declarative living is here to stay.

Static Structure

This pattern has two static views. The first, shown in Figure 7-39, is a simple view in which a user (actor) interacts with a resource and makes declarations about the resource. Via these declarations, people express themselves and aspects about how they perceive their existence. This, in itself, is similar to the Collaborative Tagging pattern. However, it is specific to instances in which a human actor is involved and making the declarations, whereas the Collaborative Tagging pattern is agnostic in terms of which actors may make such declarations.

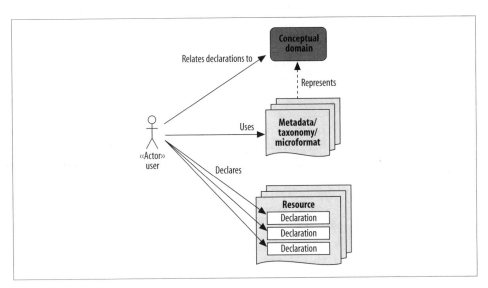

Figure 7-39. The Declarative Living pattern

A second static view of this pattern corresponds to the aspect of tag gardening. This is where declarations may be subsequently harvested and/or aggregated (see Figure 7-40).

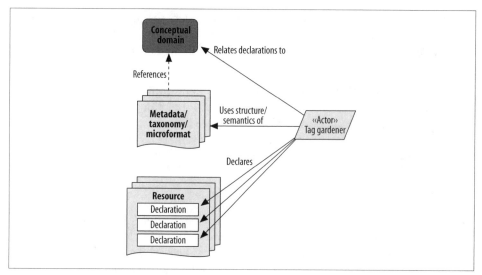

Figure 7-40. The Tag Gardening pattern

Note that the tag gardening actor can be a human, a machine, or another type of actor. Once harvested, declarations can be represented in many forms, as noted earlier.

The conceptual domain shown in Figure 7-39 refers to a higher-level abstract concept of the instance coupled with an alignment in the first order(s) of logic (FOL). Several upper ontologies embrace this in the best way they can, and you can use the work of the upper ontologies as a platform to build mid-level ontologies and more domain-specific taxonomies. Figure 7-41[§] illustrates the relationships between the FOL and domain-specific ontologies.

The ability to link semantic declarations to higher-level concepts is still in its infancy; however, it has become an area of interest in some ontology circles, including the Ontolog Forum.[‖] You can reach SUMO creator Dr. Adam Pease, of Articulate Software, via the Ontolog Forum, alongside ontology gurus and notables such as Professor Bill McCarthy, Dr. Matthew West (Shell), John Sowa, and others.

Dynamic Behavior

The dynamic aspects of the Declarative Living and Tag Gardening pattern are roughly equivalent.

[§] (courtesy of SUMO, *http://www.ontologyportal.org*)

[‖] See *http://ontolog.cim3.net*.

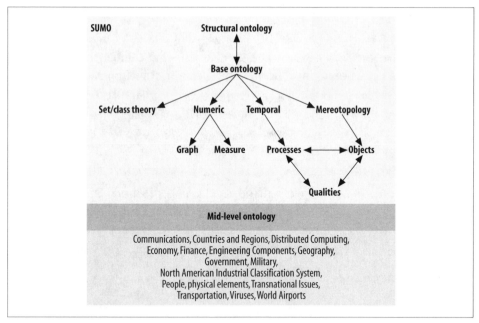

Figure 7-41. The relationship of SUMO's first order of logic to mid-level ontologies

Implementation

There is a fair amount of overlap between the Collaborative Tagging and Declarative Living and Tag Gardening patterns.

The two patterns do, however, have some differences in terms of analysis. Tag gardening offers some specific approaches: tag metadata can, for example, be expressed with user interface patterns such as tag clouds, as shown in Figure 7-42.

The tag cloud in Figure 7-42 comes from Flickr, and it represents many people's first exposure to the term. In a tag cloud, the more popular a term is, the bigger and bolder it becomes. Essentially, this represents a garden of tags used to declare aspects of digital images referenced within Flickr.

Although people don't generally consider *tagsonomies* amenable to hierarchy, hierarchies do emerge. Paul Lamere, a researcher at Sun Microsystems, has done some very interesting work using a search engine to analyze tagsonomies and extract hierarchies from them (see Figure 7-43).[#] As in taxonomies, these hierarchies usually convey the knowledge aspects of inheritance as well as polymorphisms and dependencies. They also can represent the relationships where one concept splits into other concepts due to the child descendents being *disjointed*. Disjointed binary relationships are sets in which each sibling has an exclusive characteristic that is in contrast to the others. For

[#] Courtesy of Paul Lamere's website, *http://blogs.sun.com/plamere/entry/metal*).

Figure 7-42. A tag cloud

example, you could note the class of all humans, and then make further distinctions based on humans who are female and others who are male. With the exception of a small transgender community, these subclasses are considered disjointed.

Given that most systems employ some form of automation of access, avoiding complexity in any API would be a good strategy for those offering services to collect declarations. Most developers find SOAP to be overly complex, let alone other flavors of XML web services, Corba, or RPC. Delicious only offers the ability to GET the value of a resource or PUT a new resource, using a RESTful approach (for more on REST, see "Also Known As" on page 190).

Business Problem (Story) Resolved

When it comes to declarative living, the proof is very much in adoption behaviors. Although Twitter is not a tag-based system per se, it may morph into one: microformat support is one possibility currently being discussed, and the service already supports map coordinates for user locations. But Twitter is certainly a declarative living engine, and its adoption has been explosive.

At the time of this writing, business problems are still evolving at a rapid pace, and nothing less than the need for community and clarification of digital assets is required in our age of disintegration.

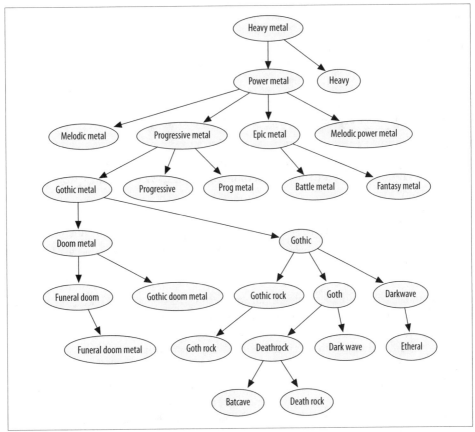

Figure 7-43. Representation of a hierarchy automatically extracted from a number of tags about different styles of heavy metal music

Specializations

Humans think in a manner that is conducive to implementing this pattern. Our sub-conscious thoughts often try to make meaning out of the situations we encounter, and by analyzing the tags any specific human applies to a variety of resources, you can determine a lot can about that human.

Declarative living(i.e., the act of making explicit declarations about resources we encounter) can be specialized in many ways. Music tagging, for example, represents a rich field for tag-based systems. An entire science is now being established to deliver musical recommendations to users based on gardening their tags. The main fight is between Rhapsody, which makes music recommendations by algorithmically breaking down music into constituent parts and recommending that which is similar, and Last.FM, which offers recommendations based on tag gardening the collective intelligence of its users. Last.FM and Rhapsody both offer surprisingly accurate recommendations, with some key differences in the "look and feel" of the app. Rhapsody is like a radio station that only plays the music you like, whereas Last.FM is like going back to college and hanging out with lots of cool people with great music collections, some of which you find utterly amazing and some of which you abhor. Both services can be tuned to give you more of what you want, but Last.FM is more likely to throw something unexpected into the mix. CBS has great ambitions for Last.FM; one obvious possibility is to turn it into a TV, rather than audio, recommendation service.

A number of additional specializations can be applied to this pattern:

Book tagging

> A great deal of Amazon.com's success is predicated on getting customers to write reviews for others to read, and its recommendation service uses tag gardening very effectively.

URL tagging

> A number of URL tagging services exist. How many times have you wondered, "Oh no, what was that link again?" That's the problem these services are designed to handle.

Search

> The most powerful example of tag gardening in action is Google PageRank. Though not usually thought of in relation to URL tagging, Google's spiders effectively crawl the Web looking for links to other sites. Google treats these links much like tags of interest, which can then be parsed for authority.

Photo tagging

> Flickr really did write the book here. Steward Butterfield and Caterina Fake beat their competitors by making user-generated content the core element of Flickr's photo storage and sharing services. The mechanism for letting users do amazing things with Flickr, such as creating recipe books, making games, illustrating poems, and so on, was the humble tag.

RFID mashups

> It's really too early to define winners in this space, but there are some interesting implementations out there. London's Oyster card, for example, is a card that offers cheap passage on public transportation in London. As you move around the city, fares are automatically deducted from your prepaid RFID-enabled card; the optional auto top-up feature ensures that you never get stranded. Users can also query the system to see where they have been traveling. This is a very different example from the others listed earlier, and that difference is intentional. Machine tagging (in this case, geographical) is an important element in the future of the Declarative Living and Tag Gardening pattern.

Distributed development repositories

> Distributed development repositories also replicate this pattern and specialize it for the field of software development—most commonly, to enable people on different continents to check in and check out code using the same interface to the

versioning system. Developers working on large-scale open source projects typically use such content versioning systems to avoid overwriting each other's work, and to track the state of the overall project.

Location-based declarations

Several mobile and laptop hardware platforms already include GPS sensors that can be used to augment any declaration and make it geo-spatial specific. This trend is manifesting as massive growth in commercial applications for things such as finding nearby restaurants or gas stations, remembering where you took photographs, and more.

Offline access to online web applications

This was discussed in the earlier section on the Synchronized Web pattern (under "Specializations" on page 111).

Known Uses

Delicious (*http://delicious.com*) is minimalist and is primarily used by a geeky, developer-centric crowd. Ma.gnolia (*http://ma.gnolia.com*) is a bit prettier and is more widely used by web designers, though data corruption brought it to a sudden halt in early 2009. Functionally, it is similar to Delicious in that members save websites as bookmarks, like they would in their browsers. The users also tag the websites, assigning semantically meaningful labels to make them easy to find again. Other users may search via Ma.gnolia and find sites that others have deemed worthwhile, based on the tags they have applied to those websites.

Digg (*http://www.digg.com*) is a community site where users can flag URLs as interesting. By combining all declarations of usefulness, compiling a list of sites that are really of interest to a large segment of society is easy. Since 2007, many people have used Digg as a verb ("Can you *digg* this blog post?").

Twitter (*http://www.twitter.com*) is both the ultimate declarative living site, allowing people to make declarations about any aspects of their lives that they wish to make public, and one of the best places to harvest those declarations (other users can subscribe to your updates to see what you've been doing). Some users have fanatically embraced this site, whereas others have labeled it one of the most annoying uses of technology of all time (a poll was set up at *http://wis.dm/questions/37343-do-you-find -twitter-annoying*). Using the poll to declare your answer is in itself a manifestation of this pattern.

Dopplr (*http://www.dopplr.com*) is a great site that can be used for declaring and harvesting travel information for people in your social circles.

Consequences

If you minimize the complexity of the tagging infrastructure and the API, the declarative living service and its associated tag garden can quickly scale and attract new users. The size of the community alone is no guarantee of income, but attention can always be monetized. If you have enough eyeballs, a business model will emerge; ad sales are one obvious opportunity.

If tags make the user experience better, they encourage community, which in turn encourages more attention, and so increases the possibility to make money, or at least deepen community ties. In the case of Delicious, for example, its owner (Yahoo!) has chosen not to try to make money directly from the service.

References

Josh Schachter is an evangelist and a great storyteller. He has done as much as anyone to define the Declarative Living and Tag Gardening pattern. See, for example, his Future of Web Apps 2006 presentation,[*] from which this section borrows heavily.

Other references include the following:

- Search Inside the Music (the blog of Paul Lamere, who works in research at Sun Microsystems)—*http://research.sun.com/spotlight/2006/2006-06-28_search_in side_music.html*
- *Ambient Findability*, by Peter Morville (O'Reilly)
- Clay Shirkey, various essays
- David Weinberger, various essays
- *The Search: How Google and Its Rivals Rewrote the Rules of Business and Transformed Our Culture*, by John Battelle (Portfolio)

The Semantic Web Grounding Pattern

Also Known As

The Semantic Web Grounding pattern is related to several patterns and concepts discussed in this book:

The Collaborative Tagging and Declarative Living and Tag Gardening patterns, among others
> This pattern draws upon several related patterns, including the Collaborative Tagging pattern, the Declarative Living and Tag Gardening pattern, and various other search and retrieval patterns.

Adaptive software
> Adaptive software is a term used to describe a pattern that employs the grounding aspect to "understand" semantic declarations.

---

[*] See *http://redmonk.com/jgovernor/2006/02/08/things-weve-learned-josh-schachter-quotes-of-the-day/*.

Some consider the overlay of a good semantics mechanism to be the harbinger of the next generation of the Internet, known as either "the Semantic Web" or "Web 3.0." For the record, we do not like to use the term Web 3.0 and would encourage everyone to stop this convention. Semantic mechanisms are complex to understand, but they are already part of the Web today.

Business Problem (Story)

A government agency archives hundreds of thousands of data sets submitted from various public and private sector organizations. To make the archives useful, a search facility should exist to allow users to search for and retrieve the data sets they require.

Unfortunately, many data sets are likely to match any specific search request, making it hard for the searchers to find the exact data sets they want. A sorting and ranking algorithm can make preliminary search results somewhat more relevant; however, the thousands of records returned for each search make the retrieval of data sets slow and inefficient.

Some sort of system is needed to aid those searching for specific data sets. To implement such a mechanism, you need a set of search and query algorithms that can rapidly locate the specific data set required.

Some form of semantic declaration about web resources can aid entities wishing to find resources that are relevant to their requirements. These declarations can come from many sources (a folksonomy approach) or a single source. The core problem is that regardless of a resource tag's origin, most semantic work is not grounded in real-world post-interaction analysis. To rectify this, the Semantic Web Grounding pattern includes a secondary step whereby an application can inspect the claims made about a resource's semantics and compare those claims to real-world patterns of interaction with the resource or its attributes. No matter where the tags come from, subsequent to the tagging activity, monitoring the patterns of interaction with resources and correlating those actions to the tags used can help refine the relevancy of semantic search and retrieval, enabling applications to adaptively infer desirable results and best choices for future searches.

Context

This pattern can be used wherever large numbers of resources exist and some form of declaration about what they represent is required to aid entities wishing to locate specific resources. The pattern implies that the metadata declarations are not made using some pre-agreed form of semantics; hence, an adaptive mechanism is required for semantic reconciliation. A metadata declaration is nothing more than the application of a label, or tag. The meaning of that label, however, can vary greatly depending on the context (a concept known as pragmatics).

Derived Requirements

To facilitate the Semantic Web Grounding pattern, you need a mechanism for structured exchange of metadata that allows claims to be made about resources. The claims must be in a syntax that is universally parsable by all entities of a fabric. In this context, the term *fabric* is used to denote all accessible points on any given network, regardless of protocols used (this is akin to the use of the word in the phrase "fabric of space" to denote the universe). It could refer to a Bluetooth short-reach network or even to the Internet, and it is used to ensure that the pattern can be applied to the widest possible range of situations. The claims must be linked to specific resources, and each resource must be uniquely identified.

The entities using the claims should employ some mechanism to reconcile them against the observable real-world effects of interactions with those resources to facilitate cause-and-effect auditing. This mechanism should allow adaptive inferences about future resource claims based on a history of claims versus real-world effects. For example, you could find a way to track search engine users to see how they interact with resources returned for specific search terms. If a user interacts with a resource and then seems to be finished with his search (as evidenced by not searching for the same topic again), an observer could conclude that resource is more relevant than another resource that the user visited only briefly before returning to the search engine and clicking on another search result. Conversely, if the user clicks on more than one search result, you could infer that the first resource visited was not sufficient and potentially lower that resource's "score" for the search term. Such observations by application monitoring searches could lead to the conclusion that these resources did not fulfill the user's needs.

Generalized Solution

The generalized solution for this pattern is a mechanism whereby resources are tagged with metadata that relays claims about them to entities seeking a specific resource or set of resources. Entities that interact with those resources are also able to add tags.

Static Structure

Figure 7-44 illustrates the simple pattern for resource claims and reconciliation with real-world effects. An entity that has an interest in a specific class of resources can inspect the claims made by other entities about a given set of resources. These claims generally describe what the resource is or some aspects about unique instances of that class of resources. The entity's interaction with any given resource can form part of a real-world effect that may be of interest to other entities seeking the same type or class of resources. These interactions are the basis of this pattern. Without being grounded in a real-world effect, the claims are essentially unquantifiable in terms of accuracy.

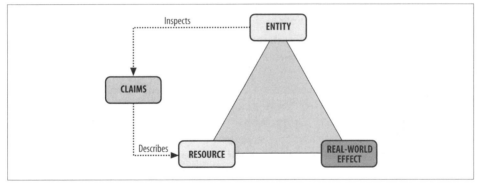

Figure 7-44. The core of the Semantic Web Grounding pattern

Implementation

You can implement this pattern using a simple word-tagging mechanism in which any entity that interacts with the resource can declare what tags it believes are relevant to describe the resource. Subsequent entities first parse those tags (claims), and then interact with the resource itself. A post-mortem analysis of the relationship between the declared metadata and the real-world effect of the interaction is then carried out. This is done to determine whether the resources are relevant for the terms with which they are tagged.

In the real world, search engines that index large numbers of HTML files perform in this manner. First, entities (in this case, the authors of HTML pages) use metadata declarations to indicate what their web pages are about. These declarations are often nested inside an HTML `meta` element. When the search engine first builds an index of resources, it may use these tags to create relevancy rankings for the web pages.

As subsequent entities (for example, other human actors) come to perform searches, they are presented with results based largely on a combination of the actual metadata claims and an index of relevancy to specific terms. The index of relevancy is a mechanism that keeps a score of the relevance of a resource, much like Google PageRank. The search engine returns a list of options to the entity performing the search and monitors the entity's interactions with the resources. In most cases, search engines return results in a format that allows tracking of which resources the entity visits. The search engine also provides the entity with a cookie to determine whether the entity returns to the search utility after visiting an external resource.

An inference engine is fed data about the real-world effects, and the search engine learns from observing the behavior of multiple entities. Over time, a pattern starts to appear regarding what resources are most relevant for entities searching for specific terms.

Business Problem (Story) Resolved

This pattern creates a dynamically adaptive approach to the semantic web and learned behavior by grounding semantic claims in an audit trail of real-world interactions between entities, claims, and resources. When this pattern is adopted, implementations of it will continue to adjust their inferences as usage patterns emerge.

Specializations

We'll consider two specializations of this pattern. First is the use of tagging to provide metadata for resources. On the Slashdot website, for example, members can add descriptive tags to each story that's published. For example, a recent story on using cell phones as servers[†] was tagged with the terms *stupid*, *apache*, and *nokia*.

Another specialization is to add information about the entity's context to create another layer of predictive semantic behavior. For example, if the visiting entities' IP addresses are tracked as part of each interaction with a resource, patterns may emerge indicating that IP addresses in certain geographical regions prefer one resource or set of resources, whereas addresses in a different geographical region prefer a second set.

Known Uses

Adobe's XML Metadata Platform (XMP) is a prime example of a toolkit that allows resources to be tagged with metadata claims. Several online systems, including Technorati and Google Search, also adopt this pattern to some degree. We describe Google Search's use of the pattern in the following paragraphs.

Google uses an adaptive learning mechanism to track search terms entered by entities seeking resources, observing the entities' behavior to determine whether the claims made about the resources are meaningful and useful. When Google returns a search page, even though the actual resource URLs are shown on the page, Google tracks the entity's choices amongst the search results by following each choice back through a Google-controlled URL and matching it against the searcher's unique IP address. A URL on the search result page can be inspected to reveal this behavior. For example, a search for "Mackenzie-Nickull" yields this return choice:

> *http://www.google.com/url?sa=t&ct=res&cd=1&url=http%3A%2F%2Fwww.nick ull.net%2Fwork%2FMacKenzie-Nickull_ArchitecturalPatternsReferenceModel-v0 .91.pdf&ei=17aBRKOuCaz6YJ7Nje8L&sig2=pdt4i7x6oSVZA1xdObv6ig*

Google uses the entity's interactions with this URL to determine which results are most relevant, and an algorithm adjusts the results for the next searcher. If enough people select a certain resource's URL, eventually that resource is inferred to be most relevant

---

[†] See *http://hardware.slashdot.org/article.pl?sid=06/06/03/1311231*.

for others searching on the same search term and it is filtered to the top of the list of results.

Clearly, this is far more advanced as a pattern than the simple string matching employed by search engines in the late 1990s.

Consequences

In this pattern, applications still rely on individuals who may have widely differing worldviews. Differences in culture, upbringing, and natural language make many people think differently about the labels they attach to objects. Folksonomies are about diversifying tags and catering to a wide range of points of view, while simultaneously enabling the building of applications that can filter out the list of tags that are of most interest to any given segment of society.

You may also note that Google's adaptive learning algorithm caters only to the majority, and there will always be a minority of the population that it does not serve well. Although that could be an issue, an additional mechanism Google uses ties the search terms into an upper ontology and attempts to provide contextualized result sets based on what the search engine knows about its users. This system seems to ensure that a balanced list of search results is always returned.

References

For more on the Semantic Web Grounding pattern, visit the following websites:

- Google's search engine—*http://www.google.com/intl/en/help/features.html*
- SUMO—*http://www.ontologyportal.org*
- Adobe's XMP—*http://www.adobe.com/products/xmp/*

The Persistent Rights Management (PRM) Pattern

Also Known As

Digital Rights Management (DRM) is often thought of in the same manner as Persistent Rights Management (PRM). However, DRM is only a small subset of PRM aimed at preventing unauthorized use or placing other constraints on the capabilities of an entity, such as locking a file format to a specific hardware/software platform. DRM has been widely criticized by many people. Much of the ado is because of a perceived intrusion upon the rights of those who have paid for content but have to pay again if they want to port it to another technology platform. For example, if you bought a song on LP, then bought it on tape, then again on CD, and finally on iTunes, you might still not legally be allowed to play the song on a non-Apple MP3 player. Many people consider this a violation of their rights.

Business Problem (Story)

Many digital assets and resources are connected to or can be made widely available on the Web via a variety of methods. Inherit policies and owners' rights on most of these resources can easily be observed and enforced in the tangible world of paper documents, yet they are extremely difficult to enforce in the digital world. Additionally, owners of digital assets are technically required to control certain aspects of their functionality, but doing so can be difficult when there are multiple copies of a resource or asset.

One problem that may occur is when people participating in a review cycle examine a copy of a digital asset that is either the wrong asset or an older version of it. Continuing to work on an older version when a newer one exists might happen for a multitude of reasons, and it is a persistent and expensive problem. Another scenario might involve a person accidentally releasing a document and then wishing to recall it, erasing all traces of its existence.

Often, owners of sensitive or copyrighted resources place them in a secure location and allow access only via some form of authentication. This solution does not address the post-retrieval aspects of the digital asset owner's rights, however. As shown in Figure 7-45, once an asset is out of the secure location, there is almost no way the owner can control it. This problem is amplified by the sheer ease with which a digital asset can be copied and sent over the Internet.

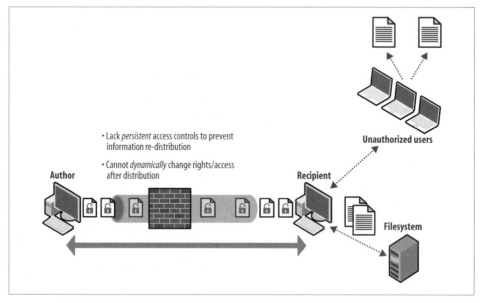

Figure 7-45. Shortcomings of the old approach to rights management

Context

The Persistent Rights Management pattern may be of interest in any environment in which digital assets or files are distributed electronically and where the owners or stewards of those artifacts wish to exercise post-distribution management rights.

Derived Requirements

The technical requirements for this pattern are:

- Digital assets must be able to be linked to a centrally controlled policy.
- The policy must be explicitly and inalienably linked to the digital asset in such a way that no application can ignore the policy.
- The link to the policy should be traversable so that applications dealing with the digital assets can gain access to the policy logic and information regarding how to set up and enforce a policy decision point (PDP) to evaluate claims made in efforts to comply with the policy. For example, if the policy involves authenticating someone against a corporate directory, it is essential that that information be available to the application so that the application can collect the tokens required for authentication and forward them back to the rights management server.
- The policy itself should be mutable so that asset owners or stewards can modify it based on their requirements and changing circumstances.

Generalized Solution

The generalized solution for the Persistent Rights Management pattern is to wrap the digital asset in an outer envelope that either is linked to the actual policy or can be used to reference the policy. The outer wrapper represents a policy decision point that cannot be traversed without the policy being adhered to, thereby forming a contract. The outer wrapper must persist in all copies of the digital asset so that it protects each and every copy.

The wrapper must be written in a manner that lets software agents attempting to interact with the digital asset understand that the asset has a policy on it and how to satisfy the policy requirements.

Static Structure

Each artifact that will be enhanced with rights management requires an outer wrapper that can relay information about the rights enabled on the digital asset. This includes information about the algorithm used to encrypt the asset, a link to any policies or other conditions that must be met to access the resource, where to obtain the key, and possibly what tokens or other information needs to be collected from actors wanting to present claims to satisfy the policy or policies. A *policy repository* is a component of a rights management infrastructure where policies are stored. It will likely be linked to other components of the infrastructure that enable the functionality shown in Figure 7-46.

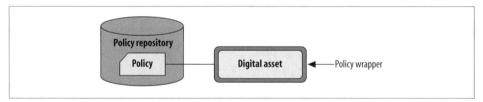

Figure 7-46. A static view of the PRM pattern

An architecture that reflects this pattern should include, at a minimum, the following components:

- Client application software
- File formats for persistent rights management
- A policy repository and server
- Services for authentication of users
- Interfaces for asset owners to manage their rights and set up and manage policies
- A communications protocol for secure communications between the client application software and the policy server
- A format for declaring policies that is independent of the actual file formats being protected
- A strong encryption mechanism to protect the digital asset if the policy is not satisfied

Dynamic Behavior

In the pattern shown in Figure 7-47, asset owners access policies via a special server. The asset owner then uses an application to wrap the digital asset in such a way that the wrapper protects it by encrypting the contents and links the opening of the contents to a specific policy in the server. The asset owner can then distribute the digital asset. When another application attempts to open the asset, it encounters the outer wrapper that links to the policy. The policy has a set of conditions that must be satisfied in order for access to the asset to be granted. This pattern does not get into the specifics of the types of conditions the policy may impose; however, there are many possibilities. For example, the policy could be linked to the ability to authenticate a specific individual, or it might specify the exclusive date and time range during which the asset owner will allow the asset to render for interactions. Other facets of rights management might include the ability to constrain certain types of interactions for specific classes of viewers. For example, asset owners might want to disable printing for most viewers, yet

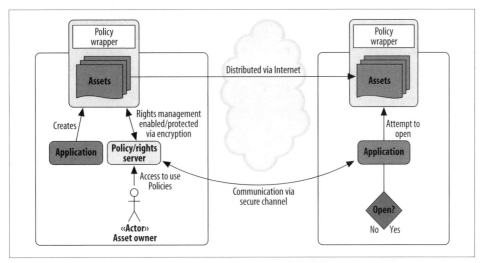

Figure 7-47. Deployment infrastructure for the Policy Rights Management pattern

enable low-resolution printing for a small class of viewers. Concurrently, the owner might choose to disable the ability of all viewers to copy and paste text from the asset.

Once the application understands what the policy represents and what must be done to satisfy it, it may take steps to try to satisfy those requirements until it ultimately reaches a decision regarding whether or not to open the asset. The decision control point may be outside the application's domain, in which case the application will likely be unable to access the asset without the server providing a key. In this manner, you can keep absolute control.

Implementation

When implementing this pattern, you must keep in mind several important design considerations. The communication channel between the clients and the policy server component might be a weak link, subject to back-channel attacks, replay attacks, or even denial-of-service attacks that might prevent legitimate access to assets. Hence, that communication channel must be protected against a multitude of attacks.

The outer wrapper must be in a format that can be parsed and inspected even if the asset itself remains out of reach. This ensures that applications attempting to open the asset will be able to understand what is happening when they encounter a cyphertext file instead of the asset. *Cyphertext* is the array of bytes that results when an asset is encrypted. It generally appears as a nonsensical, random array of characters bearing no resemblance to the original asset; hence, it is difficult to rearrange as the original asset if you do not possess the key to unlock it.

The encryption used must be strong enough to guard against brute-force attacks and sufficient for the purposes of the assets it will be protecting. Typically, the more important it is that a resource remain protected, the higher the level of encryption should be. Implementers should attempt to understand the consequences of the system failing, in terms of illegitimate access to assets and denial of access to legitimate users of the assets. The general rule most cryptography workers follow is to find an algorithm that would take all the computing resources in the world one year or longer to crack via a brute-force attack (iterating through every possible key) for basic assets, and longer depending on the useful life of the asset.

A method of authenticating users must be linked into the policy server.

Asset owners should be able to change policies after distributing assets to reflect new conditions such as a newer version, the fact that an asset has expired or is no longer meant to be in the public domain, and so on.

Business Problem (Story) Resolved

By encrypting the digital asset, wrapping it in the policy envelope, and linking it to a policy that ensures potential users cannot modify it, you have protected the asset. If asset owners can dynamically change the policies or aspects of them, the system has bestowed dynamic rights management capabilities upon these owners.

Specializations

You can specialize this pattern to handle certain file formats for assets or to use only a subset of its capabilities. For example, iTunes uses a DRM-type system to protect against copying, but this does not reflect the PRM pattern's full capabilities. Other systems, such as Adobe's LiveCycle ES Rights Management solution, work well with only certain file types.

In the future, we anticipate that other file formats may be rights-management-enabled by this pattern, including video and audio files.

Known Uses

Many companies have implemented this pattern. Here are a few of the more notable ones:

- Adobe Systems has implemented this pattern in its LiveCycle ES Rights Management server,[‡] a J2EE server that protects assets in the PDF, Microsoft Word, Microsoft Excel, and CATIA file formats as of this writing.

---

‡ See *http://www.adobe.com/products/server/policy/*.

- Microsoft has implemented a pattern similar to this in its Rights Management Server,§ which works with RMS-enabled applications to help safeguard digital information from unauthorized use.

Consequences

The use of this pattern may result in confusion for those whose applications do not understand the wrappers used to protect assets. Additionally, users may experience issues opening documents when they are not in a network-connected environment and/or if the implementation does not allow for an "offline" lease period for digital assets or other means of nonnetwork use.

It's hard to support searching if bots that index the assets cannot access the actual assets to extract metadata, such as word counts for relevancy scores. A good implementation might allow for encryption of the document, yet still expose some metadata for spiders and other search bots to use.

Rights management in general continues to be controversial, often seen as getting in users' way rather than helping them accomplish what they hope to do. Apple has removed DRM from its iTunes store, but there are still battles around DRM on Amazon.com's Kindle and related eBooks platforms, as well as in video streaming. At about the time this book goes to press, Adobe Systems's Flash platform will introduce DRM-style functionality into the Flash video (*.flv*) format.

References

For more on the Persistent Rights Management pattern, visit the following websites:

- Adobe LiveCycle ES Rights Management server—*http://www.adobe.com/products/livecycle/rightsmanagement/* (you can also use this server via the Software as a Service pattern at the Adobe Document Center, at *http://createpdf.adobe.com*)
- Microsoft's Rights Management Server—*http://www.microsoft.com/windowsserver2003/technologies/rightsmgmt/default.mspx*

The Structured Information Pattern

Also Known As

Terms associated with the Structured Information pattern include:

---

§ See *http://www.microsoft.com/windowsserver2003/technologies/rightsmgmt/default.mspx*.

Fine-Grained Content Accessibility and Granular Data Addressing
> The concept of structured information has been described by people such as Tim O'Reilly as *fine-grained content accessibility*. This pattern is a specialization of a well-known generalized pattern called the Whole-Part pattern, which they extend with some specific nuances.

The Declarative Living and Tag Gardening pattern
> The Declarative Living and Tag Gardening pattern, discussed earlier in this chapter, is highly relevant; the Structured Information pattern is one way in which finer aspects of declarative living can be implemented.

Microformats
> The term "microformat" generally refers to a small snippet of syntax that can add self-declaring metadata within existing content. Examples include marking up contact information, calendar events, and other fragments of an existing HTML web page. For more on microformats, see *http://microformats.org*. The larger notion of a "markup language" is a pivotal concept that many implementers of this pattern use.

Business Problem (Story)

A lot of largely unstructured content exists on the Internet. Most of this content is captured and presented as HTML documents, with author-supplied data forming part of a web page and the markup forming the other part. These documents are considered to be largely unstructured in terms of finding specific chunks of data within them. If someone wanted to scrape a collection of web pages to find only certain types of data, he would need a consistent syntax and mechanism to reach specific places in the documents and grab the content. Such scraping might be done for a variety of business reasons, including to repurpose content for some other use. (As discussed earlier in this chapter, content repurposing, or "mashing," is a popular Web 2.0 pattern.) Sometimes it may be desirable to retrieve the content without any extraneous elements that pertain to it. For instance, you could use just the plain text from a PDF document without needing any data regarding how the text should be displayed (font, color, size, etc.).

It is fairly impossible, though, to create a system for deterministically grabbing content from large collections of pages. Scraping and grabbing tend to be fragile processes, breaking frequently when the underlying markup changes.

Structured Versus Nonstructured Markup

Although some have argued that HTML is structured, most people who have compared it to XML and other languages consider it unstructured. The main quantifier for structured data is the ability to programmatically query or address it in a manner that is consistent and deterministic across all artifacts of the general class. From that definition alone, you can't consider HTML structured, as you cannot write an application that will retrieve information about "subject X" from all HTML pages. HTML pages have

---

no general rules regarding where or how relevant information is located within the HTML document.

Some people assert that programmatically accessing certain components of an HTML document is possible, and that the structure allows consistent access. This statement is true in some cases; however, HTML is far more generic than a language built using the XML syntax standard. Yes, you could theoretically write a program that grabs `//HTML/Head/title` and returns the document's title as a string. Most programming languages have libraries that you could use to construct such a program and account for the lax rules of HTML, such as not enforcing case, having closing tags for all opening tags, and so on. But how do you then qualify which titles you want out of a collection? If you want all the titles, it will work, but keep in mind that the titles array returned from querying a collection will be nonspecific to any one author or subject.

An XML document, by comparison, might allow generic queries based on finding namespace-qualified elements of a certain type, and an XQuery or XPath statement can be written to locate those items if they occur across all documents in a collection of the XML type. XML is far terser than HTML and has much more structure, but it never got the browser support for styling and linking that it needed to become a common web format.

Context

HTML is ubiquitous, but content stored in HTML is difficult to reuse. What's more, people creating with HTML are often less than enthusiastic about changing their work processes in order to support reuse. Other factors, such as cross-browser compatibility of creation, are generally much higher priorities.

Requirements

f content pages must have a language to use to mark up (tag) various parts ontent in a manner that will allow applications to consistently retrieve indices of that content. In other words, you have to develop a syntax that lets ablish information that contains declarations pertaining to its inner structure. *re*, any such markup declarations must be in a format that has meaning to others who may attempt to leverage those declarations to address content at the fragment level.

Supplementary mechanisms and methodologies must also exist to guide authors in how to mark up the content in a way that those who later wish to retrieve fragments of that content will understand. This process therefore crosses into the realm of *taxonomy creation*, or the development of specific structures or hierarchies to guide the authors of the documents.

Generalized Solution

The generalized solution for this pattern is to employ syntax to mark up the data in accordance with the rules of a specific vocabulary, syntax, and/or taxonomy. The markup language used can mark up content in such a way that it is logically divided into smaller pieces, each of which is tagged with a label that provides a way to identify the content fragment. Content fragments must be much smaller than HTML web pages, and may be as small as one or a few bytes or characters.

Ideally, the syntax for the markup language will be similar to existing markup languages yet simplistic enough to enable large-scale adoption by authors and developers.

Taxonomy developers will use the markup language syntax to create vocabularies for specific purposes. The taxonomy will include various tags that have corresponding annotations to help others understand their semantics or intent.

Another potential solution is to divide web pages into smaller logical chunks and assign URIs to each of them. This solution allows users to find and use the smaller fragments with great ease using HTTP get() requests.

Static Structure

The static structure view of the solution incorporates the new syntax to declare fragments smaller than the parent container. It is depicted in Figure 7-48.

Each piece of content within the parent container might logically be a candidate for markup by one or more microformats. The marking up of smaller chunks of data allows other agents or system actors to access or address content at a more atomic level than is possible by deterministically accessing the content at only the parent container level.

Dynamic Behavior

Several workflows for authoring and marking up data are possible. In general, once the author has prepared the content, it can be marked up with microformats to allow addressing at a much finer-grained level. When the marked-up content is published and made available over the Web, it can be retrieved by the normal means of content acquisition and parsed with the normal methodology. For most of the Internet, this means applying the rules of HTML. When the content is parsed for general purposes (including common tasks such as building a graphical representation for a user or consumption via an application), special handlers can be registered with the parser to do something special with the marked-up fragments within the parent content.

In Figure 7-49, such special handlers are assumed to be registered with the parser. During the parsing process, event notifications are sent to the handlers registered for specific types of events. After processing an event notification, the handler may take the optional step of talking to the parser (or possibly other software components) and giving it special instructions based on the content detected.

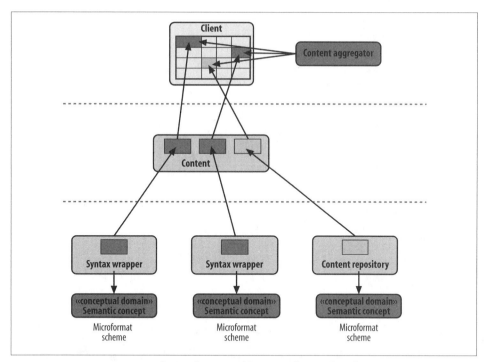

Figure 7-48. Component view of microformats adding metadata at the subparent container level

A simplistic example might be a browser with a plug-in to detect a microformat. When the browser begins streaming a new HTML page, the HTML is fed to the browser's parser. The HTML parser in the browser has an internal handler for the HTML syntax, as well as other handlers (some internal, some via browser plug-ins) to deal with extensions to HTML or other technologies that commonly work with HTML, such as Cascading Style Sheets, Flash, and JavaScript.

Plug-ins may exist for microformats that can register handlers, so that they are notified when a microformat is detected within the HTML syntax. When the microformat is sent to the handler, the handler might take additional steps, such as providing the parser or the parent browser with instructions based on user configuration and preferences. In the case where vCard syntax is used within an HTML web page, for instance, the browser may be given special instructions to highlight the contact information in yellow and show a tooltip (e.g., "This is a contact card. Right-click to input this card to your address book."), and some dynamically created JavaScript may be registered to fulfill that functionality when the user interacts with the content in the manner specified.

Alternatively, the parser may simply pass the microformat or small syntax snippet to the handler, and the handler may never talk to the browser's parser again. In fact, a browser does not even need to be involved. Spammers often write "email harvesters" that use HTTP GET requests to grab content, parse the HTML looking for syntax that indicates that an email address has been found, and then pass links back to the queue

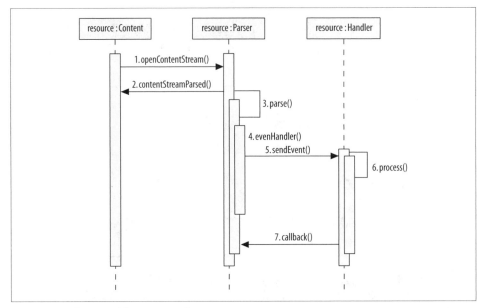

Figure 7-49. One possible sequence of events

for the HTTP GET implementation to retrieve. The balance of the HTML may be completely dropped from memory.

Both these examples illustrate possible sequences for processing content marked up at a more fine-grained level than the parent container as a whole in what is called a "deterministic" manner. The processing result is consistent, and all examples of the inner content will be found regardless of the structures of the parent container and the inner marked-up child.

Implementation

When implementing such a solution, if syntax is used that a parser interpreting the parent container understands to mean something different from what you intended, the smaller marked-up chunks of data may disrupt the display. It's important to avoid possible confusion between declarative syntaxes. One way to do this is to namespace-qualify the markup so that parsers will not confuse microformat markup with the parent container's markup language. For example, suppose both markup languages used an element that looked like this:

```
<bold>some content</bold>
```

but one had the semantics of making the graphical text appear in bold type and the other had the semantics of making it appear with "brave" or "strong" formatting, which might be rendered differently. Namespaces are often used in markup languages to avoid conflicts such as this, and the microformats community has embraced this usage.

In the process of marking up fragments of content, content owners will want to carefully consider the needs of the stakeholder communities. Before embarking on creating a syntax, it might be necessary to create a formal standards group and to reach a consensus on the higher-level models of use. This will allow stakeholders to raise issues that could affect the syntax (such as including non-North American address formats).

Implementers who work with microformats commonly embedded in HTML web pages might want to implement their applications as plug-ins to existing browsers so that they do not have to duplicate their efforts.

Business Problem (Story) Resolved

The use of microformats within content available on the Internet enables deterministic accessing or referencing of small fragments of content. This mechanism enables several other patterns—including the Declarative Living and Tag Gardening pattern and the Mashup pattern, among others—to be implemented in a common manner.

Specializations

You can specialize this pattern in several different ways. For example:

Automation

Content can be automatically marked up via an application that intercepts the content as it is being published, or when the original content is aggregated. Several software vendors have experimented with combining composite documents and other aggregations of information into existing content collections.

Specialization by type

Various methods and syntaxes exist to allow markup of very specialized types of data. For example, Adobe's XML Metadata Platform lets users mark up metadata of various types of files using a multitude of schemas and includes the option to extend the infrastructure to incorporate custom schemas.

Known Uses

Visit *http://microformats.org* for more information regarding known uses of the Structured Information pattern.

Consequences

Implementers of the Structured Information pattern must carefully assess the risks posed to forward compatibility by embedding markup languages in their documents. They need to take special care to avoid potential future conflicts or collisions of syntax and semantics. If someone designs a new microformat and uses a tag such as foo, it may clash with later versions of HTML if those versions also contain a foo element. You can avoid this danger by using namespaces to qualify elements; however, there is no way to guarantee that your namespace qualifiers will be unique other than using your unique domain name or universally unique identifiers.

Designers and implementers must also consider, when designing their microformats, at what level of granularity things become semantically meaningful. For example, an address may have subelements for street, city, region, country, and postal/zip code. Some of these may be further decomposed. For example, the street address 3347 West 6th Ave. contains four pieces of information that may be semantically meaningful to different people. Microformats should be designed to account for further optional decomposition that may require careful data modeling. The street address element, for instance, could contain a choice of character data or four subelements that each contains character data.

References

For more on the Structured Information pattern, visit *http://microformats.org*.

Summary

The patterns discussed in this chapter have captured information based on consistencies in things generally deemed to be Web 2.0. This set of patterns is by no means exhaustive or complete, and new patterns are bound to pop up in the near future. Still, this represents a start toward defining a concrete set of Web 2.0 patterns.

To complete this book, the next chapter takes a look at some of the phenomena that we anticipate will be features of the years ahead.

CHAPTER 8

Where Are We Going from Here?

"Where do we go from here? Try to find a better place,
but soon it's all the same. What once you thought was
a paradise is not just what it seems"

—Chicago, "Where Do We Go from Here"

Often it seems as though you can't turn around without discovering some great new pervasive online software. But the core ideas of Web 2.0 are also spreading at a surprisingly rapid pace into a wider community that's applying them to different contexts. The patterns described in this book are already being applied to new problems in different spheres, while new solution patterns are being invented by combining technology and social tendencies in new ways.

Web 2.0 Offshoots

Increasingly, we have been encountering new movements directly triggered by Web 2.0 ideas. They range across the spectrum of human endeavor. For example, a few years ago *Law Practice Today*, a journal of the American Bar Association, ran a detailed story on Web 2.0 and its tie-in with the law.* Why do lawyers care about Web 2.0, you ask? As it turns out, Web 2.0 has spawned a relatively full-blown movement: Law 2.0.

---

* See *http://www.abanet.org/lpm/lpt/articles/tch01061.html*.

Law 2.0 is a conceptual departure from the law business of yesteryear. Like other aspects of Web 2.0, some claim it's in beta right now. There is already a Law 2.0 application called Wex,[†] (a legal wiki encyclopedia available to everyone). Document management, a common challenge for lawyers, is evolving rapidly into document engineering. Integrating existing technologies such as PDF into document-centric processes has been a key focus of evangelists such as Lori Defurio (Adobe) and Bob Glushko (Berkeley University), who cowrote what we consider the definitive book on the subject.[‡]

Law 2.0 is built on the premise that current law practices are insufficient, as they describe problems to be solved and the solutions to those problems. In theory, law should reflect its real-world, multidisciplinary existence and should rely on more than the treatise-reporter-practice law triangle,[§] an established pattern within the law community. Law 2.0 is really about building law practices that recognize the capabilities that technology offers society today.

A primary example of a case where law did not reflect reality pertains to a struggle over copyright of content for the popular cartoon series "Dilbert." While existing copyright law made it impossible for someone to serve up a website with a Dilbert cartoon from a server that was not authorized by United Feature Syndicate, Inc., a clever user wanting to get around the logistics just had to serve up a web page template that referenced the Dilbert cartoon from United's server. The existing law was totally unprepared to deal with this in 1999, as technically no physical bytes representing Dilbert cartoons would ever be placed on the user's server. The owners of the Dilbert franchise have since readily embraced Web 2.0, and at *http://www.dilbert.com* you'll find things like mashups, Dilbert widgets, blogs, and various examples of harnessing collective intelligence and other Web 2.0 patterns. Perhaps this is Cartoons 2.0? The movement seems to be spreading; companies like Pixton.com are already building user-generated comic strips into platforms and deploying them to the Web.

Law 2.0 and Cartoons 2.0 are just the beginning. The interrelated, mutually reinforcing concepts in Web 2.0 (such as true disintermediation, customer self-service, and harnessing collective intelligence) are resonating with many other industries, as shown in Figure 8-1. As it turns out, these industries are all in the process of being transformed by technologies that facilitate the relentless collapse of formal central controls, pervasive web usage, rapid technological change, and more. These communities seem to crave a new model for collaboration, relevance, and usefulness. Web 2.0 gives them a beacon to rally around, as well as a useful set of practices that they can use for constructive reinvention.

[†] See *http://www.law.cornell.edu/wex/index.php/Main_Page*.

[‡] *Document Engineering: Analyzing and Designing Documents for Business Informatics and Web Services*, by Robert J. Glushko and Tim McGrath (MIT Press).

[§] See *http://proxy.seattleu.edu:2048/login?url=http://ilrweb.com*.

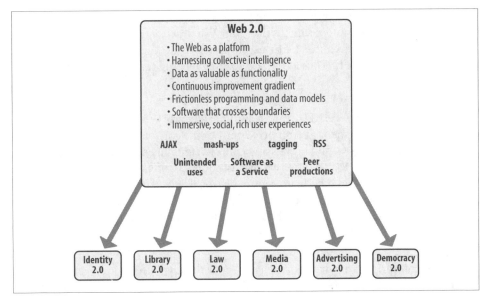

Figure 8-1. Web 2.0 offshoots

The following list of Web 2.0–related movements offers a sampling of what other communities are striving for. Although some, such as Library 2.0, are well underway, other movements, such as Media 2.0, are still quite nebulous:

Identity 2.0

Widely covered by numerous periodicals and even at the Web 2.0 Conference, Identity 2.0 is an intriguing concept most commonly identified with Sxip (*http:// www.sxip.com*) and its CEO, Dick Hardt. Dick gave a keynote presentation at the 2005 O'Reilly Open Source Convention (OSCON)[||] in which he outlined several key advances in identity management that represented disruptive influences on the existing identity industry.

Library 2.0

Library 2.0 is a very Web 2.0 view of library resources that emphasizes the two-way flow of information between library users and the library itself. Library 2.0 embraces many of the patterns and technologies described in this book (specifically, Participation-Collaboration, Mashup, and SOA) and has many proponents. You can read more about it at *http://www.libraryjournal.com/article/CA6365200 .html*.

Media 2.0

The Web is revolutionizing the content-delivery models of newspapers, magazines, and other print media (and not only for the better, in some cases). Still, some folks believe in a second coming of media—both old and new—known as Media 2.0.

[||] See *http://identity20.com/media/OSCON2005/*.

This new media conceptually embraces issues such as democracy, distributed aggregation, identity, and contextualization. We described some of these issues in the preface and in Chapter 1 of this book; however, the body of knowledge far exceeds the scope of this book. A good starting place to learn more is *http://media2.0workgroup.org*.

Advertising 2.0

Advertising 2.0 is a Web 2.0 approach to participatory, scalable advertising. Like the Media 2.0 movement, it embraces many of the core concepts of Web 2.0, such as knowing your users and harnessing collective intelligence, along with such specific patterns as RUE and those we discussed in Chapter 1. Even the core models for television are changing from sequential display of advertisements (you watch a show, which is interrupted to display some ads) to a model of concurrent display of advertisements (ads are splashed up on the screen but do not entirely displace the television content).

Enterprise 2.0

Large enterprises are trying to engage more robustly with their target audiences. Enterprise 2.0 is a recognition that today's web users demand more and will not be as forgiving as they were a decade ago. Enterprises that are scared by how rapidly young startup companies can upstage incumbent forces (e.g., MySpace.com becoming the most popular web destination within three years of its launch, followed by Facebook's similar trajectory) are studying the patterns in this book to see how they can adapt, and which patterns they can adopt.

Government 2.0

Years of pressure on governments to share more information with their citizens and the 2009 arrival of the largely sympathetic Obama administration in the U.S. have fueled efforts to reinvent government. Transparency—"sunshine"—is a key ingredient of most Government 2.0 efforts, but developers are also looking for better ways to gather and present citizen input for government processes.

Democracy 2.0

A grassroots attempt to repair perceived problems with old-world, representative democracy, Democracy 2.0 is working to ensure that a wide range of individuals can contribute to the creation of our nation's laws through Web 2.0. Although perhaps idealistic, it is an interesting exercise to try to understand what laws would be made if a truly democratic country were created today.

Music 2.0

Music 2.0 is more than just a revolution in how we distribute and listen to music; it shakes the existing music industry to its very core. The rise of small, independent providers of audio content from independent artists is a trend that will likely continue. Even the creation of music, which historically has been done in a recording studio with audio tracks laid down one at a time, is being challenged by startups such as Mix2r.com and MixMatchMusic.com, where people can go online and contribute audio tracks to existing works or remix other people's audio tracks to essentially create new pieces of music. Combined with democratic licenses and community features, this movement is embracing most of the core patterns of Web 2.0 in this book.

What do these offshoots have in common? For starters, they all embrace one or more of the patterns in this book. In all cases, people seem to be questioning the status quo, asking "What can we do differently?" or "Why are we currently doing this [function, task, or activity] the way we are?" The evolution has started a revolution.

In the IT world, the pendulum is swinging rapidly away from centralized IT command and control (the push model of management) and toward a more scalable and effective decentralized model of IT self-service (the pull model). The push model is one in which digital information or functionality is provided by a centralized authority and fed outward. The pull model, by contrast, is a versatile pattern that is closely aligned with web services' basic request/response model, in which decentralization is a key feature.# Thanks to their modular design and decentralized platforms, pull systems connect a far more diverse array of participants.

The offshoots described here are all about the pull model: they all use a form of marketing, termed "viral," in which participation spreads rapidly based on a model of outsiders wanting to join in. The push model, a relic from broadcasting days, is expensive by comparison and is the least targeted in terms of reach and true connections. Whichever model you choose, it is hard to ignore that it would take millions of dollars to rival the success of something like Twitter or Drupal, and even then your success is not guaranteed. Understanding what makes something a target for viral adoption is a holy grail to many in the IT industry.

Readers might want to ask themselves, "What can happen in my industry?" or even go further and ask why their industries exist today or whether they will exist in the future. Some industries might dwindle if disruptive new models become the norm for society. However, regardless of what industry you're involved in, some things never go out of style. We will study one of those things in the next section.

A Timeless Way to Build Software 2.0

This book's authors have all been software architects by trade. We've been witnessing the creation of software for more than 20 years and have experienced movement after movement, from object-oriented design in the 1980s–1990s to component-based design, distributed objects, web-based software, Service-Oriented Architecture (SOA), and too many others to mention. In general, the problems that the previous generation of techniques couldn't solve are only marginally more solvable by the next (which is invariably developed to "fix" the earlier problems). A genuinely better mousetrap is really hard to invent.

See *http://www.w3.org/TR/2002/WD-ws-arch-scenarios-20020730/*.

Logically, if you couldn't do whatever you wanted to do with the previous generation of techniques, it's unlikely that you'll succeed with the next generation if you use the same flawed design process. Certain software problems remain hard to solve, and in general, the evolutionary path mysteriously happens to involve the juncture between technology and people in some way. Software and the techniques used to create it get better fairly constantly, but people remain the same.

Every once in a while, though, something new and big comes along—or at least something that looks new and big. One of the big new things that came along about 10 years ago was the concept of design patterns, as we've discussed throughout this book. Despite the perpetual changes in technology, many software design problems have certain timeless solutions. Some things that get "discovered" are in fact not new at all and have been working well for years. The design patterns concept was a revelation a decade ago, and the writers of the book that explained it to the world became both famous and very successful.* Why? Because these design patterns really worked. The patterns were there well before a book documented them; the revelation was in making everyone aware of them, and enabling understanding of their use in the software design process.

Design patterns are a solution to a problem within a context. We are starting to grasp the context and even the outlines of the patterns of this "new" generation of software, but we have a long way to go. The Web is a monstrously big space with big problems, and it's not getting any easier to grasp. Clearly, understanding what it takes to create great online software that is successful, useful, and vibrant will be an ongoing challenge for a long time to come.

People want software that does what they want and is available when they need it. They want software that grows with them, that helps them and teaches them and lets them do the same with others. They want software that gets out of their way, disappears, and is convenient. And they want to pay as little as possible for it. They are willing to have software get right into the middle of their lives—but only if it's the right software. People have always wanted all of these things from their software, and now, they might actually start to get them.

Concepts like harnessing collective intelligence and the continuous improvement gradient are applicable for all software development and have been around since the dawn of the software industry. Their large-scale implementation has only really become possible during the last decade, though. Continuous improvement has always been a goal of most software companies, but only recently have they increased the release cycles of software to, in some cases, nightly builds rather than year-long release cycles for improvements.

---

* Chapter 6 of this book discussed the Gang of Four and Christopher Alexander in greater detail.

The Timeless Way of Building Software: Inspiration for the Next Generation of Web Software

This section is our reinterpretation of the first chapter of Christopher Alexander's *The Timeless Way of Building* (Oxford University Press) as it applies to software. Once you've read it, ask yourself these questions: Are we yet at a place where we can really identify the design patterns in Web 2.0? And are Web 2.0 patterns in fact old patterns that we have been using all along, with new implementations?

There is one timeless way of building software. It is decades old and is the same today as it's always been. Because it is timeless, it will always remain this way.

The great software of our time has always been created by people who were close to this methodology. It isn't possible to create great software—software that is satisfying, useful, and makes itself a natural extension of life—unless you follow this way. This way will lead anyone who looks for it to elegant, vibrant software that is itself timeless in its form.

It is the process by which the function of a piece of software grows directly from the inner nature of people and naturally out of the raw bits, the otherwise meaningless digital medium, of which it is made.

It is a process that allows the life inside a person, or a group of people, or a community, to flourish, openly, freely, and so vividly that it gives rise, of its own accord, to the natural order that is contained within it.

This methodology is so powerful and fundamental that with its help you can create software that is as beautiful and enriching as anything else you have ever seen.

Once you understand this way, you will be able to create software that is alive, and intertwined comfortably with your life and the lives of others. You will design worlds in which you and others will want to work, play, and coexist; beautiful places where you can sit and dream comfortably.

This way is so powerful that with its help, hundreds or thousands, or even hundreds of thousands, of people can come together to create software and a community that is as alive and vibrant, peaceful and relaxed, as any living experience has ever been.

Without the central control of authorities and experts, if you are working in this timeless way, a genuine place will grow right from underneath your fingertips, as steady as the grass in the fields or the trees in your backyard.

And there is no other way to make software that is fundamentally good. That doesn't mean that all ways of making software are identical. Quite the contrary, it means that at the core of all successful software and at the core of all successful processes of creation and evolution, one fundamental invariant feature is responsible for their success. Although this way has taken on a thousand different forms at different times, in different places, still there is an unavoidable, invariant core to all of them.

Take a look at some of the great web software, such as Google's search page, Flickr, or Delicious. They all have that unique yet unhurried grace that comes from perfect ease and natural balance. But what do they have in common exactly? They are beautiful, ordered, and harmonious. But especially, and what strikes to the heart, is that they live. They are the perfect blend of logic and emotion, of the machine and the human experience, intrinsically intertwined and symbiotically embracing each other.

Each one of us yearns to be able to bring to life something like this, or to just be a part of it somehow. It is a fundamental human instinct, a funtion of our desire to be part of something greater than ourselves. It is, quite simply, the desire to make a part of nature, to complete a world that is already made of mountains, streams, stones, buildings, ourselves, our living systems, and our increasing connectedness.

We all have the potential to make a living world, a universe, and a place of our own for us to share with others. It is within our hearts. Those of us who have trained as software designers, developers, or architects have this desire perhaps at the very center of our lives; that one day, somewhere, somehow, we will build a software experience that is wonderful, beautiful, and breathtaking; a place where people can go and live their dreams.

In some form, every person has some version of this dream; whoever you are, you may have the dream of one day creating a most beautiful place, virtual or otherwise, where you can come together with others and freely share your knowledge, learn, participate in your community or government, and otherwise conduct your daily interaction with the rest of the world.

In some less clear fashion, anyone who is concerned with communities and other large group efforts has this same dream, perhaps for the entire world. There is a way that software can actually be brought to life like this. A definable sequence of activities is at the heart of all acts of software design, and it is possible to specify, precisely, under which conditions these activities will generate software that is alive.

Consider the process by which a group of independent people can make software become alive and create a place as real as any other. There is a definable sequence of activities that are more complex than old-school software creation approaches at the heart of new collective processes of software creation. These processes can be made so explicit and so clear that any group of people can use them.

This process is behind the design of community-built software such as Linux, Apache, Wikipedia, and many others. It was behind the design of the great virtual places for people to live and work: the Internet, Usenet, *World of Warcraft*, *Second Life*, and the World Wide Web. It was behind the creation of simple, satisfying software of the kind that powers the iPod, the BlackBerry, and Firefox; of SourceForge and BitTorrent. In an unconscious form, this way has been behind almost all ways of creating software since the beginning.

Now we can identify the methodology and process behind these inventions by going to a level of analysis that is deep enough to show what is invariant in all of the different versions of this way. This hinges on a form of representation that reveals all possible design processes as versions of one of the most fundamental sets of patterns.

First, we have a way of looking at the ultimate constituents of the environment: the ultimate "things" that a piece of software is made of. Every piece of software makes use of entities known as *design patterns*, and once we understand software in terms of its patterns, we have a way of looking at them that makes all software, all of their parts and functions, members of the same class of thing.

Second, we have a way of understanding the generative processes that give rise to these patterns: in short, the source from which the ultimate constituents of software come. These patterns tend to come from certain combinatory processes, which are different in the specific patterns that they generate but always similar in their overall structure and in the way they work. The patterns are essentially like languages. And again, in terms of patterns, all the different ways of building software, although different in detail, become similar in general outline.

At this level of analysis, we can compare many different software creation processes. Once we can see and distinguish their differences, we can identify those processes that make software vibrant, alive, and useful, and those that make them the opposite.

Upon examination, it turns out that behind all processes that let us make great software, there is a single common process. The correct path is operational and precise. It is not merely a vague idea, or a class of processes that we can understand: it is concrete and specific enough to function practically. It gives us the power to make software and virtual communities. It is a method inasmuch as a discipline that teaches us precisely what we have to do to make our software what we want it to be.

Although this method is precise, we cannot use it mechanically. The fact is that even when we have seen deep into the processes by which it is possible to make software, this awareness only brings us back to that part of ourselves that is forgotten. Although the process is precise, it becomes valuable because it shows us what we know already.

This timeless way of software architecture represents a more complete reconceptualization of what we thought we knew. We can give this place, where common sense and logic collide with humanity and society, a name.

We call that place Web 2.0.

Creating Open Services That Last (and That Anyone Can Use)

Developers everywhere have started to access the thousands of terrific open Web 2.0 software services available on the Web, using them either to create new Web 2.0 software or to weave them into their own organizations' systems. Mashups and web service reuse are intriguing grassroots phenomena that continue to grow.

The Web is now the world's biggest and most important computing platform, in large part because people providing software over the Internet are starting to understand the law of unintended uses. Great websites no longer limit themselves to a single user interface. They also open their functionality and data to anyone who wants to use their services as his own. This allows people to repurpose and reuse a thousand times over another service's functionality in their own software for whatever reasons they want, in unforeseen ways. The future of software will encompass combining the services in the global service landscape into new, innovative applications.

Writing software from scratch will become rarer and rarer, because it's often easier to recombine existing pieces. This echoes the revolution of the object-oriented approach for software development a few decades ago, when software developers began building small, self-encapsulated chunks of software that could be used over and over again. Service-Oriented Architecture expands that evolution over disparate domains of ownership, and across functional and technical boundaries of operation. The proliferation of truly amazing mashups, among them Facebook, is another symptom of change. Although Facebook started as a social networking site, its developer infrastructure allows a variety of services to be aggregated and mashed up from multiple sources.[†] Facebook now describes itself as a "platform."

Figure 8-2 shows a mere fraction of the technology and architectural choices facing those who develop services. Consider that Facebook alone now supports ActionScript (the scripting language behind Adobe's Flash, Adobe Integrated Runtime, and Flex), multiple AJAX combinations, ColdFusion, Perl, PHP, and other languages.

The world of traditional software integration has long had its favorite tools, including SOAP and JMS. Vendors have provided integration platforms for those developing services, helping the average coder to develop, test, and deploy services very rapidly. One problem is that regardless of the underlying platform or technology, these types of service tend to impose a large amount of complexity on the client side of the conversation. Advanced services generally require special, often expensive, tools. The web services family of technologies now includes WS_Addressing, WS_Trust, WS_Secure-Conversation, WS-ReliableExchange, and a wide variety of other technologies. Just recognizing these and being able to parse an incoming SOAP message to understand what the other side is trying to communicate is a daunting task.

If you want your services to be adopted by the masses and to withstand the test of time, you need to make them simpler and cleaner. A stripped-down service interface that allows the average developer to write usable code within an hour will make users happy. Making the complexities optional will win over the many people who have no need for enterprise functionality in their mashups. Low barriers to reuse, frictionless integration, and widespread reuse: these are the mantras of Web 2.0.

[†] See *http://developers.facebook.com*.

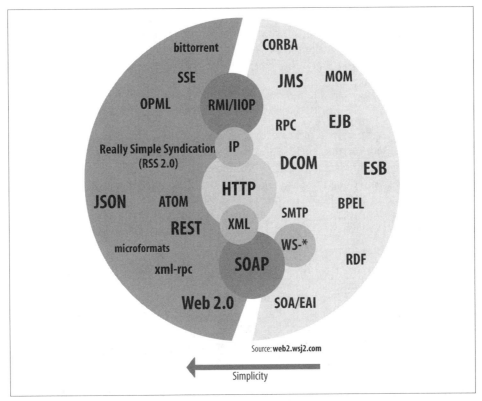

Figure 8-2. The wilderness of service models…what to choose?

So, how do you deliver an API for your services that lasts and that anyone can use? There are a few approaches you should consider:

Simplicity and scalability

Simpler interfaces are easier to support and easier to scale than complex multilevel systems that have to pass messages through multiple layers before figuring out what they mean. Interfaces that stay close to the HTTP protocol—notably REST-style interfaces implemented over HTTP—can take advantage of years of work that have gone into making HTTP request handling efficient and easy to scale. HTTP isn't always the answer, of course; extremely scalable peer-to-peer architectures like BitTorrent require their own protocols and different, more complex, data structures.

Ease of consumption

Developers will almost always prefer data that arrives in easily processed (and easily debugged) forms. Text-based formats have a natural advantage here for many kinds of data, though graphics and multimedia generally require binary formats for efficiency. XML offers structure and readability, though JSON offers a lighter-weight approach that minimizes the need for tools. Even fragments of HTML may be useful, depending on the circumstances. Similarly, for the Flash, Flex, and AIR crowd, the Action Message Format (AMF) is by far the most efficient and easiest to integrate. Heavier-weight approaches like SOAP and the WS-* family of specifications may be useful if your customers want them. James Ward has built a RIA testing application to compare many of the remote service technologies; you can find it at *http://www.jamesward.org/census/*.

Tool support

Most people prefer to avoid reinventing the wheel. Good libraries and tools can help to connect servers, clients, and peers with minimal tweaking, and as long as you can count on your prospective customers having and wanting to use those tools, they can reduce the costs of connecting to your systems. While SOAP had an early lead in tools, JSON requires few tools, plain XML tools are now common, and support for REST keeps growing with projects like the Restlet library for Java.[‡]

Security

Security is an issue that never goes away. SOAP certainly has the goods here, but really good encryption toolkits are doing just fine. As a general rule, adding security into applications increases the processing and bandwidth overhead as well as the complexity of integration on the client side.

XML over HTTP, REST-style services, and, where appropriate, Really Simple Syndication (RSS) are usually the lowest common denominator for Web 2.0 communications. Organizations experiencing the outside-in forces that David Linthicum[§] talks about are going to have to figure out how to bring in these simpler services and trust them. Lightening the weight of enterprise systems will become more important as the boundaries between IT systems, the Web, and mobile devices start to blur seriously over the next few years.

Scalability will be the most difficult issue for successful Web 2.0 software. You'll need to plan for radical decentralization early if you're going to survive your own growth curve. Fortunately, genuine BitTorrent support for web services is finally becoming available; an example is Prodigem's mind-blowing Auto RSS Torrent, which takes RSS feeds and turns them into BitTorrents. This service isn't exactly REST or SOAP with BitTorrent behind it to make it infinitely scalable, but it's a start. Expect lots more as the service worlds not only collide, but turn upside down as well.

Web 2.0 into the Uncertain Future

So what Web 2.0 phenomena will persist? We would like to think that all the patterns we've explored (both the larger explicit patterns covered in Chapter 7 and the smaller

---

[‡] eWeek.com has an article on the merits of this library at *http://www.eweek.com/article2/0,1895,2113997,00 .asp*.

[§] David Linthicum is an SOA guru currently working at analyst firm ZapThink (*http://www.zapthink.com*).

implicit patterns readers might pull from this book) are durable and will survive well into the future. While some pundits and analysts declared SOA dead in January 2009, we believe the style of architecture using services will likely be around a decade from now, and beyond.

Never before has it been so important for companies to understand the patterns that have driven their tactical behavior. If optimizations can be made, now is the time to make them. If processes can be made more efficient, saving from the bottom line now might make the difference between surviving or not. The future brings uncertainty. Having the mindset and mental discipline to recognize new patterns before your competitors do might make the difference between just surviving or being the biggest player in the space.

The Rich User Experience pattern, which often manifests as Rich Internet Applications (RIAs), is probably one of the hottest patterns today. The reason for this is that on the Web, your competition is only a few clicks away. The quality of the user experience matters now more than ever. While some companies might consider cutting back on customer service to conserve cash, now is probably the worst time to cut back on customer experience enhancements. If you have a RIA plan, put it into effect now. Seize the opportunity to innovate and improve.

Being the first to recognize patterns gives you a huge advantage. If you observed the first Internet boom before 2001 and noticed that a pattern that almost always turned out to be a mistake was to launch and then let competitors come in and undercut you, and you noticed the pattern of socially generated collaborative music emerging in 2007 but thought the first two companies in the space were priced too high, you had an opportunity to put those two patterns to use and launch a competitive enterprise. When you recognize the new patterns first, you have the natural advantage of a faster time to market over those who take longer.

Patterns continue to evolve and grow, and it's not yet clear which will persist. While researching this book, we uncovered many other prospective patterns, including the following:

Architectures of Participation and A Platform Beats a Website
> Architectures that leave a platform open to participation by thousands of users and developers end up creating ecosystems that may eventually allow members of the community to earn a living. *Second Life* is a primary example of Architectures of Participation. Instead of expecting a site to provide everything its users need, these approaches leave room for users (and sometimes even competitors) to figure out what they want and provide it themselves.

Plug-in Business Models
> Sites like eBay and Amazon.com allow people to create their own virtual stores and make a living from their involvement. Architecting a platform to be open, attract users, and scale is a skill that we think will persist as a cornerstone of IT for some time to come.

The Biggest Pile

If you were going to sell something today via an online auction, where would you go, and why? The answer you probably chose is "eBay," and the reason is that it attracts the largest number of buyers. Now consider where you would go if you wanted to buy something via an online auction today. Again, the answer is likely to be eBay; however, the reason probably is that it has the most amount of goods for sale. eBay has locked in the two groups—buyers and sellers—because it has the "Biggest Pile." This prevents any competitor from challenging eBay's dominance without spending a lot of money. This pattern can be the key to long-term success.

Opting Out, Not Opting In

By default, you are "in" and have to take specific action to opt out. The Web itself is built on this axiom: if you have an image file publicly available on a web server, for example, anyone can link to it.

We hope you have enjoyed this book and that it has helped you understand some of the fundamental concepts of Web 2.0. We hope you now possess the skills to think like an architect and seek patterns where they exist. We hope you have had some great new entrepreneur moments and have ideas for new startups. If so, we hope you will lend someone else your copy of this book to help pass on the enlightenment.

Index

We'd like to hear your suggestions for improving our indexes. Send email to *index@oreilly.com*.

derived requirements, 146
DoubleClick/Google AdSense comparison, 30
dynamic behavior, 147
functionality, 4
generalized solution, 146
implementation, 148
known uses, 150
personal websites/blogs comparison, 52
references, 150
specializations, 149
static structure, 147
Atom format
blog subscriptions, 53
functionality, 24
Atwood, Jeff, 74
authentication
HTTP support, 21
TLS support, 22

B

bandwidth alternative solutions, 38–41
banner ad placement, 30–34
barcodes, 73
Battelle, John, 202
Beck, Kent, 8
Biddulph, Matt, 183
BitTorrent
Akamai comparison, 38–41
pattern considerations, 102
reference architecture and, 88
Blogger software, 53
blogosphere, 78
blogroll, 53
blogs
Participation-Collaboration pattern, 143
personal website comparison, 52–54
Boucher, Marcel, 86
BPM (Business Process Management), 57
Briet, Suzanne, 194
Britannica Online/Wikipedia comparison, 50
bus, 17
Buschmann, Frank, 103
Business Process Management (BPM), 57
business rules, 90
Butterfield, Steward, 200

C

CAP (Common Alerting Protocol), 127
Carr, Nick, 79
Cartoons 2.0, 224
Cascading Style Sheets (CSS)
AJAX support, 71
functionality, 24
cause-and-effect auditing, 204
Chong, Fred, 132
client tier (Reference Architecture)
communication services, 94
components supported, 93–95
controller, 93
data/state management, 94
defined, 86
rendering and media, 94
security container/model, 94
virtual machines, 94
client/server model
capabilities, 67
client tier, 74
connectivity/reachability, 71–74
evolution, 65–67
Internet and, 11
services tier, 67–70
user considerations, 75–78
cloud computing, 41, 127
CMS/wiki comparison, 57
collaboration
Britannica Online/Wikipedia comparison, 50
Ofoto/Flickr comparison, 35–38
Collaborative Tagging pattern
also known as, 184
Britannica Online/Wikipedia comparison, 50
business problem (story), 184
business problem (story) resolved, 188
CMS/wiki comparison, 57
consequences, 190
context, 185
derived requirements, 186
directories/tagging comparison, 58
dynamic behavior, 187
functionality, 5
generalized solution, 186
implementation, 187
known uses, 189
MP3.com/Napster comparison, 41

service interactions, 70
WS-S (Web Services-Security)
    evolution of standards, 71
    functionality, 22
WS-SX (Web Services-Secure Exchange)
    functionality, 22
    reference architecture and, 88
WSDL (Web Services Description Language),
    57

X

XAML (eXtensible Application Markup
    Language), 96
XFN format
    functionality, 23
    Structured Information pattern, 6
XForms, 97
XML (Extensible Markup Language), 23, 214
XML Infoset, 57, 99
XML Metadata Platform (XMP), 206, 220
XML Remote Procedure Call (XML-RPC), 35
XML User Interface Language (XUL), 97
XML-RPC (XML Remote Procedure Call), 35
XMLHTTPRequest object
    browser flexibility, 21, 71
    functionality, 23, 24
XMP (XML Metadata Platform), 206, 220
XUL (XML User Interface Language), 97

Y

Yahoo!, 32, 59
Yegge, Steve, 97
YouTube website
    file distribution and, 45
    Participation-Collaboration pattern, 8
    pattern considerations, 102
    Semantic Web Grounding pattern, 8
    Viral Marketing pattern, 8

Z

Zachman Framework for Enterprise
    Architecture, 164